"A collection of the greatest thinkers in business today, every chapter of this book will inspire you to be a better leader and a better person."

—Chester Elton, bestselling author of *The Carrot Principle*, *All In* and *The Best Team Wins*

"In our divided and distracted world, it can feel difficult to find our calling, make a positive impact on others, and contribute to a more collaborative world. *Work is Love Made Visible* should be required reading for every leader who wants do just that."

—Tasha Eurich, *New York Times* bestselling author of *Insight* and *Bankable Leadership*

"Frances Hesselbein exemplifies the notion of a life well lived. It's impossible to imagine a finer tribute to her magnificent work and life than this inspiring and beautifully titled volume."

—Sally Helgesen, coauthor of *How Women Rise* and author of *The Female Advantage*

Work Is Love Made Visible

FRANCES HESSELBEIN
MARSHALL GOLDSMITH
SARAH McARTHUR

Foreword by ALAN MULALLY, Former CEO of Boeing and Ford

A Collection of
Essays About the Power of

Work Is Love Made Visible

Finding Your Purpose from

the World's Greatest

Thought Leaders

WILEY

For general information on our other products and services or for technical support, please contact our Customer Care Department within the United States at (800) 762–2974, outside the United States at (317) 572–3993 or fax (317) 572–4002.

Wiley publishes in a variety of print and electronic formats and by print-on-demand. Some material included with standard print versions of this book may not be included in e-books or in print-on-demand. If this book refers to media such as a CD or DVD that is not included in the version you purchased, you may download this material at http://booksupport.wiley.com. For more information about Wiley products, visit www.wiley.com.

Library of Congress Cataloging-in-Publication Data

Names: Hesselbein, Frances, editor. | Goldsmith, Marshall, editor. |
  McArthur, Sarah, editor.
Title: Work is love made visible : a collection of essays about the power of
  finding your purpose from the world's greatest thought leaders / Frances
  Hesselbein, Marshall Goldsmith, Sarah McArthur, editors.
Description: Hoboken, New Jersey : John Wiley & Sons, Inc., [2019] | Includes
  index. |
Identifiers: LCCN 2018028401 (print) | LCCN 2018029391 (ebook) | ISBN
  9781119513575 (Adobe PDF) | ISBN 9781119513643 (ePub) | ISBN 9781119513582
  (hardcover)
Subjects: LCSH: Leadership.
Classification: LCC HD57.7 (ebook) | LCC HD57.7 .W668 2019 (print) | DDC
  655.4/092--dc23
LC record available at https://lccn.loc.gov/2018028401

Printed in the United States of America

V10004557_091418

*This book is dedicated to our friend and mentor
Peter Drucker whose teachings and encouragement
are the inspiration for this book.*

Work is love made visible. And if you can't work with love, but only with distaste, it is better that you should leave your work and sit at the gate of the temple and take alms of the people who work with joy.

—Kahlil Gibran

Contents

Contents

Foreword

When Frances Hesselbein, Marshall Goldsmith, and Sarah McArthur asked me to write the foreword for their edited compilation book, *Work Is Love Made Visible*, my answer to their request was a heartfelt and enthusiastic, "Yes!"

What an honor for me to be part of the latest creation from three of my heroes, whose work and leadership I admire and have benefited from so much.

I immediately read the book from start to finish and was deeply struck by its leadership messages and the way the book was organized. These leadership messages cause us to reflect on our purpose and our passions. It is about what matters so much to each of us that we want to share it with others. And the book is organized in such a way that each contributor's reflections on Frances's question, "What is it you see when you look out the window that is visible but not yet seen by others?" supports one of Frances's five philosophies on leadership:

- Leadership Is a Matter of How to Be, Not How to Do
- To Serve Is to Live
- Defining Moments
- Be Ye an Opener of Doors
- Bright Future!

Reading each contributor's reflections inspired me to answer Frances's question myself!

When I look out the window, what do I see that is visible but not yet seen by others? I see talented and motivated people working together for the greater good. I see three elements that are absolutely critical to the true success of any venture, company, product, or life: humility, love, and service. And I see the unique contribution of leaders to hold themselves and their leadership teams responsible and accountable for creating smart and healthy organizations that are delivering value for the greater good.

Reflecting on Frances's question invited me to reflect about my own leadership journey and how it might serve to help you uncover and realize your own purpose as you study this book.

Alan's Story

Growing up, we lived with very modest means. Even so, I was incredibly fortunate because my parents loved me and believed that I could make a significant difference and contribution to our world. To this end, they taught me the following lessons that I have carried with me throughout my life:

- The purpose of life is to love and be loved, in that order.
- To serve is to live.
- Seek to understand before seeking to be understood.
- It's nice to be important, but more important to be nice.
- By working together with others, you can make the most positive contribution to the most people.
- Lifelong learning and continuous improvement.
- Respect everyone, we are all creatures of God, and worthy to be loved.
- Develop one integrated life to deliver your life's work.

And, like all kids, I wanted to fit in. I wanted a pair of Levi jeans, some Weejuns penny loafers, and a car and college some day. So, with my parent's teachings and encouragement, I decided my way forward was to serve and maybe I could earn those special jeans.

I started "work" with *TV Guide* and newspaper routes and then a lawn mowing business. I was a bagger, checker, and then night manager at the Dillons grocery store. I was a carpenter, ranch and farm hand. I played sports and was my college fraternity rush chairman and president. All the while I learned aerospace engineering at the University of Kansas and summer jobs at Beechcraft, Cessna, and Boeing.

Starting with my very first "work," I became very aware of the power and advantages of "working together" with all the stakeholders associated with my service ... my customers, parents, family, employers, employees, suppliers, communities, competitors, bankers, and investors.

I looked at each "work" as service and I loved serving! I loved asking my customers what they wanted and valued the appreciative smiles on their faces for my service. I loved learning and growing and exceeding their expectations! And I loved the satisfaction I felt when I meaningfully contributed to making people's lives better. I loved working together with all the stakeholders to create value for everyone. And I continued to refine and improve my following working together principles and practices through my "work."

- People First
- Everyone Is Included
- Compelling Vision, Comprehensive Strategy, and Relentless Implementation
- Clear Performance Goals
- One Plan
- Facts and Data ... We Can't Manage a Secret ... The Data Sets Us Free
- Everyone Knows Plan, Status, and Areas That Need Special Attention
- Propose a Plan ... Positive "Find-A-Way" Attitude
- Respect, Listen, Help, and Appreciate Each Other
- Emotional Resilience ... Trust the Process
- Have Fun ... Enjoy the Journey and Each Other ... and No Humor at Another's Expense

As the scope of my service grew with the teams at Boeing and then later at Ford, I developed and continued to refine my following working together management system to implement my working together principles and practices for the product programs and businesses I supported and led.

- Our Governance Process
- Our Leadership Team
- Our Working Together Principles and Practices
- Our Creating Value Roadmap Process

- Our Business Plan Review Process
- Our Leadership's Unique Responsibility and Contribution

My working together management system proved to be a very reliable process with clear expected behaviors to manage our organizations, to include all of our stakeholders, and to sustainably deliver value for the greater good in our rapidly changing world.

This, my life's work, the working together principles, practices, and management system, is how I have made my love visible. It is a system that leaders can use to work together for the greater good. And it is this book based on Frances's inspired question that has led me to take the next steps in my journey, to make my love visible yet again by sharing my working together principles, practices, and management system in this brief foreword.

I hope you will read this book and soak it all in! Take in everything that these wonderful thought leaders and contributors have to teach us. Then ask yourself Frances's question, "What is it you see when you look out the window that is visible but not yet seen by others?" Ponder, analyze, and reflect on your purpose. Explore and discover what is important to you and then do that at work and in your actions. When you do, you will find that your love is visible to you and to others, and you will be well on your way to being a leader who is helping us all work together for the greater good!

Thank you Frances, Marshall, and Sarah for inspiring each of us to discover and make our love visible!

Alan Mulally
Former CEO of Boeing and Ford

Preface

Most of us who will read this book have heard of Peter Drucker. Many of us even call him the "the founder of modern management." In fact, shortly before Peter Drucker died in 2005, *Business Week* magazine claimed him as "the man who invented management." A renowned teacher, writer, and guru, Peter himself would say, "They call me guru because 'charlatan' is too hard to spell."

It is with this matter-of-factness that Peter described his uncanny ability to describe the future of management, "I never predict. I just look out the window and see what's visible – but not yet seen."[1] This description is just one of the gifts that he left us with and it is the central focus of this book.

Fast forward to 2011 at The Four Seasons Restaurant in New York City. Frances Hesselbein, whom Peter Drucker said is the "greatest leader he had ever known," and I (Sarah) are sitting to have lunch for the first time since we have met. A wonderful discussion ensues of life, work, and purpose.

Mid-lunch, Frances looks me directly in the eyes, puts her hand on my arm, and asks me poignantly, "What is it you see when you look out the window that is visible but not yet seen by others?" I stop. This is a question that does not have a quick or rote answer. It asks me to examine my view of the world and I find no easy answer pops to mind. A few years later at lunch again with Frances, I am finally able to formulate an answer that makes sense to me, and that answer is my chapter in this book. Frances's answer is her chapter. Marshall's answer is his chapter. And so on ...

With its title taken from a favorite saying of Frances, "Work is love made visible," the idea of this book came about in November of 2016, after a lovely dinner with Frances. The United States was just about to elect its 45th president. Change and uncertainty were in the air. Everyone had something to say about the future, outcome, and implications should either candidate be elected; in essence, everyone was looking out the window.

When change is happening it's hard to be passive, even if we are not (as Peter Drucker would say) the *person with the power to make the decision*. We look at who is making the decisions and the actions being taken and think about how we could do better. Yet, for most of us it is impossible to reflect upon the entire system and envision a better path of action for the whole of society. So, we do it in parts, each of us holding a different view, and then through dialog with our friends we try to integrate those views as much as possible into a working, functioning vision. Integration requires teamwork, participation, and leadership – all of which we must learn to do if we are to succeed as a global society.

So, when Frances and I met that fateful day in November, her question, "What is it you see when you look out the window that is visible but not yet seen by others?" rang loudly in my head. What I see that is invisible to others is my unique gift to society, my area of concentration, my purpose, my expertise, my inherent knowledge, my *call to service*.

How can each of us recognize what we see when we look out the window? In our earlier years, most of us would have no idea how to do this and many have never even given it a thought. We are not taught to do this when we are growing up or as we go through school, and if we aren't one of those fortunate people who knows their calling from an early age, we can spend years living lives without direction and purpose. Then again, for those more established, who may have stumbled upon or chosen a path, it may be time for a change. How do we decide our next steps, how do we know which direction to choose, how do we know if it will be fulfilling and meaningful in the next phase of our lives?

We, the editors and contributors to this book, think this should be part of the learning that all of us receives: how to recognize our call, our gift, our purpose, at any point and at different points of our lives. It is crucial that each of us understands how to identify our purpose in order that we can focus our studies, make our decisions, choose our passions, and play our part in the societal system toward what drove Peter Drucker to do all that he did, *create a functioning society*. One route to accessing this understanding is to answer for ourselves Frances Hesselbein's insightful question.

And therein lies the twofold purpose of this book: (1) to teach individuals to ask themselves Frances's question and discover their purpose, passion, and calling, and (2) to illuminate the inherent gifts that each of us has so that we may contribute our talents to the advancement and healthy functioning of our global society.

To help us fulfill our book's purpose, we have asked some of today's and tomorrow's greatest thought leaders to give us their answers to the question: "What is it you see when you look out the window that is visible but not yet seen?"

This question, so profound and provocative, requires us to explore our deepest thoughts, concerns, fears, and hopes for our society. And, for those of us who are contributing to this work, it also challenges us to offer encouragement, ideas, and solutions for what we see.

On a global scale, there is no better time than now to collectively connect to our purpose. We need to ask ourselves: What is our purpose and how can we as a global society work together toward a bright future for all, despite our differences?

In the United States, for instance, during the past decade, we've seen our country divided over who will lead us and how we will be led. This division caused a standstill in our movement forward as a society. How many times have you heard, "It's impossible to get anything done in government"? This standstill has led many people to have to choose a side, whereby rather than working together for the benefit of all, we are hoping our side will win so we don't lose what's ours. This is a purpose. However, we don't believe it's a common purpose that serves all of us, as we explore and define it in *Work Is Love Made Visible*.

As individuals, finding our purpose, understanding our calling, grappling with and committing to what we inherently know that others may not and to serving that purpose, can be the challenge of our lives. It can also be the opportunity of our lives. We look to those who understand their purpose and who have made it their life's work, to role model for us what it is to live a life that has meaning. Thus, in *Work Is Love Made Visible,* we start the conversation by asking some of the world's greatest thought leaders and leaders of the future to tell us what they see and how this vision shapes their lives, their decisions, and their contributions.

Our book is structured into five parts based on the leadership philosophy of Frances Hesselbein.

Part I: Leadership Is a Matter of How to Be, Not How to Do. Leadership is not about title or destination; it is about our character. Good leaders have strong characters. What does it mean to be a great leader?

Part II: To Serve Is to Live. For those called to serve, the joy and responsibility of being of service goes beyond our current condition or place of employment.

Part III: Defining Moments. Defining moments are those experiences we have when we become aware of something of which we previously had no consciousness. These moments shape our character and are the inspiration for many of our choices in life.

Part IV: Be Ye an Opener of Doors. What does it mean to open doors – for ourselves and for others – through which we can walk together toward a shared and positive vision of the future?

Part V: Bright Future! In this section, we share our hopes for tomorrow and solutions to challenges arising today that will lead us toward the bright future that we envision.

You can read this book one chapter after the next in order, you can peruse the Table of Contents for writings from your favorite thought leaders, or you can jump to a section that strikes you, for instance, Bright Future!, and read the authors' ideas, thoughts, and contributions on this subject.

Work Is Love Made Visible comes at a time in human history when working together toward a cooperative future is critical. We recognize that such working together requires us to share our insights into what we see as our greatest challenges and opportunities as a global society and how we can address these issues going forward. Working together requires us to look out the window and see what is not yet seen by others, to share what we see with our fellows, to listen to others as they share their views, and from this build a healthy, functioning global society based on inclusion and cooperation.

Notes

1. www.forbes.com/forbes/1997/0310/5905122a.html.

Acknowledgments

We are deeply grateful to Peter Drucker, whose simple observation, "I don't predict. I just look out the window and see what's visible but not yet seen," is the foundation of this book.

We would like to thank all of our wonderful contributors whose unique and thoughtful answers are leading us toward a bright future, as well as the publisher for bringing this book to its audience, and to all those behind the scenes – editors, production staff, and copyeditors – who have helped bring this work of love to life. And we are extremely thankful to our families, friends, teachers, and mentors for their support and encouragement throughout our lives and especially in the creation of this book.

Special thanks from Sarah to my dearest friend and inspiration, Frances Hesselbein, to Marshall Goldsmith, Laurence S. Lyons, Nathan Lyons, Taavo Godtfredsen, Doug Baker, the George Washington University, and to my wonderful and supportive husband, Monty Brewer, without whom this book truly would not have been possible.

About the Editors

Frances Hesselbein

From her Pennsylvania beginnings as a volunteer Girl Scout troop leader to her rise as the CEO of the largest organization serving girls and women in the world – the Girl Scouts of the USA – Frances Hesselbein has always been mission-focused, values-based, and demographics-driven. For her transformation of the Girl Scouts in the 1970s, former president Bill Clinton awarded Frances the country's highest civilian honor, the Presidential Medal of Freedom. For more than 25 years, Frances has been at the helm of a very small but strong organization based in New York where she continues to train a new generation of leaders through leadership education and publications. She is chairman of the Frances Hesselbein Leadership Forum, part of the Graduate School for Public and International Affairs, Johnson Institute for Responsible Leadership at the University of Pittsburgh, and editor-in-chief of Leader to Leader. *Frances is the recipient of 21 honorary doctoral degrees, the author of 3 autobiographies, and the co-editor of 30 books in 30 languages. Frances has traveled to 68 countries representing the United States, and* Fortune *magazine named her one of the "World's 50 Greatest Leaders."*

Marshall Goldsmith

Dr. Marshall Goldsmith is the world authority in helping successful leaders achieve positive, lasting change in behavior: for themselves, their people, and their teams. He was recently chosen as the inaugural winner of the Lifetime Achievement Award for Leadership by the Harvard Institute of Coaching. Dr. Goldsmith is the only two-time *Thinkers50 #1 Leadership Thinker in the World. He has been ranked as the World's #1 Executive Coach and Top Ten Business Thinker the past eight years.*

Dr. Goldsmith is the author or editor of 38 books, which have sold over 2.5 million copies, been translated into 32 languages, and become listed bestsellers in 12 countries. His three New York Times *bestsellers are* Triggers, MOJO, *and* What Got You Here Won't Get You There.

Dr. Goldsmith is one of a select few executive advisors who have been asked to work with over 150 major CEOs and their management teams. He is a fellow in the National Academy of Human Resources and winner of the Lifetime Achievement in Teaching Award from the Institute for Management Studies. His work has been recognized by almost every professional organization in this field.

Sarah McArthur

With more than two decades of experience in publishing, most prominently as a writer, editor, and writing coach, Sarah McArthur is continually striving to enhance her knowledge and expertise about the rapidly changing business of publishing and to share it with those who have a message to spread.

COO of Marshall Goldsmith Inc. and Founder and CEO of *sdedit, Sarah's fields of expertise are management, leadership, and executive and business coaching. She manages the daily operations at Marshall Goldsmith Inc. and has co-authored and co-edited numerous books including, Coaching for Leadership: Writings on Leadership from the World's Greatest Coaches *with Marshall Goldsmith and Laurence S. Lyons and* The AMA Handbook of Leadership, *co-edited with Marshall Goldsmith and John Baldoni (chosen one of the Top 10 Business, Management, and Labor Titles of 2010 by Choice).*

In addition to her own works, Sarah has played significant roles in many other book projects including Marshall Goldsmith's New York Times *bestseller* Triggers; *all three editions of the best-selling management classic* Coaching for Leadership; *and Marshall's Amazon.com, USA Today, and Wall Street Journal #1 best-seller,* What Got You Here Won't Get You There.

Sarah holds a Masters in Publishing from George Washington University and a BA in English and Environmental Studies from the University of Oregon.

Leadership Is a Matter of How to Be, Not How to Do

In her work as a leader and writer, Frances Hesselbein reminds us that *leadership is a matter of how to be, not how to do.* Leadership is not about title or destination; it is about our character. Good leaders have strong characters. They are mission-focused, values based, and demographics-driven. They manage for the mission, for innovation, and for diversity.

In the first part of our book, our contributors use this definition as a stepping off point to explore leadership through their unique perspectives: what it is, what it isn't, and how to be a great leader in this time of massive change.

Frances Hesselbein leads the section with a recounting of the influence of Peter Drucker on the development of her own brand of leadership. She discusses the importance of mentorship and of clearly defining one's leadership values and principles. Marshall Goldsmith then takes us on a brief walk through the evolution of leadership from the days of cave people to the professional managers of today by revealing common characteristics of leaders of the past and then sharing seven key trends for leaders of the future. Dave Ulrich advocates viewing your organization from the outside observer perspective of an anthropologist studying an unfamiliar culture. He describes the wisdom of shifting how you look and listen at your organization and the value of considering different perspectives, demonstrating how this can lead to far greater insights and effectiveness for human resources professionals and leaders. Whitney Johnson applies the image of waves to S-curve models, extrapolating from their uses in describing *disruptions* – new product innovations and ideas in markets – to the analysis of human disruptions in the patterns of our careers and lives. She emphasizes the need to "catch a new wave" on a fairly regular basis and offers suggestions for navigating wave cycles. Patrick Lencioni shows how engaging in some serious self-reflection about what leadership truly means to you and your own sense of identity can reveal some often-difficult truths, but ultimately opens a path to greater satisfaction and effectiveness. Taavo Godtfredsen identifies some tangible action steps that leaders can take to better *scale* their intentions with their actions so as to optimize their impact on members of their teams. And finally, Susan Scott contemplates the role of *obsession* in entrepreneurship and leadership and identifies the key obsessional ideas that fueled the creation of her company, Fierce, Inc.

1

My Journey with Peter Drucker

Frances Hesselbein

From her Pennsylvania beginnings as a volunteer Girl Scout troop leader to her rise as the CEO of the largest organization serving girls and women in the world – the Girl Scouts of the USA – Frances Hesselbein has always been mission-focused, values-based, and demographics-driven. For her transformation of the Girl Scouts in the 1970s, former president Bill Clinton awarded Frances the country's highest civilian honor, the Presidential Medal of Freedom. For more than 25 years, Frances has been at the helm of a very small but strong organization based in New York where she continues to train a new generation of leaders through leadership education and publications. She is chairman of the Frances Hesselbein Leadership Forum, part of the Graduate School for Public and International Affairs, Johnson Institute for Responsible Leadership at the University of Pittsburgh, and editor-in-chief of Leader to Leader. *Frances is the recipient of 21 honorary doctoral degrees, the author of 3 autobiographies, and the co-editor of 30 books in 30 languages. Frances has traveled to 68 countries representing the United States, and* Fortune *magazine named her one of the "World's 50 Greatest Leaders."*

■ ■ ■

We transformed the organization using his principles.

Six years after coming to New York to serve as CEO of the Girl Scouts of the USA in the late 1970s, I received a letter from John Brademus, then the chancellor of New York University, inviting me to a dinner at the University Club to hear Peter Drucker speak. I had never met Peter Drucker but had read every book he had ever written.

I knew that in such a large group I would not have an opportunity to meet him, but I would have the opportunity to hear him live – Peter Drucker, the great thought leader who had influenced the volunteers and staff in the largest organization for girls and women in the world.

The invitation read, "5:30 p.m. reception." Now, if you grew up in western Pennsylvania, 5:30 is 5:30; so when the evening came, I arrived on time, walked into the reception room, and found myself alone with two bartenders. I turned around. Behind me was a man who had just walked in. He said, "I am Peter Drucker." (Obviously, if you grow up in Vienna, 5:30 is 5:30.) I was so stunned that instead of saying "How do you do," I blurted out, "Do you know how important you are to the Girl Scouts?" He said, "No, tell me."

"If you go to any one of our 335 Girl Scout councils, you will find a shelf of your books. If you read our corporate planning and management monographs and study our management and leadership structure, you will find your philosophy," I replied.

"You are very daring," Peter replied. "I would be afraid to do that. Tell me, does it work?"

"Superbly well," I told him, adding, "and I have been trying to get up enough courage to call you, and ask if I may come to Claremont and have an hour of your time?"

Peter said, "Why should both of us travel? I'll be in New York next month, and I will give you a day of my time."

Before we met again, Peter studied us at the council level – on the ground where the girls and leaders were – as well as our circular governance and management systems, and declared the Girl Scouts of the USA the best-managed organization in the country. "Tough, hardworking women can do anything," he said. I wasn't sure about tough, but hardworking, yes!

So, in 1981, the great day for our meeting arrived. The national board and staff members were in the boardroom. I am sure they expected him to comment on the results of the past five years, for these remarkable people with their partners in local councils had transformed the organization using Drucker's principles. He stood before us and thanked us for permitting him to join us, and then he completely surprised us. "You do not see yourselves life size," he said. "You do not appreciate the significance of your work, for we live in a society that pretends to care about its children, and it does not." I wanted to rise and refute this, but could think of nothing to say. He continued, "And for a little while, you give a girl a chance to be a girl in a society that forces her to grow up all too soon."

After that first transformative day, he gave the Girls Scouts two or three days of his time each year. He studied us, talked with us, advised us, and wrote about us for the next eight years.

When I left the Girl Scouts of the USA in 1990, I bought a home in Easton, Pennsylvania, promised a publisher I would write a book on mission, and wasn't going to travel so much.

Six weeks later, I flew to Claremont, California, to brainstorm a way to permeate the nonprofit, social sector with Peter's works and philosophy. Long story short, six weeks after leaving one of the largest voluntary organizations in the world, I found myself the CEO of one of the smallest foundations in the world – the Peter F. Drucker Foundation for Nonprofit Leadership – with no staff and no money, just a powerful vision shared with cofounders about bringing Peter to the wider world and transforming the social sector. The rest is history. Our organization's name has changed over the years, and our resources and publications are well documented on our website (www.Hesselbein Forum.org), in our 30 books in 30 languages traveling around the world, and in our quarterly *Leader to Leader* journal. We are in our 27th year fulfilling our mission of strengthening the leadership of the social sector and their partners in business and government.

Leadership Is a Matter of How to *Be*, not How to *Do*

When I was the CEO of the Girl Scouts of the USA, I knew I had to define leadership on my own terms and in my own language, in ways that would communicate and embody the heart and the spirit of the leadership we were called to provide. After a long, difficult introspection, I developed my definition of leadership: "Leadership is a matter of how to be, not how to do."

All of the *how to* advice in the world won't work until *how to be* is defined, embraced by leaders, and embodied and demonstrated in every action, every communication, and every leadership moment.

The leader of today, and in the future, must be focused on how to *be* – how to develop quality, character, mindset, values, principles, and courage. The *how to be* leader knows that people are an organization's greatest asset and in word, behavior, and relationships, they demonstrate this powerful philosophy. In all interactions, from the smallest to the largest, the behavior of the *how to be* leader will demonstrate a belief in the worth and dignity of the men and women who make up the enterprise.

You and I spend most of our lives learning how to do and teaching others how to do, yet we know that, in the end, it is the quality and character of the leader that determines the performance – and the results.

How to be qualities are not baskets of skills; rather, they rise in miraculous ways to comfort, to sustain, to challenge, and to embrace. I believe passionately in the *whys*: the values, principles, and beliefs that define who we are, what we believe, what we do, and how we work with others, our fellow travelers on a shared journey to leadership in an uncertain world.

My definition of leadership defines who I am, why I do what I do, and what I believe. I test it over and over. Leadership is a matter of how to be, not how to do.

A Call for Leaders of the Future

Today, we need leaders who help distill Peter's concept and language of *mission*: why the organization does what it does, its purpose, its reason for being. Leaders of the future must invest in building a mission-focused, values-based, and demographics-driven organization, reflecting the many faces and cultures of our country.

We need leaders who communicate with the people and the customers of the organization and the many audiences with whom we engage – always reflecting in our communications that, "Communication is not saying something; communication is being heard."

Now, may I share a secret with you? I have two tattoos – invisible ink, of course – you can't see them, but they are there. First, Peter Drucker's admonition to *Think first, speak last.* My second tattoo is also Peter's: *Ask, don't tell.*

We need leaders who practice the art of listening. We need leaders who use listening to include, not exclude – to build consensus, appreciate differences, and find common concepts, common language, and common ground.

We need leaders who in their own lives try to find work–life balance and make that balance a reality in the lives of those with whom they work. If you think that this is a lovely ideal, but not a realistic one in today's tough world, try comparing the productivity and morale of a workforce that is encouraged and supported in finding this rare work–life balance with those of a dispirited workforce where such balance is not a consideration, and *take no prisoners* is a valued management style.

Today, perhaps most of all, we need leaders who share successes widely while accepting responsibility for shortfalls and failures. These leaders take a tough measure of their own performance, aware that their language, behaviors, and actions are measured against their self-proclaimed values and principles.

Reflection Questions

1. Can you recall a defining moment or mentor who propelled you into your career in leadership?
2. How do you define leadership?
3. What is your mission?

2

The Evolution of Leadership – Yesterday, Today, and Tomorrow

Marshall Goldsmith

Dr. Marshall Goldsmith is the world authority in helping successful leaders achieve positive, lasting change in behavior: for themselves, their people, and their teams. He was recently chosen as the inaugural winner of the Lifetime Achievement Award for Leadership by the Harvard Institute of Coaching. Dr. Goldsmith is the only two-time Thinkers50 #1 Leadership Thinker in the World. He has been ranked as the World's #1 Executive Coach and Top Ten Business Thinker the past eight years.

Dr. Goldsmith is the author or editor of 38 books, which have sold over 2.5 million copies, been translated into 32 languages, and become listed bestsellers in 12 countries. His three New York Times *bestsellers are* Triggers, MOJO, *and* What Got You Here Won't Get You There.

Dr. Goldsmith is one of a select few executive advisors who have been asked to work with over 150 major CEOs and their management teams. He is a fellow in the National Academy of Human Resources and winner of the Lifetime

Achievement in Teaching Award from the Institute for Management Studies. His work has been recognized by almost every professional organization in this field.

■ ■ ■

Think back on our history as human beings. Many of our stereotypes of leadership are from a past that no longer exists. They come from a yesterday that is very disconnected from today and miles from the world of tomorrow. These images from the past are reinforced in our literature, TV, movies, video games, and art, and they can prevent our understanding of what great leadership is today and what it will look like in the future.

For instance, here's a brief walk through the evolution of leadership.

The Cave People – Leadership Through Physical Strength: Thousands of years ago, our ancestors lived in a brutal and harsh world. Small clans grouped together in caves to protect themselves from the elements. Leaders were usually strong, young men and ruled through physical strength.

The Land Owners – Leadership Through Control of the Land: As we evolved, humans began to gather and store crops. Ownership and control of the land became the key to power. Leaders were not necessarily the strongest physically; they were the people who controlled the land. Control of resources became the key to power.

The Royalty – Leadership Through the Family: For the last few thousand years, the source of most leadership was often the family. Kings and queens ruled with no need to justify their power, since they were declared to have been descended from God. The simple solution for anyone who criticized or challenged royalty was to kill them.

The Church – Leadership Through the Religion: Historically, the church provided spiritual leadership for the people and supported the royal families. Often members of the royal family, the Church had the ability to determine what was right or wrong, and criticism of its doctrine was not tolerated. Critics were referred to as *heretics* and were susceptible to excommunication, torture, or even death.

The Military – Leadership Through Power: While the Church provided the moral case for royalty, the military provided the power needed to keep the members of the ruling class on their thrones. In the world of kings, the strongest army won. Military leaders were often related to the ruling families, but not always. Sometimes generals worked their way up the hierarchy and were rewarded for their loyalty, bravery, intelligence, and competence.

The Academy – Leadership Through Education: Until very recent times, the best formal education was largely reserved for the elite. Liberal education separated the elite from the masses and along with the Church and the military, reinforcing the status quo of the country.

The Master – Leadership Through Skill: As the merchant class began to rise, a new type of leader emerged, the master. The master was typically an expert in a certain trade who taught his skills to a younger apprentice. The apprentice practiced the craft, and eventually became the master to a new apprentice.

The Politician – Leadership Through Support: Eventually the subjects of royalty and the colonists of royalty rebelled. In the early democracies, the power and control was in the hands of an elite group. Only in recent years, and in some countries, has democracy evolved to a level of true representation of the people. Politicians, like kings and queens, have historically been more focused on maintaining power than on building collaborative relationships.

The Business Owner – Leadership Through Control of the Corporation: With the advent of capitalism came the rise in business. While these early entrepreneurs may not have been descended from royalty and wealth, they were able to acquire wealth and pass it on to their family members. Since they owned the controlling interest in the stock of the corporation, they maintained ultimate decision-making power.

The Manager – Leadership Through Promotion: As organizations grew and the families of founders became less focused on leading their companies, a new class of leaders emerged – professional managers. The key role of these managers was to protect and grow the assets of the owners. These managers typically worked their way up through the company and were rewarded by promotion for their effort, achievement, and loyalty.

Common Characteristics of Leadership in the Past

As we look at leadership in the past we can see that leaders historically had the following common characteristics:

- *Leadership was local.* From the tiny world of the cave, to the village, to the city, to the country, the history of leadership has almost all been domestic.

- *Leaders managed uniformity.* Throughout history almost all leaders have been men who represented the ruling class of their countries. Women were not even considered for most leadership roles, or even many occupational roles. Along with being the same sex, leaders were the same race and religion and were brought up in the same culture.
- *Leaders managed very slowly changing technology.* Throughout most of history, leaders managed technology that did not change at all, or changed very slowly. Revolving masters could prosper for generations without being concerned about the impact of new technology.
- *Leaders knew the answers and did not encourage differing opinions.* Religious leaders, masters, academics, and generals were assumed to have the right answer. Followers who disagreed with authority were often punished severely by being fired, excommunicated, ostracized, or even killed.
- *Leadership was top down.* Most leadership involved immediate control over direct reports, as opposed to team building or building peer relationships. Being able to influence colleagues without direct-line authority was not a skill that was required for success.
- *Leaders were bosses.* From kings to generals to managers, leaders had one important quality in common. They had clear power over the people whom they led. They could easily punish those who did not demonstrate loyalty. Once they acquired power, they usually did their best to keep it. One definition of *boss*, as a noun, is "a person who makes decisions, exercises authority, and dominates." Another definition, as a verb, is "to order about" or "to be master over." The leader of the past was clearly the boss!

These characteristics of leaders may (or may not) have been effective in the past. In practical terms, it doesn't matter. These characteristics will not work for the most important leaders of the future.

The one over-arching theme from studying leaders of the past is that, in some very important way, *leaders were supposed to be superior to the people they were leading.* Kings were descended from God, clergy were closer to God, masters were more skilled, academics had more knowledge, generals had more experience, owners had more wealth, politicians had more support, and cave leaders had more strength.

Almost all movies, videos, TV shows, and games reinforce the concept that great leaders are, in some way, superior to the people that they lead. Looking at the history of leadership, it is very easy to understand why *servant leadership* is such a recent concept: managers were actually referred to as "superiors"!

As the world and its people are evolving, so is leadership. The leader of the future will have qualities that are clearly different from the leader of the past, and many of the characteristics of yesterday's leader will not work for tomorrow's leaders.

The Leader of the Future

Accenture invited me to partner with them in a two-year research project that compared the qualities of leaders of the past with those that would be required of leaders in the future.[1] Instead of interviewing *current* CEOs and leaders, who would not be leading the organizations of the future, we interviewed 200 *future* CEOs from around the world. A few qualities were seen as clearly more important than the leader of the past. Looking back on this study years later, I find the *direction* of the predictions from these high potential leaders to have been proven to be amazingly accurate. If anything, the *degree* of change, or the speed of change in the importance of new leadership qualities may have been understated.

Combining this research with all that I've learned since the study's completion, I can share seven key trends that have emerged and will dramatically impact the leader of the future, why the changing world calls for an end to old assumptions about leadership, and how a new model is emerging to fit today's world.

1. From Thinking Locally to Thinking Globally
   Globalization is a trend that will continue to have a major impact on the leaders of the future. Even 20 years ago, leaders in some huge companies could focus on their own countries or, at most, their own regions. Those days are rapidly screeching to a halt! The trend toward globally connected markets and globally integrated organizations is going to become even stronger in the future.

2. From Requiring Uniformity to Seeking Diversity
   In the past, seeking diversity was not even 'on the radar screen' for most leaders. In fact, the leaders of the past usually required uniformity in the workforce – and eliminated the possibility of diversity. As the importance of globalization continues to increase, leaders will need to appreciate and strive for diversity in new and different ways. They

will have to understand not only the economic and legal differences, but also the social and behavioral differences that are part of working around the world. *The most effective leaders of the future will understand that developing an understanding of other people and other cultures is not just an obligation; it is a requirement. Even better, it is an opportunity!*

3. From Understanding One Technology to Becoming Technologically Savvy

   In the past, the core technology of organizations changed very slowly or, in many cases, not at all. Leaders of the past could understand their company's core technology, develop enough expertise in this technology to lead their people, and stay as current as they needed to without a huge effort. That is not the case with the rapid pace of technological change today. This does not mean that every future leader will be a gifted technician or a computer programmer. It does mean that leaders should understand how the intelligent use of new technology can help their organizations; recruit, develop, and maintain a network of technologically current people; know how to make and manage investments in new technology; and are positive role models in leading the use of new technology.

4. From Leader as Knower to Leader as Learner

   In the past, leaders generally knew more about what they were doing than the people they led. That is why masters were called masters and apprentices were called apprentices. In the future, the most important leaders will be managing people who know far more about what they are doing than the leaders do. In the new world with its global organizations, diverse stakeholders, and rapidly changing technology, the leader often knows less than the people he or she leads. The higher the leader moves up the organizational chain of command, the more this is true.

5. From Eliminating Challenge to Encouraging Constructive Dialogue

   Leaders of past went out of their way not only to discourage challenge, but also to *eliminate* challenge. For instance, providing negative feedback to landowners could lead to starvation and providing negative feedback to royalty could lead to execution. In a world where leaders knew more than their followers, the drawbacks of leading by intimidation were not nearly as great as they are today. Today, leaders who cut off the flow of constructive dialogue run the risk of becoming obsolete in a very short period of time.

6. From Leading in the Hierarchy to Building Alliances and Teams
   Leadership has traditionally been thought of as a top down, hierarchical process. In the world of the past, with leaders controlling knowledge and subordinates doing what they were told, this model seemed to make sense. It is becoming increasingly hard to determine these roles and in industries as diverse as energy, telecommunications, and pharmaceuticals, the same organization may be your customer, supplier, partner, *and* your competitor. In this new world, building positive, long-term, win-win relationships with many different types of stakeholders is critical.

7. From the Leader as Boss to the Leader as Facilitator
   As we consider all of the trends listed, it becomes clear that the leader of the future needs very different skills and qualities than the leader of the past. The *leader as boss* told people what to do and how to do it. In the old world, for all of the reasons that we discussed, this was understandable. The leader of the future will not have all the answers. The leader of the future is not only *learning* as opposed to *knowing*, the leader of the future is a facilitator who is helping everyone on the team learn.

One of, if not *the*, greatest leader I have ever met is Frances Hesselbein. Frances retired after serving for 14 years as the CEO of the Girl Scouts of America. Peter Drucker said that Frances was the most effective executive he had ever met, and Peter Drucker never made remarks like this casually. Frances did an amazing job of changing an organization that was, for a time, mired in the past and not moving toward the future. As the CEO of the Girl Scouts, she developed a wonderful doctrine, *Tradition with a future!* She never demeaned the past; in fact, she celebrated the wonderful traditions of the past. On the other hand, she did not live in the past. She realized that, in her organization, the leader of the future would have to be very different than the leader of the past.

As a CEO, Frances was remarkably ahead of her time. She coined the phrase *circular leadership* to describe her leadership style and the style that she wanted to promote in all of her leaders. She envisioned herself as a person in the center of circular relationships, not as a boss sitting on top of a hierarchy.

Frances saw herself as a servant leader who was there to facilitate the success of her team — not as a boss who was there to tell people what to do and how to do it. She was constantly learning and helping others learn. She encouraged constructive disagreement. She did an amazing job of building alliances inside and outside the organization.

As you think about your role as the leader of the future, remember the *Frances Doctrine* of tradition with a future. Whatever you have done in the past – or other leaders have done in the past – is over. Recognize all that the leaders you have known in the past have done right. Appreciate what you can learn from their mistakes.

Focus on the future! By understanding the past, you can see why leaders ended up being the way they were, you can also see how leadership needs to change in order for organizations to thrive in the new world – a world where leaders do not strive to be superior to the people they lead – a world where leaders strive to develop people who will become, in many ways, superior to the leader!

Work Is Love Made Visible is a wonderful title for this collection of essays. In our new world, the role of a leader will be *earned* not *granted*. Leaders will manage knowledgeable workers who know much about what they are doing – more than their leaders know. In the new world of leadership, great leaders will be facilitators who love the process of leadership – not experts who know more than their co-workers. Great leaders will create an environment for learning where each member of the organization can work – and make their love visible – in a world that respects them for their unique contributions.

Reflection Questions

1. Think about your leadership journey, as a leader or as one being led, which qualities and characteristics do you find most valuable in leaders – those of the leaders of the past or those of the leaders of tomorrow?
2. Who do you think is a good role model of tomorrow's leaders? What qualities do they exude?
3. How can you enhance your own leader of the future qualities?
4. Why is creating an environment where work is love made visible even more important for leaders of the future than it has been for leaders of the past?

Note

1. The result of this project was the book *Global Leadership: The Next Generation,* which I coauthored with Cathy Greenberg, Alastair Robertson, and Maya Hu-Chan. Valuable contributions to the research were made by Warren Bennis and John O'Neil.

3

Leaders Who Become Organization Anthropologists

Dave Ulrich

Dave Ulrich is the Rensis Likert Professor of Business at the Ross School, University of Michigan, and a partner at the RBL Group (www.rbl.net). He has published over 30 books and 200 articles/chapters that have shaped the fields of leadership to deliver results, of organizations to build capabilities, and of human resources to create value where he is the known as the "father of modern HR." He has been named a top management thought leader in Businessweek, Fortune, Financial Times, The Economist, *and* People Management, *and is the recipient of many awards, including a Lifetime Achievement award from ASTD (now ATD). He has consulted and presented in about 90 countries and with over half of the Fortune 200. He has been repeatedly named to the Thinkers50 list of thought leaders and is now in Thinkers50 Hall of Fame.*

■ ■ ■

Decades ago when I took my first OB course, I called my parents and told them I was shifting from studying law to studying OB. They thought I would become a doctor, but then asked, "What is OB?" I could not fully explain, but my psychologist wife realized I had OCD, or *organization* compulsive disorder. I started to observe organizations, from restaurants where we ate to stores where we shopped to athletic teams where I played to churches where I worshipped and so forth.

My organization passion led to a PhD and dozens of major research projects where we have theorized, collected data, analyzed results, and offered advice on organizational practices.

But in the process of studying organizations, I have realized that much of the organizational phenomena I care about are not in spreadsheets or open to statistical analyses. Much of what I learn about organizations comes from careful observation. My experience is confirmed in conversations with Professor Wayne Brockbank,[1] a thought leader in how organizations access and use information. He has reported that only 20% of information is structured and embedded in traditional numbers that are susceptible to spreadsheets and statistics. But 80% of information – that which comes from day-to-day living, experience, and observation – is *unstructured* and not easily quantifiable.

Quantitative data (the 20%) identifies themes and offers empirical insights and should be supplemented with qualitative data (80%), which works with observation, discontinuities, and requires judgment.

Leaders and human resources (HR) professionals who I counsel must recognize and use structured data, and most of them have acquired these skills. The most successful leaders and HR professionals appreciate and rely even more on unstructured data. In Peter Drucker's terms, they look out the window at that which is visible, but not often seen. I call them *organization anthropologists*, who seek ambiguity and are constantly exploring questions that are not yet or not easily answered. What do these leaders do that makes them effective organization anthropologists?

Listen for Things That Seem Counterintuitive

I interviewed a new head of HR who came from outside HR. He discovered that his professionals were superb at managing talent: bringing good people into the organization and moving them through. But he said that the organization was facing major strategic changes and that the real problem was finding the right people for the future and then creating a culture where they did their best. After our discussion, we found that his department's *talent* practices were 70% to 80% up the *S-curve* of effectiveness, but the organization's *culture* practices were only 20% up the curve. This experience (and others) has led me to exploring culture as an organization capability.

We found in our market valuation studies that two firms in the same industry with the same earnings might have up to a 40% difference in market value.[2] At first, this did not make sense, so we explored more and discovered both intangibles and then the leadership capital index.

In both of these cases, I was listening to things that were a bit different and even counterintuitive.

Leaders generally are in positions of influence because of what they know. With their accepted knowledge, they should be very attuned to questions or experiences that challenge them or give them new insights. In one company, a leader recognized that the innovation and culture in emerging markets was much higher than in his home country. He started to create an organization learning model to move knowledge from new to old markets more than in the reverse direction.

Leaders sometimes hide behind titles, offices, and roles. Leaders in organization anthropology spend time outside their comfort zone.

Surround Yourself with People Who See Things Differently

Insecure leaders often surround themselves with people who think like them but may not be quite as good as them. By doing so, they boost their own self-image through knowing more than others and receiving approval for their insights. Effective leaders, on the other hand, spend time with people who are different and who offer new and challenging ideas.

In my career, I have formed partnerships with remarkable colleagues whose ideas complemented mine. I have coauthored all but 2 of the 30-plus books I have written, with the goal of learning from my coauthors. When doing my PhD, I formed a partnership (called *applied quantitative research*) with a statistician colleague who could perform the right data analysis. I learned from Roger Bolus how to access and manipulate data. I continued to learn about finance by working with a finance professor (Ray Reilly) at Michigan who taught me to turn data into managerial insight. I partnered with C.K. Prahalad to think about how to help leaders recognize and shape new business realities. Our 20-year business partnership at the RBL group combines my more abstract thinking with Norm Smallwood's discipline to turn ideas into action.

In consulting, I work at the intersection of HR issues (e.g., talent, leadership, and capability) and marketing to link to customers (*Leadership Brand*[3]and *HR from the Outside In*[4]) and investors (*The Leadership Capital Index*[5]). Effective leaders have both the self-confidence and the curiosity to surround themselves with people who have new ideas and fresh insights. One of my favorite leadership coaching questions is *What do you think?*

Experiment – Be Willing to Fail – Learn

I worked in a company where we developed this mantra: Think Big, Test Small, Fail Fast, Learn Always. This company was constantly innovating products, services, business models, and leadership actions. They found that they (and many other companies) were pretty good at thinking big and testing small. They were not as good at failing fast and learning always. When failure was reconceptualized as opportunity, the company began to increase innovation because people were not hiding from mistakes but sharing and learning from them.

As organization anthropologists, leaders are constantly observing what people do, and then testing if these observations are generalizable. Leader–observers recognize that failure is a great opportunity to learn. Leaders celebrate the lessons of success as much as the lessons of failure. Another favorite leadership probe: *What did you learn from the last experience that you can adapt going forward?*

Leaders who observe see individual actions as a series of experiments. They are *donut-hole* leaders who don't control people by telling them what to do, but are open (hole in the donut) to seeing what others are doing and connecting them with one another. One anthropologist leader who traveled would encourage leaders he met in location A to talk to leaders in location B or C who were facing the same problem. Instead of the leader giving solutions, he encouraged others to connect in order to learn from and share with each other.

Another leader who ran a top management annual meeting started to invite 10 innovative (often high-potential) employees who were not in the meeting by title, but by activity. These innovators were identified by the senior leaders' observations of their new ideas. After one meeting, the top leader decided that, in future meetings, 5 of the 10 invited would have succeeded in their innovation and 5 would have failed, but learned. This leader observed new ideas and propagated those ideas to others through getting people to experience them by attending senior leadership meetings.

Continually Navigate Paradox

In our leadership studies,[6] we find that people seek the holy grail of being an effective leader by attempting to find a single underlying factor that will ensure leadership effectiveness. In recent years, leaders have been encouraged to have emotional intelligence, then learning agility, grit, resilience, growth mindset, and perseverance. In our research, navigating paradox has become the next wave in the evolution of leadership effectiveness.

Paradoxes exist when seemingly contradictory activities operate together. When these inherent contradictions work together, success follows. Instead of focusing on *either/or*, paradoxes emphasize *and/also* thinking.

In my personal work, I have learned to observe, accept, and navigate paradoxes. I see them as representing the guardrails that guide leadership behaviors. Leaders should be both long- and short-term, top-down and bottom-up, directive and engaging, relishing the past and creating the future, global and local, able to zoom out and zoom in, and so forth.

Paradox navigation requires asking questions more than giving answers, as well as not judging on a single dimension, but rather seeing the combination of ideas.

I encourage leaders as observers to identify paradoxes. As soon as they see a new answer, they must recognize and accept the other guardrail, then think about how to navigate between these guardrails. Such leaders know when to converge and focus and when to diverge and encourage variety. By observing an organization's predisposition, a leader can encourage the paradox that leads to innovation and success.

Conclusion

Being an organization anthropologist requires a commitment to learning and letting go of relationships and ideas that don't work. In my teaching work, I find I need to have 20% to 25% new material every two years. This sounds easy, but over the decades is enormously demanding. This requires letting go of ideas I might like and constantly acquiring new stories, creating new tools, and asking new questions. Leaders who constantly unlearn end up learning. My OCD (organization compulsive disorder) has only intensified as I continue to look for things others may not yet see.

Reflection Questions

1. How would you describe the culture of your organization? Do this from the perspective of an anthropologist discovering a completely new and strange *tribe*.
2. How many of your colleagues and the people you lead are different from you? In what ways? Do people who are different challenge or frustrate you?
3. In what areas have you experimented in the past, and what was the outcome? What lessons did you draw from this experience?
4. Identify some paradoxes in your organization and how you navigate them as a leader.

Notes

1. Wayne Brockbank, Dave Ulrich, David G. Kryscynski, and Michael Ulrich, "The Future of HR and Information Capability," *Strategic HR Review* 17, no. 1 (2018), 3–10, https://doi.org/10.1108/SHR-11–2017–0080.
2. Dave Ulrich, *Leadership Capital Index: Realizing the Market Value of Leadership* (San Francisco: Berrett-Kohler Publishers, 2015).
3. Dave Ulrich and Norm Smallwood, *Leadership Brand: Developing Customer-Focused Leaders to Drive Performance and Build Lasting Value* (Cambridge, MA: Harvard Business Review Press, 2007).

4. David Ulrich, *HR from the Outside In: Six Competencies for the Future of Human Resources* (Columbus, OH: McGraw-Hill Education, 2012).

5. David Ulrich, *The Leadership Capital Index: Realizing the Market Value of Leadership* (Oakland, CA: Berrett-Koehler Publishers, 2015).

6. Dave Ulrich, David Kryscynski, Michael Ulrich, and Wayne Brockbank, "Leaders as Paradox Navigators," *Leader to Leader*, September 2017.

4 | Waves

Whitney Johnson

Whitney Johnson brings a strategic eye and long-range vision given her multifaceted professional experience. In addition to great success as a Wall Street investment equity analyst, she cofounded (with Harvard Business School's Clayton Christensen) and managed Rose Park Advisors – Disruptive Innovation Fund. As a classically trained pianist, she has special insight into discipline, practice, and perseverance.

Whitney is an expert on disruptive innovation and personal disruption and specializes in equipping leaders to harness change by implementing the proprietary framework she codified in the critically acclaimed book Disrupt Yourself: Putting the Power of Disruptive Innovation to Work. She's been named a Thinkers50, Leading Business Thinker Globally, and a Finalist for Top Thinker on Talent, 2015. Her guests as host of the Disrupt Yourself Podcast include such luminaries as Patrick Pichette, former CFO of Google, and Garry Ridge, CEO of WD-40.

Whitney coaches C-Suite executives across a variety of industries, and has a deep understanding of how executives can create or destroy value. Her approach to coaching is grounded in the disruptive innovation theory, based on the premise that the individual is the fundamental unit of the disruption. Building on this foundation of personal accountability, she works with executives using the stakeholder-centered coaching approach devised by Marshall Goldsmith: Change must come from within, but it is facilitated by the ecosystem.

■ ■ ■

In my early school years, I learned that the earth has five oceans. I was growing up near the largest of these, the Pacific, which covers more than 30% of the planet; an area greater than the landmass of all the continents combined. The Atlantic is next in size, then the Indian, Southern, and Arctic oceans.

Later, I learned that oceans and seas aren't really the same thing; each ocean encompasses numerous seas – and straits and gulfs and bays. I discovered that tides and currents have a singular impact on weather systems and life generally, the world over.

And later, still, I became aware that all of this water can't really be clearly demarcated this way; the five oceans in all their parts are really one great ocean, rolling continuously over almost three-quarters of the earth's surface, one into the next and then the next.

These days, I see waves.

I live on the other side of the North American continent from where I passed my youth, a solid half-day's drive from the Atlantic coast. In the busy ebb and flow of my work and personal life, I haven't made it to the shore in ages. Nevertheless, I see waves. Every day. Everywhere.

I could be standing in Lebanon, Kansas, the designated geographic center of the United States, and about as far from an ocean as one can be in America, and I would still see waves. Not just "amber waves of grain" either, although those probably riffle and sway in Lebanon, Kansas.

Let me explain:

In 2007, at the Disruptive Innovation Fund that I cofounded with Clayton Christensen, we employed the S-curve model, popularized several decades ago by E.M. Rogers,[1] to inform our investment decision making. This model has traditionally been applied to gauge the rate at which new ideas and innovative products – disruptors – will be embraced and how rapidly they will penetrate cultures and markets. In the beginning, at the base of the S, progress is slow; eventually, a tipping point is reached. Hyper-growth follows: acceleration up the steep back of the curve. At the top, progress slows again as market saturation nears, flattening the top of the S.

I began to realize that this model can also be usefully applied to human disruption, supplying a pattern to understand the unpredictability of human growth, change, and development – in careers, but also across our lifespans and in other realms.

I think of these S-curves as waves – thrilling, challenging opportunities we can successively surf to new learning and competency. I see S-curve waves everywhere and believe we need to catch a new wave, or waves, on a more-or-less regular basis. Brain science strongly suggests that cognitive challenge in the form of new things to learn and problems to solve keeps our brain lubricated with feel-good dopamine, elevating our mood, our sense of well-being, and ultimately, staving off the onset of cognitive decline. We are more productive and remain more actively engaged in our careers and our lives for a longer period of time.

Waves Within Waves Within the Wave

Let's picture it this way: Our lives follow an S-curve. At the low end, we are infants, children, and adolescents. There is an enormous amount of learning to do. At some point in early adulthood, we have hopefully achieved a sufficient level of understanding and competence that we reach the tipping point; what follows are many years of productive work, exploration of personal interests and talents, additional education, family and community building, and valuable contributions – ideally, a lengthy prime spent scaling the exhilarating steep back of our personal wave. Eventually, our progress slows as the top-end plateau is reached; some degree of decline will ultimately follow for most of us.

But as with our planet's single great ocean, composed of the five named oceans and their smaller watery components, this life-cycle S-curve is made up of several distinctive contributing waves. Career is one of these, the one I am most focused on in my coaching, writing, and speaking, but it's not the only one. We may pursue ambitions and objectives on multiple fronts throughout our lives or during discrete stages thereof. Parenting, for example, is a significant personal life wave: for new parents there is a low-end learning challenge, a lot of skills to master. But infants and toddler are soon schoolchildren, presenting a new curve for parents to scale, and then there is the super disruption to the S-curve of adolescence. Anyone who has parented teenagers knows that it requires an almost entirely different skillset than parenting an infant. Then the kids grow up, and defining the relationship with adult children presents a new opportunity, unique from those that have come before. Parenting is a wave composed of smaller successive learning curve waves simultaneously flowing into the overriding wave of our lifespan, which will also include a career wave, hobbies, talents, volunteerism, extended family, and spirituality; there is an ocean of possibilities to explore.

In times past, our career wave may have taken shape with a low-end, entry-level position, perhaps preceded by formal education but in many cases not, followed by a promotion or two, occasionally more. But a career was often spent in a single place, with a single employer performing, for lengthy stretches of time, a single task set. Not so anymore. Successfully managing our careers in today's rapidly changing work environment requires an understanding and acceptance of the value of personal disruption – periodically leaping from peak performance on one wave to catch the low-end of the next – and agility at making these sometimes daunting leaps from confident, expert competence to once again becoming a novice on a new learning curve. Chances are, if we don't disrupt ourselves, choosing our own waves to surf, we will be disrupted at times and in ways we do not prefer – firings, layoffs, feeling left behind by the constant unfolding of new technologies – aimlessly adrift like flotsam on the currents or washed ashore and then abandoned like the ocean wrack on the beach when the tide recedes.

Making the Most of Your Wave

I have articulated seven accelerants of personal disruption that can help us successfully navigate these tricky moves from wave to wave; here is a summary description of these essential touch points:

1. Take the Right Risks
   Evaluate the type of risk your career leap will entail. I advocate seeking market risk, which means you find a wave to surf that isn't already occupied by someone else. When you can create or step into a role (or innovate a new product, service, business, etc.) that meets a presently unmet need, you greatly increase your chances of success. Unlike competitive risk, which requires going head-to-head against established competitors in an already-defined market, being the first surfer on the wave gives you the advantage over all who might challenge you later.

2. Play to Your Distinctive Strengths

   Do you have a super power? I'm not just talking about the things you're good at; I'm focusing on the thing(s) you are uniquely good at, the things that those around you handle less adeptly or even struggle to accomplish. It may be a skill acquired through education/experience, but it is just as likely something you have done well your entire life, something that may even have made you a little weird to your peers during childhood – or presently. Think about a compliment you frequently receive and dismiss, because you take for granted your ability in that area; it comes so naturally to you. Or watch for the things that irritate you in other people; we are prone to annoyance when activities that are quick and easy for us are less nimbly accomplished by others.

3. Embrace Constraints

   Our initial response to the word *constraint* is usually a negative one. A constraint is a limitation of our freedom. But when we start out on the low end of a new S-curve there are inevitably limitations – too little time, money, expertise, buy-in. In fact, unlimited options can be paralyzing, an impairment to good decision making. Constraints help mark the path we need to follow to reach our goals; without them, we can be lost in the weeds without a clear direction. With fewer options available to us, we are forced to be more resourceful and more innovative. We have fewer variables to solve for as we strive toward that all-important tipping point on our wave. We are also able to get rapid feedback on our progress. Quickly discerning what doesn't work aids us in more rapidly discovering what does.

4. Battle Entitlement

   Entitlement is the sneaky saboteur of personal disruption. Entitlement takes the stage in the guise of complacency, the sense that we deserve the privileged position we've attained on the cresting high end of our S-curve wave. Good things should always roll our way. Or, conversely, the bitter attitude that we've been denied the things we were owed. Perhaps we were passed over for promotion or accolade, or credit for our ideas or efforts has been hijacked by another. Entitlement robs us of the energy we need to disrupt ourselves from positions of relative comfort to take on the challenges of a new learning curve. Sometimes, when success has led to the dissolution of resource constraints, we must impose new constraints ourselves in order to make progress. Death by success is a common career and business casualty; combat entitlement to avoid it.

5. Step Back to Grow

An S-curve model of career development is nonlinear; forget what you've always thought about the corporate ladder. Up is not the only way up. Sometimes we may move sideways, backwards, even downward to find ourselves positioned at the high-learning end of a new wave. Think of a slingshot or catapult; it's the pull back that generates the high-energy propulsion forward. To remain engaged in the work we do, we need to be learning new things and confronting significant and demanding problems to solve. To battle entitlement, we have to relinquish our handle on the wave we've mastered and step back into a role that allows us room to grow.

6. Give Failure Its Due

Failure is the great instructor and, thankfully, the death of a dream is not terminal. There is a cosmic abundance of dreams to pursue and contributions to make. When one avenue of endeavor comes to a dead end, successful disruptors will pocket what they've learned and carry on to greater achievement on the next wave. I love the example of professional golfer, Jordan Spieth. Going into the final round of the 2016 Masters Golf Tournament, he was in the lead. He'd won the event in 2015 and had outstanding performances throughout that year. Victory was within his grasp for a second straight year, but Spieth faltered. By the time he recovered, it was too late.

A few days after the event his caddie, Michael Greller, made a memorable post to Facebook: "There have been tough losses and will be more. We won't get stuck in this moment, nor should you. We will work harder, fight harder and be better for it. We will bounce back as we have done many times. A wise coach reminded me recently, winning shows your character and losing shows ALL your character." Bravo, failure.

7. Be Discovery-Driven

When we first decide to surf a wave, we often don't know how it will develop. Flexibility is a key virtue of successful disruptors. Most of the celebrated explorers of the globe were not prepared to meet the challenges that arose on their journeys. They required tremendous levels of improvisation, adaptation, and resourcefulness. They learned as they went and what they learned was often a product of failure. Personal disruption requires the same willingness to launch ourselves into the unknown and discover our wave as we ride it, innovating as circumstances present themselves.

Catch the Wave Before It Catches You

In the early summer of 2017, I read this letter printed in the nationally syndicated advice column *Dear Abby*:

> Life has me worn out. I have accomplished more than I ever thought I could (considering my upbringing), traveled as much as I wanted, always strived to be a good husband and father, a good employer, a loyal volunteer, a supportive friend and good neighbor. I have done so many different things during my life that at this point, the thrill is gone.
>
> At 56, I am tired of working, tired of travel, bored with my hobbies, and sick of dealing with most people in general. I'm relaxed and laugh easily and have good relationships, but nothing excites me anymore. Honestly, if the Grim Reaper tapped me on the shoulder and said, "Pack your bags; tomorrow's the day," I'd just shrug and ask, "What time?"
>
> I went to a couple of therapists who told me I don't need therapy; I just need to find a new "spark." So what's a person to do? Must I keep wallowing through the days waiting for the end? Am I the only person who feels this way?[2]

He is not the only person who feels this way; people at many stages of life encounter S-curve plateaus and waning, even crashing, enthusiasm. Ultimately, in old age and/or when confronted with a serious health challenge, decline is a natural part of the S-curve of life, but at age 56? I agree with the therapist calling for a new spark. This gentleman and many like him who find themselves midlife, later career, and experiencing the gentle outgoing tide as the roller-coaster waves of daily parenting play themselves out, require new sparks – new S-curve waves to surf, to remain fresh, engaged, and relevant, living a vibrant, contributing life for the decades yet ahead. There's a reason we have developed terminologies like *midlife crisis* and *empty-nest syndrome*. I see these relatively common and similar pitfalls as manifestations of S-curve high-end full competence yielding to boredom as challenge declines and complacency encroaches.

Disrupting ourselves proactively, before stagnation takes hold, is usually easier, but we can always, with a little effort and imagination, move from stuck to unstuck through personal disruption at any stage, early or late. One of my favorite data points is this one provided by the Sports Performance Research Institute New Zealand (SPRINZ):[3] competitive surfers spend, on average, 8% of their time riding waves, 54% paddling, and 28% waiting (the remaining 10% is variable). Hopefully, our career ratio of S-curve wave surfing to treading water will be a little higher, but we would never suggest that the less-thrilling episodes of pausing, preparing, and positioning ourselves, or the inevitable waiting and wipeouts, aren't integral to ultimately catching the perfect waves.

Conclusion

I had the privilege of interviewing Bernie Swain, founder of the iconic American lecture agency, Washington Speakers Bureau, which has represented multiple American presidents and British prime ministers as well as luminaries from business, entertainment, sports, and so on. Bernie is also the bestselling memoirist of *What Made Me Who I Am*.[4] In our conversation, he suggested, "Wouldn't you like to discover, early in your life, what made you who you are? Who are you? Rather than looking back on it, and looking at a life well-spent, looking at it early and creating a life that's well-lived."[5] I advocate this approach to consciously and strategically visualizing and positioning ourselves via personal disruption to catch the S-curve waves that will carry us to the places of experience we want to visit, in our careers and otherwise. Ideally, the S-curve of life will be, on inspection and introspection, waves within waves within waves. Within *the* wave.

Reflection Questions

1. Draw an S-curve of your own life. What appears at the highest and lowest points?
2. Do you notice any intersection between high and low points on this curve in your personal versus your professional lives? How do you see the influence of one realm on the other?
3. Is it possible to change the course of an S-curve wave in one's own life? What factors make this harder or easier?

Notes

1. E.M. Rogers, *Diffusion of Innovations* (New York: Free Press of Glencoe, 1962; 5th ed., 2003); S-curve model, https://en.wikipedia.org/wiki/ Diffusion_of_innovations, accessed March 1, 2018.
2. *DailyJournalOnline*, http://dailyjournalonline.com/news/opinion/ advice/dear-abby/dear-abby/article_b43e2b41–3c64–5887-b6eb- d453f0531b5b.html.
3. Surfertoday.com, https://www.surfertoday.com/surfing/7653-surfers- only-spend-8-of-the-time-riding-waves.
4. Bernie Swain, *What Made Me Who I Am* (Brentwood, TN: Savio Republic/ Post Hill Press, 2016).
5. Whitney Johnson podcast interview with Bernie Swain, December 2016, https://whitneyjohnson.com/bernie-swain-disrupt-yourself/.

5 | Being a Good Leader

Patrick Lencioni

Patrick is the founder of The Table Group and the author of 11 books, which have sold over five million copies and been translated into more than 30 languages. The Wall Street Journal called him "one of the most in-demand speakers in America." He has addressed millions of people at conferences and events around the world over the past 15 years. Pat has written for or been featured in numerous publications including Harvard Business Review, Inc., Fortune, Fast Company, USA Today, The Wall Street Journal, *and* BusinessWeek.

As CEO, Pat spends his time writing books and articles related to leadership and organizational health, speaking to audiences interested in those topics, and consulting to CEOs and their teams.

Prior to founding The Table Group, Pat worked at Bain & Company, Oracle Corporation, and Sybase. Pat lives in the Bay Area with his wife and four boys.

■ ■ ■

Perhaps, the best lesson about leadership that I've learned during my career is one that I've only recently come to understand.

I should have learned it as a teenager the first time I flew on an airplane, because flight attendants repeat it time after time: "In the event of a drop in pressure, put your oxygen mask on before assisting another passenger with theirs." Essentially, the lesson I learned is that I can't be a better leader than I am a person, and that I can't put off working on myself in order to help others. That sounds pretty obvious, I know, but it deserves some explanation.

Early in my career, I wanted to be a good leader. It was an important priority for me, which sounds like a good thing. But I also wanted to be known as a good leader and manager, and that was the problem. `

I was intentional in how I cared for my employees, and I did good things for them. I took an interest in them, their families, and their careers. I sacrificed for them often, putting their needs above my own. I championed them and encouraged them to become more than they thought they could become. And I celebrated them.

But deep, *deep* down inside I measured my success and worth as a leader by what I believed my people thought of me. Though I didn't understand or admit it at the time, being a good leader wasn't really as much about them as it was about my own identity and self-worth.

Some might be tempted to accuse me of being overly scrupulous in my self-analysis. They might say, "What is the harm in this, as long as the people you were leading were getting what they needed?" I contend that the harm was subtle, but very dangerous; it threatened my own peace of mind, as well as the sustainability of any goodness my employees were receiving from me.

See, when things went well, I felt a sense of satisfaction. But it never lasted long. I was always thinking about what else I needed to accomplish, and how I could continue to prove my prowess as a leader and a professional. At the end of the day, I would find myself feeling a little empty.

When things went poorly, I found myself disproportionately upset. Why? Was it because my employees were impacted by something gone wrong? As much as I wanted to think so, looking back, I know it was because my world was not right. My identity was at risk.

It was only as I grew older, and started to understand the true definition of humility, that I understood how to improve. Until I separated my identity as a professional from my definition as a person, I could not be a truly good leader. So I began to go deeper in my faith in God, then in my roles as a husband and a father and a son and a friend. It wasn't that I was indifferent to these things before. In fact, I was extremely involved in my home life. It was my identity that I struggled with and that I needed to get right.

I wish I could say that all this happened in my early thirties and that I've been living this way for the past 20 years, but it wasn't until my mid-forties that I fully made this critical realization. I can tell you that the people who have worked with me both before and after I made this realization saw a big change in me. I'm far from perfect now. Still learning lessons. But I'm definitely less stressed. Less invested in work. More thoughtful. More measured. And much more effective as a mentor, strategist, and manager.

My message to those who are reading this book in order to become better leaders is simple. *Be a whole person first.* Get your priorities in order. Know that neither your job nor your leadership defines you. Ask yourself if it might be better to set this book down to invest in your faith, your marriage, or your parenting. If you do, you'll come back better able to digest and apply the principles of leadership for the right reasons, and with better prospects for long-term success.

Reflection Questions

1. What do you consider the qualities of a good leader to be?
2. How do you evaluate yourself as a leader? How much do you rely on the opinions of others in making this judgment?
3. How much is your personal sense of identity linked to your perception of yourself as a leader? What other roles do you have that provide you with a sense of identity? How hard is it to separate your identity from your roles?

6

Scaling Your Impact as a Leader

Taavo Godtfredsen

Taavo Godtfredsen is an executive coach, speaker, and is currently an advisor to the Marshall Goldsmith 100 Coaches organization.

Taavo has spent more than 20 years in the leadership development field as a successful business leader and practitioner. He has traveled the world interviewing and collaborating with hundreds of the most recognized CEOs, best-selling business authors, and top business school faculty. With both a breadth of experience and depth of knowledge in the leadership development field, Taavo has remained on the cutting edge continuously working with executives as they adapt to a changing business environment. As a pragmatist, Taavo's methodology zeroes in on the most innovative and time efficient leadership actions that yield the greatest impact.

Taavo was the originator of Five@5:00™ and co-created the Leadership Development Channel™. Taavo began his career at Linkage Inc., and held various senior roles leading both functions and business units. He later helped to grow Targeted Learning Corporation, a private company sold to Skillsoft Corporation. Taavo is the chair and founder of the CEO Advisory Group, a private equity only CEO group; a certified and experienced executive coach; and holds an MBA from Babson College.

■ ■ ■

There are three things extremely hard: steel, a diamond, and to know one's self.
                                                    —Benjamin Franklin

What I have come to learn from working with hundreds of executives is that your success as a leader is not based on your intentions, as most leaders want the very best for their people and organization. Rather, your success is based on your *impact*. When there is a misalignment between your intentions and your actions, you can be operating at a fraction of your capability as a leader. This is the single greatest leadership challenge I see today – the lack of awareness in leaders of the gap between how they *intend* to lead and how they *actually* lead.

Let me put a face to this astounding leadership challenge. The example below involves a coaching client from a Fortune 100 company.

I will never forget coaching Adam. He was an incredibly successful senior leader working for a major global industrial organization who was viewed by senior leadership as *hitting it* [the numbers] *out of the park*. Adam was leading a high-growth business and his executive team brought me in to help him accelerate the revenue of the business. In parallel, they wanted me to support his advancement to the executive level and work with him on how to avoid burnout. They saw a looming cliff on the horizon if Adam didn't change course. He was going too hard and too fast and his people couldn't keep up.

In getting to know Adam, it appeared he simply didn't have an *off* button. He was your classic *drive-for-results* type of leader. He was bright, competent, and dedicated. Early in the coaching process, I asked him a question (which I will be coming back to later): "How do you want your people *feeling* as a result of your leadership?" I thought he would stew on this for a bit, but without any hesitation and with a voice of conviction two words popped out: "passionate and energized." Right then I knew Adam had a long road ahead because I had already interviewed his direct reports, manager, members of the senior team, and close colleagues. As one of his direct reports shared with me, "He sees himself one way and the reality is different. He is not being perceived as the person he thinks he is."

In fact, people who worked for Adam felt the exact opposite of how he wanted them to feel: "exhausted," "underappreciated," and even "used." Fighting back tears, one of Adam's direct reports told me, "He has taken years off my life." I don't know about you, but there isn't a leader I have met who would want to be having this type of impact on his people.

The leadership practices Adam had been employing simply did not align with his intentions for leading a high-growth business. Just imagine the impact Adam could have on the organization and his team's performance if his leadership had been in the same ballpark as his intellect and intent. He was already highly successful despite the chasm between how he intended to lead and how he actually led.

What do you think are the primary reasons we, especially senior leaders, can be out of step with our intentions?

There are a few primary reasons. One of them (and this was true of Adam) is that we don't create a safe space for people to provide us with feedback on how we show up as leaders.

A second reason, and I am going to quote my friend Dr. Peter Fuda,[1] is that "We judge ourselves by our intentions and everyone else by their actions." You see, we have high standards for everyone around us, but we don't always hold ourselves to the same high standards. Meanwhile, because you are a leader, everyone is judging you by your behavior – watching your every move – and they will look to see if you hold yourself to the same standards to which you hold everyone else. It isn't just what you say or how you say it that affects people; it is also your body language and what you do. There is a massive echo effect in the organization based on how others perceive you.

A third reason can be attributed to the power we hold in an organization. The research has found that the more power you have – the weight your title carries – the more likely you are to be blind to your shortcomings as a leader. In fact, studies show that people in positions of authority in organizations are three times more likely to interrupt coworkers and to raise their voices. Most of us have seen examples of this type of behavior from senior leaders. A classic example of this power effect is when the most senior person in a meeting is looking at his or her phone and checking email or text while others are speaking. This individual would be appalled if others were doing it when he or she was speaking but think nothing of doing it him- or herself. To combat this, leaders must learn to control their mindset. One quick tip on how to limit this power effect when you are meeting with your team or others is to imagine that you are on the same level with everyone else in the room, that you are peers or colleagues. In other words, think and behave as if you are equals.

A fourth cause of our intent being out of step with our impact is our own perception of ourselves. Self-perception can be just that – perception and not reality. Studies show that too many of us, especially those of us from Western cultures, believe that we are better at things than we really are. It is why 88% of US drivers and 77% of Swedish drivers put themselves in the top 50% driving ability for safety. My personal favorite is that 95% of the faculty at a major US university considered themselves above average in teaching ability and 68% placed their teaching abilities in the top 25%.

Tasha Eurich, an organizational psychologist and author,[2] conducted a three-year study on self-awareness and found that 95% of people think they're self-aware, but in reality only 10% to 15% really are. She identifies seven different categories of self-knowledge that we must develop if we want to increase our self-awareness. These include: values, passions, aspirations, fit (situation/setting that is most enriching to us), personality, strengths and weaknesses, and the impact we have on others around us. All of these elements are critical for leaders to understand deeply about themselves, particularly in regard to the impact they can have on others.

Let's go back to the feeling question I asked Adam. Is the way a leader makes others *feel* really that important? Irwin Federman, a venture capitalist and the former president of Monolithic Memories, certainly believes so. As he put it to Jim Kouzes, author of *The Leadership Challenge*,[3] "Conventional wisdom has it that management is not a popularity contest.... I contend, however, that all things being equal, we will work harder and more effectively for people we like. And we will like them in direct proportion to how they make us feel."[4]

Just think back to managers you have had in the past: How much discretionary effort did you give to the one you admired the most? The least? Liz Wiseman,[5] a top authority on effective leadership, calls these types of bosses (respectively) either *multipliers* or *diminishers*. As she found in her research, diminishers get approximately 48% of the capability out of their people while multipliers get 95%. Close to a 50% difference! What percentage of capability do you think Adam was getting from his people? Just imagine him increasing the capability of his people by even 10% or 20% and what could be accomplished. And this is what he did.

Adam did not go over the cliff and was able to grow the business while avoiding burnout. The turning point to his success was his proactive and courageous step of asking for and acting on the feedback from his team, manager, and colleagues. The feedback was not easy to digest. It was so tough, in fact, that he contemplated walking out of the building because he was so shocked at the gap between how he saw himself and how others experienced him. He finally had a lens into how poorly he treated others. He learned that he needed to empower and recognize his team members in a fundamentally different way if he was to continue to successfully scale the business. Eventually, Adam received the promotion he hoped for and his division had a record sales year. His people slowly began to feel differently as they started to believe and trust in the changes he was making. They felt appreciated and could bring more of themselves to their work. They didn't view Adam's changes as superficial or inauthentic. Quite the opposite. They saw who Adam really was.

Action Steps

My goal for you, as it was for Adam, is to create a bridge to help you reach your deepest leadership aspirations. So, let me shift now to the *how* of scaling your impact as a leader. I am going to provide you with two very simple techniques that you can complete over the next 30 days. The first and most important is an action you will implement on your own to assess the size of the gap (if any) between your intentions and actions. Ultimately, your goal is to get yourself into alignment.

The second action is a fantastic team exercise you will lead to learn if everyone is clear on the most critical goal(s), top priorities, and metrics for success. This exercise will provide you with additional feedback on whether or not you have been communicating what you think you have been communicating. Teams that are not on the same page can experience a debilitating level of frustration, conflict, and wasted effort. The objective here is to understand whether your team is in alignment and make sure you get them there if they are not. Too many leaders believe that they have adequately communicated their goals and priorities and therefore assume that all their people are working under the same assumptions and that there is no confusion. This is rarely the case, from my experience.

As you will discover, the two actions outlined below will take relatively little time, are scalable, and connect to two critical areas of leadership success – continuous improvement and clarity of goals. As for the scalable part, the actions you take will have a compounding effect because you will be modeling what you expect your team members to do with their teams, allowing the high-impact leadership practices you employ to be magnified throughout the organization.

Your First Action

In order to improve and/or adapt, you have to know how you are doing. You need the data. I am going to teach you how to get it by conducting your own assessment, which can reveal how aligned your intentions are with your actions.

1. Send an e-mail letting your direct reports, selected colleagues, and manager know that you will be asking them to evaluate you as a leader and offering suggestions on what you can do moving forward to improve.
2. Follow up directly with all those from whom you have requested feedback, and do what I have learned from Marshall Goldsmith, the world's #1 executive coach:

   - Make them feel comfortable about providing you with honest and concrete suggestions.
   - Only say "Thank you" to their suggestions—do not try to evaluate or comment on any of their ideas.
   - If you are already clear on a couple of areas you will focus on, ask them for their ideas on how you can improve in those areas. Encourage them to make suggestions that are observable and actionable.
   - Follow up with them every four to six weeks to see how you are improving in those areas. Continue to ask for their ideas.

At this point, as many do, you may be feeling quite hesitant. This can be an awkward and uncomfortable exercise for all involved. It can be hard to both ask for and give feedback, but the benefits can be numerous and profound.

Your Second Action

One of the most important roles of a leader is to make sure everyone is clear on both your key goals and priorities. When teams are not clear (aligned), it can create a tremendous amount of wasted effort and conflict. I am going to teach you a simple team exercise I call "Testing Team Clarity."

In either a face-to-face team meeting (using note cards) or virtually (via e-mail), ask your team members to write their responses anonymously to the questions below:

1. What is our most important goal (this year)?
2. What do you believe are our top three priorities?
3. What are the top two or three metrics that matter most to measure our progress/success?

Once completed, pass the note cards to a volunteer who will read out the responses to the group. If done virtually, the volunteer can e-mail the aggregate responses. Ask the team (and yourself!) the following:

1. What is your reaction to what you heard from your fellow team members? Did anything surprise you?
2. Do we have the right goals and priorities? If not, what should they be?
3. Is there something we aren't measuring that we should be?

Summary

The two actions I outlined above are a small subset of the more comprehensive program in leadership development that I employ. While simple, these are a great place to start in targeting two critical leadership challenges we face: (1) fostering and modeling continuous improvement, and (2) providing clarity of goals, priorities, and metrics for success. Addressing these two challenges will provide important enlightenment and will begin to close the gap between your leadership *intent* and your actual *impact*.

Typically, after a leader has worked through these two exercises, he or she has learned more than enough to begin making the important changes necessary to achieve greater impact and success – as an individual leader, for their team, and for their organization as a whole. These changes aren't always easy. Some may be as simple as improving your communication by providing your team with more regular updates. Others could involve a much more difficult change in behavior or way of thinking, such as controlling your anger. You may even breathe a sigh of relief as one leader did when she learned that only 2 out of her 10 direct reports was in alignment with her in identifying critical goals and top priorities through the Testing Team Clarity exercise. The truth enabled her to adapt quickly to get each team member pointed in the right direction. Whatever the outcome of the exercises above, you are modeling the way forward for your team, and as a result, scaling your impact as a leader.

Reflection Questions

1. What are your most pressing leadership challenges? Do you share these with other leaders? With your team?

2. How comfortable are you in reaching out to members of your team for feedback on your leadership? What would you do with their feedback?

3. How do you set and clarify goals with teams that you lead? What measures do you use to determine how well you are meeting these goals? In light of your performance in meeting goals, do you ever revisit or reevaluate them? How do you determine if it's time to abandon some goals and set new ones?

4. How would you honestly evaluate the correspondence between your intentions and your actions? Is the correspondence different between your personal and professional lives? Why might this be?

Notes

1. Peter Fuda, www.peterfuda.com, founder and principal of The Alignment Partnership (TAP), also an adjunct professor of management at the MGSM.

2. Tasha Eurich, *Insight: Why We're Not as Self-Aware as We Think, and How Seeing Ourselves Clearly Helps Us Succeed at Work and in Life* (New York: Crown Business, 2017).

3. Jim Kouzes and Barry Z. Posner, *A Leader's Legacy* (San Francisco: Jossey-Bass, 2006).

4. Irwin Federman, *Multipliers: How the Best Leaders Make Everyone Smarter,* revised and updated ed. (New York: Harper Business, 2017).

5. Liz Wiseman, *Rookie Smarts: Why Learning Beats Knowing in the New Game of Work* (New York: Harper Business, 2004).

7

In Search of Obsession

Susan Scott

Susan Scott is the CEO and Founder of Fierce Inc., and the author of Fierce Conversations: Achieving Success at Work & in Life – One Conversation at a Time *and* Fierce Leadership: A Bold Alternative to the Worst "Best" Practices of Business Today.

Known for her bold yet practical approach to executive coaching and leadership development, Susan Scott has been challenging people to say the things that are hard to say for over two decades. Susan founded Fierce in 2001 after 13 years leading CEO think tanks, more than 10,000 hours of conversations with senior executives, and one epiphany: While no single conversation is guaranteed to change the trajectory of a career, a business, a marriage, or a life – any single conversation can. Susan continues to share her expertise with clients through her keynote presentations, bestselling books, and her company, Fierce, Inc.

■ ■ ■

Eighteen years ago, as I read Hemingway's *The Sun Also Rises* beside a crackling fire, snoring dogs at my feet, I became obsessed with an idea. The implications hinted at my *raison d'etre*. Obsession with a second idea a few months later kicked the first into motion and brought me to where

I am today. More about the ideas in a bit. First, let's talk about obsession. Dictionaries would have you believe that obsession is a problem akin to stalking:

> "A persistent disturbing preoccupation with an often-unreasonable idea or feeling"
>
> "Compulsive preoccupation with an idea or an unwanted feeling or emotion, often accompanied by symptoms of anxiety"

I prefer this definition:

"Something or someone that you think about all the time."

My obsession wasn't unwanted or unreasonable and created no anxiety in me; rather it inspired a compulsion to share it with others. To do that on a large scale required people who were, if not obsessed, at least as taken with the ideas as I was. A tribe, a company. Of course, I had to figure out if there were people – individuals, organizations – who saw the implications of my ideas and wanted what I wanted enough to pay for it. But it was my obsession that provided the emotional and intellectual velocity required to make it so, because I knew that the success I hoped for would not be handed to me by an investor or a partner. It was something I had to find and nurture on my own.

Most companies were launched by an idea – Amazon, Google, Facebook, GoPro, WhatsApp, HomeAdviser, Airbnb, GoFundMe, Uber, Miracle Mop, Stitch Fix. All of their founders had a desire they imagined others shared, and their obsessions fueled the energy to build a company, which is no walk in the park. You gotta really want it and love it, and your idea must have a clear and compelling *why* behind it. In fact, without that *why* and your obsession about it, it's possible to spin your wheels and considerable bucks on the *what* and *how* and end up frustrated and possibly broke, which explains why so many ideas never get off the ground.

The ideas that led me to found Fierce, Inc., were like kaleidoscopic pieces that, when they shifted, changed my view of the world, of myself in the world, and therefore, what was required of me. They were the *whys* with which I remain obsessed.

Idea #1

In *The Sun Also Rises,* a character is asked, "How did you go bankrupt?" He responds, "Two ways. Gradually, and then suddenly." At the time I read this, I had been running think tanks for chief executives for 13 years and had had more than 10,000 hours of conversations with industry leaders worldwide. I thought back over important events in the lives of my clients. A piece within my internal kaleidoscope dropped.

Our careers, our companies, our relationships, and indeed our very lives succeed or fail, gradually and then suddenly, one conversation at a time.

On the failing side, sometimes the questions were: How did we manage to lose our biggest customer – the one that counted for 20 percent of our net profit? How did I lose my most valued employee, for whom I had great plans? How did I lose the cohesiveness of my team? Why are we experiencing turnover, turf wars, rumors, departments not cooperating with one another, unengaged employees, long overdue reports and projects, strategic plans that still aren't off the ground, and lots of very good reasons and excuses why things can't be any different or better?

And on a personal note: How did I lose an 18-year marriage that I was not prepared to lose? How did I lose my job? How is it that I find myself in a company, a role, a relationship, a life from which I've absented my spirit? How did I lose my way? How did I get *here?*

Once the members of my CEO groups reflected on the path that led them to a disappointing or difficult point or place in time, they remembered, often in vivid detail, the conversations that set things in motion, ensuring that they would end up exactly where they found themselves. They lost that customer, that employee, the cohesiveness of their team, their marriage, their joy – one failed or one missing conversation at a time.

On the positive side, *here* was a pretty amazing place when a company finally landed that huge customer, the one their competition would kill for. Or successfully recruited a valuable new employee. Or a leader discovered that her team was committed to her at a deep level. Or a team blew their goals out of the water. And personally, celebrating another happy year of marriage.

My CEOs got to these good places in their lives, these amazing achievements, these satisfying career paths, these terrific relationships, gradually, then suddenly, one *successful* conversation at a time. And they were determined to ensure the quality of their ongoing conversations with the people central to their success and happiness.

Imagine you are standing on a game board – the game of life. *Your* life. How did you arrive at this square on the board, with all of your current results – professional and personal – spread out in front of you, some you like and some you don't? You arrived here one conversation at a time. And when you project yourself into an ideal future, how will you get from here to there? Same way you got here. One conversation at a time.

Idea #2

Shortly after the gift of Hemingway, I heard Yorkshire-born poet and author, David Whyte, speak at a conference about a young man, newly married, who is often frustrated, even a little irritated, that his lovely spouse, to whom he has pledged his troth and with whom he hopes to spend the rest of his life, wants to talk – yet again – about the same topic they just talked about last night, and last weekend. The topic? The quality of their relationship. He wonders, "Why are we talking about this again? I thought we settled this. Could we just have one huge conversation about our relationship and then coast for a year or two?" Apparently not, because here she is again.

Around age 42, if he's been paying attention, David suggested, it dawns on him. *David smiled. He was 42 and married.* "This ongoing conversation I have been having with my wife is not about the relationship. The conversation *is* the relationship."

The conversation is the relationship.

To say this landed with me would be an understatement. The idea was simple, even obvious, but I had missed the formula. Conversation = relationship.

As the idea dropped, my internal kaleidoscope shifted. I had just left a long-term marriage and was deeply sad. I felt David was talking just to me and learned later that all 400 people in the room felt the same way. We all had a strong desire to run out into the parking lot and phone home.

If you recognize that there may be something to this, that the conversation is the relationship, then you must know that if the conversation stops, all of the possibilities for the relationship become smaller. All of the possibilities for the individuals in the relationship become smaller as well, until one day we overhear ourselves in midsentence, making ourselves quite small, behaving as if we're just the space around our shoes, engaged in yet another three-minute conversation so empty of meaning it crackles.

For me, this is a seriously big deal. Our most valuable currency is not money, nor intelligence, attractiveness, fluency in three-letter acronyms, the ability to write code, or analyze a P&O statement. Our so-called pedigree doesn't get us as far as we might hope. Our most valuable currency is relationship, emotional capital, without which we have nothing, and accomplish nothing. Superficial relationships – the "How are you? I'm fine" variety – are not gonna cut it. It is the depth of our relationships that determines the meaning of our lives, and the depth of our relationships is created gradually, then suddenly, one conversation at a time. Each conversation we have, each phone call, each email or text enriches a relationship, flatlines it, or takes it down. In other words, we are building relationships that thrill or disappoint us one conversation at a time. I founded Fierce, Inc., due to my obsession with these two ideas, having become hyper-tuned to how conversations profoundly impact our lives. In this world of asynchronous communication, where we are face down in our screens trying not to be distracted by what's happening around us, it seems that when we speak, we skim along the surface of a topic and/or withhold what we're really thinking and feeling, so that we say nothing of interest, really. And we say it over and over. Even when we recognize our prejudices as prejudices, we continue to feud. Consequently, nothing of value emerges and today is a lot like yesterday.

Sad to say, most people mistake talking for conversation. The usual chitchat doesn't get us much. A cacophony of voices attempting to peddle self-serving agendas does not advance us. We want to be ourselves, to be heard, yet growth is the process of extending our views, seeking to understand the views of others, and abandoning views that no longer serve us, so we can embrace the possibilities no single person—except a few great minds such as Einstein—could have grasped. I am not an Einstein. I need input and if you've got a clear and compelling case, I'm not that hard to persuade, especially if you're obsessed with your idea.

I am always interested to know if people have something in their lives they love beyond all reason. A person, a place, a product, an activity — cooking, painting, hiking, traveling. Or an idea. The problem is that our ideas, our obsessions, are often degraded by our rational minds. We talk ourselves out of our ideas, which leaves the field open for others to capitalize on them. Don't let this happen to you. And don't listen to naysayers. A relative, who supposedly had my best interests at heart, advised me not to write a book, as no one would publish it. A business colleague suggested I would never join the C-Suite because I wanted it too much. Wrong and wrong. Ha! If you're obsessed with an idea, if you have a passion for something that has been calling to you all of your life, if you hunger for something different, something more, then obey your instincts and do something about it. Otherwise, you are starving a little every day.

Where to begin? A fierce conversation with yourself. *Where am I going? Why am I going there? Who is going with me? How will I get there?*

Reflection Questions

1. What thought or idea has been your most frequent companion?
2. Is there a compelling *why* connected to your idea?
3. If someone else has created a business around your idea, is there a missing piece? Is there room to improve and enhance such a business? Or room to implement your idea and improve things right where you are?
4. What are you waiting for?

PART

II

To Serve Is to Live

"You and I do not retire. You and I are called to serve, and we will serve until the pine box lid is closed upon us." This quote from Frances Hesselbein is about being dedicated to our purpose. For those of us who serve, we embrace a life and attitude of being of service that goes beyond our current condition or place of employment. As Frances would say, *We are called to serve.*

In this section of our book, our contributors explore their calls to service, what they are, how they heard the call, and what it means to heed the call. We begin with Jim Yong Kim, 12th president of the World Bank, who describes his leadership journey, on which he often reminds himself and others, "No matter how holy you think your mission might be, it does not make you immune from bad leadership." Margaret Heffernan recounts her painful decision as a CEO to request that her CFO shut down their company rather than allow it to suffer and die a "death from a thousand cuts" during the dot.com bust and 2008–2009 economic recession. In describing the surprisingly positive outcomes of her decision, she demonstrates the importance of honesty and integrity for leaders. Eric Schurenberg offers historical lessons about leadership from George Washington as he led his troops in the battle for American independence during the Revolutionary War. He outlines ways that contemporary leaders can similarly motivate and inspire others. Mark C. Thompson reflects on some critical lessons that he learned about leadership from these two inspirational men, particularly about the importance of having a mission, learning from failure, admitting that you don't know all the answers, not succumbing to distractions, and letting go of perfectionism. Stephanie Pace Marshall recounts lessons learned among the Pitjantjatjara Aborigines of Australia to demonstrate the critical importance of story, map, and landscape to any organization. She discusses implications for leadership and suggests ways to enhance your role as a storyteller and mapmaker in your organization. Mel Spiese draws on his personal experiences as a proud United States Marine to disavow the notion that his organization has any problem with "workplace disengagement" among contemporary recruits who are Millennials and members of Generation Z. He identifies characteristics of this new demographic of Marines that make them particularly prone to success in the Corps—or in any other organization or workplace. And wrapping up this section is Jack Zenger, who cites an incredibly painful personal experience – his son's death from a rare form of cancer – to reveal the importance of honesty and integrity for leaders. He also identifies five behavioral indices that correlate with these key leadership skills.

8

A Call to Create Positive Change on a Global Scale

Jim Yong Kim

Jim Yong Kim, MD, PhD, is the 12th president of the World Bank Group. Soon after he assumed his position in July 2012, the organization established two goals to guide its work: to end extreme poverty by 2030; and to boost shared prosperity, focusing on the bottom 40% of the population in developing countries. In September 2016, the World Bank Group Board unanimously reappointed Kim to a second five-year term as president.

Kim's career has revolved around health, education, and improving the lives of the poor. Before joining the World Bank Group, Kim, a physician and anthro-pologist, served as the president of Dartmouth College and held professorships at Harvard Medical School and the Harvard School of Public Health. From 2003 to 2005, as director of the World Health Organization's HIV/AIDS department, he led the "3 by 5" initiative, the first-ever global goal for AIDS treatment, which

December 2, 2017, Marshall Goldsmith interview with president of the World Bank Group, Jim Yong Kim, for the WBECS 2017 Online Summit. To view the full interview, go to https://www.youtube.com/watch?time_continue=7&v=FzIX4hqpMS8. Interview edited for *Work Is Love Made Visible* by Sarah McArthur.

helped to greatly expand access to antiretroviral medication in developing countries. In 1987, Kim cofounded Partners in Health, a nonprofit medical organization that now works in poor communities on four continents.

Kim has received a MacArthur "Genius" Fellowship, was recognized as one of America's "25 Best Leaders" by U.S. News & World Report, *and was named one of* TIME *magazine's "100 Most Influential People in the World." Kim was named the world's 50th most powerful person by* Forbes *magazine's List of The World's Most Powerful People in 2013.*

■ ■ ■

At the time of this writing, Jim Yong Kim is serving as the 12th president of the World Bank Group. Trained as a physician and anthropologist, he was born in 1959, in The Republic of Korea at a time when it was one of the poorest countries in the world. To Kim, the great irony of this is that when he was born, the World Bank refused to give loans to Korea because it thought Korea would never be able to pay back even the lowest interest loans. It wasn't until Kim was about four years old that Korea got its first loan from the World Bank Group.

Most of Kim's life was spent in some of the poorest countries and communities in the world: Haiti, Peru, Mexico, and many countries in Africa. As cofounder of Partners in Health, a nonprofit medical organization that now works in poor communities on four continents, and as director of the World Health Organization's HIV/AIDS department, Kim's focus was on providing health and education for the poorest countries – and doing so in a way that made a point. The point being that it was the responsibility of physicians, anthropologists, and academics, and in a broader sense, all human beings, to think about the lives of the poorest people and ask, "What should we do? What has to be done next to make a real difference?" One day Kim answered his own question – what has to be done next? – and decided that he needed to try to lead organizations and others to have greater impact. This is when Kim began to focus on *to serve is to lead*, a slight twist on Frances Hesselbein's famous servant leadership quote.

Kim's leadership path accelerated at Dartmouth College, where he was president for three years. It was at Dartmouth that Kim began working with executive coach Marshall Goldsmith, who he says, completely changed his life, not only in the way he thought about leadership, but also in how he could apply the lessons he learned in coaching to large organizations.

For instance, at the World Bank, Kim was confronted with a suspicion of leadership training, especially among the PhD economists. "Academics tend to have a deep suspicion about leadership," says Kim. He had come across this attitude already at Dartmouth. "When I was at Dartmouth, talking about the importance of leadership for our students, one of the professors told me, 'You know we hate leadership.' 'What do you mean you hate leadership?' I asked. 'Leadership suggests followership,' she said."

They had a point in that scholars are supposed to teach young people not to blindly follow others but to think for themselves, which can be good and bad. Good in the sense that students learn to question authority and the status quo, which supports societal growth and positive change. But in the realm of leadership, it can be bad in that people assume that they shouldn't ask for help, that they need to figure *it* out for themselves, even when they are stagnating in their own careers and damaging their people, teams, and organizations with poor leadership.

Kim believes that because of his example of working with Marshall and of bringing coaches into the Bank to work with people, the tide has turned. People who were having difficulty as leaders now ask for and get a coach and many of them have gotten better. Kim has witnessed remarkable changes and in one case, a person went from having the worst feedback ratings from their people to having the best. It takes time to change cultures and the World Bank culture is changing, thanks to leadership coaching.

One of the greatest benefits of coaching, Kim says, is being brought back to a place of humility, learning, and understanding that no matter how good he thinks he is, no matter how much he thinks he's improved, there's always room to get better. In fact, he reminds himself and others quite often, "No matter how holy you think your mission might be, it does not make you immune from bad leadership."

It's because of this awareness – that no matter how sanctified the mission and no matter how well-trained a leader is, few can sustain their best performance on their own – that Kim continues to work on his leadership skills with an executive coach and he supports and encourages others to do the same.

There is always room to improve, says Kim, whose role model for great leadership is Alan Mulally, former president and CEO of The Ford Motor Company. Alan, who transformed Ford during his tenure, did so, explains Kim, with commitment, a compelling vision and comprehensive strategy, and excellence in terms of leading an organization, not anger or toughness or ruthlessness. Alan led Ford through caring about everyone in the organization, by walking the halls, smiling and engaging everyone who worked there from executives to janitors. It was a revolution at Ford, says Kim. He's not the only one who lists Alan Mulally as one of the greatest leaders he's ever witnessed in action. Among the many accolades to Alan's leadership include *Fortune*, which in 2013 recognized Alan as #3 on its World's Greatest Leaders list, and *Time*, which recognized him as one of the World's Most Influential People.

What Kim recognized and is most in awe of was the revolution that happened at Ford, the change for the better, that was instigated and guided by Alan with "a mixture of warmth and compassion linked to an absolute set of moral and ethical standards that everyone knew they could not violate." When Kim was ready to take the World Bank Group through a huge change exercise, he asked Alan to join them for a few days. The result of the exercise, coupled with Alan's visit, was transformational and continues to spread in a positive way. And, as Marshall has done, so Alan did, charging Kim and the Bank no fee other than to "get better, have fun, and do good."

As Alan Mulally and Marshall Goldsmith volunteer and serve to support The World Bank's powerful mission, "to eradicate extreme poverty on earth by 2030," as Dr. Jim Kim devotes his life to what needs to be done next to make a difference, so you, too, can give of your time and talents if you aren't already.

"Any kind of volunteer work is good," says Marshall Goldsmith, who goes on to say, "Anybody who does any volunteer work should be praised. It's great to help in a way that you're leveraging your unique skills. Put your talents to good use. It feels good! Whatever I have done to help others has come back tenfold. And not just once, but a hundred times." Especially in nonprofit organizations, the challenge for people, according to Kim, is that "sometimes we partake in toxic behaviors excusing them because we are on a 'holy mission' that is more important than how we behave towards each other." And, because most nonprofits can't afford leadership coaching, pro bono coaching relationships such as that which Marshall and Jim have forged are the only way leaders of these important organizations are going to get the coaching necessary to transform their leadership, make massive contributions, and create positive global change.

This is why Kim encourages all of us to go out and help. He wants us to hone our skills and offer our unique talents to nonprofit organizations whose missions we can get behind. For-profits can afford to pay for the services you can provide, but nonprofits often cannot. Specifically, as it relates to coaches, the missions of these nonprofits, the Girl Scouts, the Nature Conservancy, Bookshare, the animal shelter, are just as important as those of for-profits, and the conditions the leaders of these organizations face are often far more difficult and they need help.

So, let this be your call to action – develop yourself, practice your skills, and get out there and help. Do what you do best as a volunteer in an organization whose mission resonates with you. If we all work together and help each other, we will make the world a better place!

Reflection Questions

1. What do you think we should do to create positive change?
2. What can you do to help? Which nonprofit has a mission you want to serve?
3. What do you need to do next in your own life, career?

9

Turning Defeat into Victory

Margaret Heffernan

Margaret Heffernan was born in Texas, raised in Holland, and educated at Cambridge University. She worked in BBC Radio and TV for 13 years, where she wrote, directed, and produced documentaries and dramas. She also produced music videos with the London Chamber Orchestra to raise money for Unicef's Lebanese fund.

In 1994, she returned to the US, where she served as CEO for InfoMation Corporation, ZineZone Corporation, and iCAST Corporation. She was named one of the Top 25 by Streaming Media *magazine and one of the Top 100 Media Executives by* The Hollywood Reporter.

Margaret has published five books: The Naked Truth: A Working Woman's Manifesto *(Wiley, 2004) and* Women on Top: How Female Entrepreneurs Are Changing the Rules for Business Success *(Penguin, 2007). Her third book* Willful Blindness *(Simon & Schuster, 2011) was described by the* Financial Times *as one of the most important books of the decade.* A Bigger Prize *(Simon & Schuster, 2014) looks at what it takes for individuals and organizations to be truly creative and collaborative. In 2015, TED published* Beyond Measure: The Big Impact of Small Changes, *which looks at the defining characteristics of sustainably innovative organizations. Margaret's TED talks have been seen by over 8 million people.*

Margaret mentors global businesses leaders and writes for the Huffington Post *and the* Financial Times.

■ ■ ■

The Internet bubble burst. We had always known it would. But when it finally happened, between 2000 and 2002,[1] everyone looked shocked and confused. Well, almost everyone. I knew exactly what would happen next. Businesses like mine, well-funded by a publicly traded company, would come under huge pressure to cut costs. Salami cutting, we called it. Thin slices. More thin slices. I'd seen how this played out in recessions. It was impossible to protest against small cuts – after all, every company has some fat it can afford to lose. But that's just the start. It goes on. And on. And on. Demoralizing. Debilitating. All the while, credibility and trust decline; the only growth areas are cynicism and black humor. Finally, these companies become what venture capitalists call *the walking dead*: productive enough to stay alive, but never robust enough to be valuable.

I'd seen it often and I dreaded it. So, with my CFO, I tried to reconfigure our business in such a way that it could grow and thrive in the new environment. We didn't lack the nerve to imagine a radically different company. My partner and I even modeled a company with neither of us in it. Why? Because I believed then and I still believe now that the job of a leader is to serve the business. Not oneself, not friends or families or shareholders – but to serve the idea and the people on which the business depends.

We couldn't do it. With all the mathematical, financial, technological imagination, nerve, and finesse we mustered, we could not construct a business model in which the company honored the investment of funders, employees, and customers. We spent months on planes, in ugly corporate meeting rooms, trying to find corporate parents who might find enough value in what we did to stomach the losses. We failed.

So, I went to my chairman and investor with an unusual request: shut us down. Now. He was stunned. No entrepreneur, he told me, had ever asked him to do that. Entrepreneurs typically will fight for the life of their company to their last dying breath. Was I a quitter?

No, I said. I'm not a quitter. If I thought we could succeed, I would fight until my last breath. But I could see only death by a thousand cuts that would destroy my credibility, wreck the pride and passion of my work-force, and inevitably breed disappointment, frustration, and anger. That wasn't the business I was in or wanted to be in. And as CEO of a publicly traded company, I didn't think he could, with integrity, continue to invest in a company whose own CEO could not see a way forward. So, he was perfectly at liberty to fire me. He didn't want to do that, either.

My CFO and I went back on the road searching for a strategic investor; it was our only hope. All the time we were doing this, business as usual had to continue. Employees had to stay focused and keep building the value we were trying to rescue. I had a super-smart bunch of colleagues. Some had built one of the first-ever Internet browsers. Another had sent one of the first emails in history. Their genius had made our product remarkable and brilliant. I loved them for it and they loved the company because it had given them opportunities to discover and demonstrate their immense creative capacity. I owed them respect and honesty.

As I left my chairman wrestling with his admiration for what the company had achieved and the remorseless logic of my argument, another question arose: What should I be saying to my employees? I was urged to keep mum, to say nothing. It was temptingly simple. If I'd had an office to hide in, I could have stayed there, or on planes, and hidden the truth of where we were. But I'd always worked in the center of the office and hiding had never really been my style. So, I told them the truth: where we were, what we were trying, what might happen next.

I was strongly urged not to do this. I was warned against being too honest. Some of my investor's bureaucrats adopted a patronizing tone, telling me that, having worked outside of the US, I was probably ignorant or naïve about levels of violence in America. I didn't understand the risks I was running of backlash from disgruntled employees.

I didn't care. I've always been honest with people I've worked with and this struck me as the wrong moment to change tack. I also have always believed that if you treat people as adults, they are more likely to behave that way. Many men told me I was naïve.

In the end, we couldn't find a strategic investor. I went back to my chairman: You should close us down – or fire me. His board urged him to cut his losses and close the business. Reluctantly, he concurred. The day we had that discussion was sad for both of us. I'd won the argument. We'd both lost a business we loved.

Then I had to break the news to all the phenomenal people I'd hired over the years. The one concession I made to those who had been so worried about my truthfulness was that I allowed them to install a single security guard in our company meeting. I explained where we were, what we'd tried, and where we now were. There followed questions all US companies expect: about healthcare, pay, time frames, and what would happen to our customers, partners, and suppliers. This was a grown-up, professional discussion, after which most people went home, often together, some via a bar. No one was violent, but everyone was sad.

Then, in the weeks that followed, something remarkable happened. Using the office to conduct job searches and stick together with their colleagues, employees would come in after interviews and be glowing: talking about their work in the company made them see just how much they'd learned working there and how exceptional their achievements were. Talking about the past made them proud of themselves and their teams. Instead of feeling like failures, they all carried with them an aura of victory. Sure, the company was closing, but the experiences they had gained would remain with them forever.

Meanwhile, we unwound all the contracts and deals with partners, customers, and suppliers. Closing before we had to, we had the luxury of time and the money to do so honorably. Nobody who had done business with us woke up to find themselves shortchanged or let down. One business partner said he'd never had so much respect for a deal that failed. We became, and remain, fast friends. Reputations weren't only preserved; they were enhanced.

Many of the brilliant people I worked with have gone on to create their own businesses. More than a few have continued to work together. Many stay closely connected, recommending each other for prime projects and choice assignments. And most still have and wear their company T-shirts with pride.

Intellectually and emotionally, this was the toughest time of my professional life. I found it harder to quit than it would have been to persevere. Like most entrepreneurs, I'm instantly inspired when told a goal is impossible. And I have a lot of stamina. But I came to realize that heroic actions, in this context, would be (as they often are) just a form of narcissism. True leadership required not doing the hard thing, but the right thing. Not to die trying, but to get everyone home safely. I felt then as I feel now: that the job of a leader is to do what is best for the business, for its people, and for the wider society it serves.

Today, I spend a lot of time with young people. They frequently ask me how they should think about their working lives and careers; these questions unnerve me. It is harder than it should be to recommend companies where I feel they will be treated with respect. I am challenged to identify responsible leaders.

But we need our young people to be optimistic and demanding, ambitious in the best sense of the word. So, I tell them that they always have choices. Whatever the work is, you can decide whether to do it well or badly. What you do does not define you – but how you do it does. Leaders are the people who dare to think for themselves. And they are everywhere.

Reflection Questions:

1. Have you ever had to abandon or give up on a project/business/enterprise? How did you come to your decision to end it or to persevere?
2. How did others (friends, family members, subordinates) react to your decision? Did their reactions make your decision harder or easier?
3. What lessons do you think you can learn from what might look like *failure* to an outsider? How can such failures actually foster your success?

Note

1. https://www.investopedia.com/features/crashes/crashes8.asp, accessed March 1, 2018.

10 | What I See from My Window

Eric Schurenberg

Eric Schurenberg is the president and editor-in-chief of Inc. *Before joining* Inc., *Eric was the editor of* CBS MoneyWatch.com *and* BNET.com *and managing editor of* Money Magazine. *As a writer, he is a winner of a Loeb and a National Magazine Award.*

■ ■ ■

The great Peter Drucker looked out his window and saw what no one else saw. His vision overturned centuries of thinking and led to a whole new vision of leadership. I, in turn, look out my window and, well, I daydream, mainly. The leadership canon has nothing to fear.

Still, the view out my window is pretty awesome, truth be told. My office at *Inc.* is on the north face of World Trade Center, on the 29th floor, hundreds of feet in the air over downtown Manhattan. That affords a nearly unbroken view north toward midtown and upstate New York beyond, with the gray-green moat of the Hudson River on my left.

In most of New York, it's easy to forget that you live and work on an island, founded as a seaport and river town. Looking out my window, you can't forget. The Hudson is about a mile wide where I sit, and, straight as a 10-lane highway, it beckons you into the interior. No wonder Henry

Hudson persuaded himself that this was the one (not the Delaware or the Potomac) that could lead to the Northwest Passage. No wonder everyone from the Iroquois and Lenape to the British and Americans fought to control it.

When visitors to *Inc.* marvel at the view, I often find myself saying, "Had you been looking out the window at the right moment, you'd have seen Captain Sully land his plane in the Hudson." For some reason, apparently, I need to point out that the view isn't just pretty. It's also a frame for the dramas that take place, or took place, within its range. In other words, if you know how to look, what you can see out my window are the defining moments in the history of this place, a history – and let's get to the point in a book by Frances Hesselbein – that was made possible by great leadership.

Several miles upriver, gray in the distance, stands the George Washington Bridge, connecting the town of Fort Lee in New Jersey with Fort Washington Park in New York. It makes sense that the builders would name the structure after the first president of the United States. But there's a certain irony to that, too, because the bridge joins the two points Washington probably would *least* like to be remembered for.

That's where the leadership lesson comes in.

A quick background: In the months after the signing of the Declaration of Independence, Washington and his troops fought the British for control of New York. For Washington, the campaign was an unmitigated disaster; in battle after battle, his amateur army was manhandled by the disciplined British and Hessians. By November, the Americans' only toehold in New York was an earthen fort at the northern tip of Manhattan, Fort Washington. Directly across the Hudson in New Jersey lay another patriot stronghold, named after Washington's no. 2, Charles Lee.

As the British and Hessians loped after the retreating Americans, Washington doubted that the fort bearing his name could be defended. But after wavering indecisively, he yielded to assurances from his favorite lieutenant, Nathanael Greene, that the fort could hold out. Greene was fatally wrong. When the British attack came in mid-November, the defense collapsed in a few hours, with the loss of three thousand men, many precious cannon, and thousands of tents and blankets that Washington's army would sorely miss in the winter ahead. A few days later, after the British crossed the Hudson, Washington and his demoralized troops abandoned Fort Lee in a panic, leaving behind still more irreplaceable supplies.

The loss of the two forts was the crowning catastrophe of Washington's defeat in New York. Legend has it that he turned and, in a rare display of emotion, wept "with the tenderness of a child" as the victors raised their flags over Fort Washington. Some of his most loyal allies began to question whether he was up to the job.

"An indecisive mind is one of the greatest misfortunes that can befall an army," fumed Joseph Reed, Washington's aide-de-camp and closest confidant, in a backbiting letter to Lee. Lee, in turn, scolded Washington directly. "O, General, why would you be over-persuaded by men of inferior judgment to your own?" he wrote, in a rebuke that was also a thinly veiled invitation to blame Greene.

As Washington and the remnants of his army fled through New Jersey, rarely more than a few hours ahead of the British, the war seemed all but over. The army that he commanded that summer had been reduced 70% by defeat and desertion. It was undersupplied and woefully underprepared for winter. Many civilians, figuring the cause was lost, eagerly accepted British pardons in return for denouncing the rebellion.

Quite apart from the desperate military situation, Washington had reason to feel personally abandoned. Greene, his favorite, had grossly miscalculated at Fort Washington. And when a confused dispatch rider mistakenly delivered to Washington a letter furthering that carping exchange between Lee and Reed, Washington realized that his closest allies had begun to lose faith in him.

"These are the times that try men's souls," wrote pamphleteer Thomas Paine, famously, referring to this dark moment in his new country's fortunes. Yet, it was precisely at this point that Washington proved he had the soul of a leader.

For starters, Washington never let the troops see any glimmer of despair. Indeed, he made himself more visible than he had been before. Rather than be carried in his customary carriage, for example, Washington rode with his rear guard during the retreat, closest to the pursuing British. This made an impression on, among others, an 18-year-old Virginia lieutenant named James Monroe. "I ... saw him at the head of a small band, or rather in its rear, for he was always near the enemy," he would later recall, "and his countenance and manner made an impression on me which I can never efface." (The leadership lesson apparently stuck with young Monroe, for he went on to become America's fifth president.)

In addition, Washington refused to yield to what must have been a powerful temptation to lash out at his subordinates. In his own analysis of the disaster at Fort Washington, Washington never named Greene, spurning Lee's invitation to throw Greene under the bus, and after reading the letter from Lee to Reed, Washington merely sent it on with an apology for having mistakenly opened it. He made no comment on its content.

Despite all these trials, moreover, Washington never altered his instinctive, empowering leadership style. In contrast to his opposing European generals, who were strictly conscious of rank (military and social), Washington led by consensus. He continually sought his lieutenants' opinion of his tactics and listened to their ideas, even after the disaster at Fort Washington. It was a style perfectly aligned to the principles of a nation that had just finished declaring that all men are created equal.

There are many reasons that the American cause prevailed, but one of the indispensable ones, without a doubt, was Washington's skill at motivating and inspiring his followers. While he lived in a very different century, the source of his mastery would make sense to Peter Drucker, Marshall Goldsmith, Frances Hesselbein, or any of today's great thinkers. It's not at all hard to map Washington's inclusive, trusting style to the leadership principles that the iconic CEO Alan Mulally made famous in this century, when he brought Boeing and Ford back from their own near-death experiences. Three principles in particular come to mind:

1. **Put People First.** Washington saw Greene's and Reed's devotion to the patriot cause and stood by them, despite the former's error in judgment and the latter's flicker of disloyalty. Trusting in his subordinates' better angels paid off handsomely: A month later, it was Reed who suggested that Washington cross the icy Delaware and attack the Hessians at Trenton – a victory that became the war's turning point. Later, Reed proved his loyalty to the cause by refusing a 10,000-pound British bribe, saying famously, "I am not worth purchasing; but such as I am, the king of Great Britain is not rich enough to do it." Greene, for his part, repaid Washington's faith by evolving into what historian

David McCullough called "the Americans' most brilliant field commander."[1] His flawless campaign in the southern colonies led directly to Washington's crushing victory at Yorktown, Virginia, the conclusive major battle of the war.

2. **Include Everyone.** Shortly after Washington's surprise victory at Trenton, a large, revenge-minded British force marched on the city and, having cornered Washington south of the town, encamped for the night. In his war council that night, Washington abandoned his inclination to take on the British the next day. Instead, he followed the suggestion of two junior officers to slip around their opponents' flank during the night. The British generals went to bed confident that they would destroy Washington the next morning. They awoke to an empty American camp in front of them and the sound of cannon to their rear, where the Americans were busy routing their rear guard and capturing the town of Princeton.

3. **Trust the Process and Be Emotionally Resilient.** In his own demeanor, Washington modeled the calm perseverance that he recognized was needed after his army's disastrous defeat in New York. Washington had every reason to despair, but he never let his troops see it. In reply to one of his generals who was complaining about his mediocre troops, Washington wrote that he sympathized but that "we must bear up against [our troubles] and make the best of mankind as they are, since we cannot have them as we wish."[2] As for process: Despite the almost unbearable pressures he faced, he did not abandon his inclusive style of leadership and shut himself off from advisers.

From a twenty-first-century perspective, Washington seems a distant figure, a stern-faced, bewigged curiosity who seems more granite than human. And yet from my window, it's possible to picture him as an all-too-fallible 45-year-old being rowed hurriedly across the Hudson toward Fort Lee, agonizing over his spectacular failure in his first real test, and realizing that when he got ashore, several thousand scared, underequipped men were still counting on him to lead them. That man I see out my window never had the benefit of Peter Drucker's insights. But he instinctively grasped what it took to quiet his own demons and drive men to do more than they, and the world, ever thought possible.

Like I said: It's a pretty awesome view out my window, if you know where to look.

Reflection Questions

1. What historical leaders do you most admire, and why?
2. Do you think that leadership challenges of the present are different than those of the past? If so, how?
3. Describe how George Washington was able to turn his defeats into victories. What particular leadership qualities did he display that enabled him to maintain the support of those he led? Can you think of any parallels in your own organization?

Notes

1. David McCullough, *1776* (New York: Simon & Schuster, 2005).
2. David Hackett Fischer, *Washington's Crossing* (New York: Oxford University Press, 2004).

11

Loving Work Despite the Odds

Secrets from Sir Richard Branson and Nelson Mandela

Mark C. Thompson

Mark C. Thompson is a New York Times *bestselling author, coach, investor, and advisor to leaders who are transforming their companies – from Virgin's Richard Branson and Apple's Steve Jobs, to Pinterest founder Evan Sharp, LYFT founder Logan Green, author Tony Robbins, and World Bank President Jim Kim. At Schwab, Mark reported to founder Charles "Chuck" Schwab as senior vice president/executive producer of Schwab.com, and later global retail and enterprise chief customer experience officer for The Charles Schwab Corporation.*

Mark is founding patron and leadership advisor to Richard Branson's Entrepreneurship Centers – more than 400 companies operate under the Virgin brand. He was founding advisor to the Stanford University Realtime Venture Design Lab. He is adjunct faculty at Harvard McLean's Institute of Coaching and the Institute for Contemporary Leadership with Google's David Peterson. Mark has served as faculty at the World Economic Forum, World Business Forum, and Drucker/Hesselbein Leader to Leader Institute. He is a chancellor for Junior Achievement's

Success University and member of the board of trustees for the International Coaching Federation Foundation.

■ ■ ■

As Virgin America announced plans for its long-awaited IPO, Sir Richard Branson confided to me over a late-night beer[1] just how maddening it can be to launch any high-flying business, even for a serial entrepreneur with more than 350 other companies under the Virgin brand. Back when the Silicon Valley-based airline was getting started, Virgin America's competitors viciously contested the newcomer's arrival for what seemed like an eternity. Price wars, lawsuits, and regulatory battles all soaked up precious resources.

"The knee-jerk reaction you feel as a leader when you're under attack is to assume a siege mentality," Branson said. But your fight-or-flight instincts are "a self-indulgent waste of time and money." Instead, he and his partners focused on reinventing the customer experience for domestic air travel, eventually winning share in the insanely competitive airline industry. The strategy worked. While his foes fought each other, Virgin America was recently acquired at a nice profit for the legendary entrepreneur.

Branson said that rather than ever feel threatened or even sorry for himself, he's always comforted by five principles that guided his mentor, Nelson Mandela, whose circumstances were obviously far more desperate than any of us will ever experience.

1. Let Your Mission, Not Your Nightmare, Define You

"Resentment is like drinking poison and then hoping it will kill your enemies," Mandela once said. Vengefulness and victimhood would not erase the crimes done to him in the past, nor would they help him build a better future. Mandela could have emerged from decades of jail "still imprisoned by bitterness," Branson said. "Instead he devoted every ounce of creativity to building a lasting legacy."

When Branson's house burst into flames during a hurricane a few years ago, actress Kate Winslet and her family, along with Branson's 90-year-old mom, Eve, fled to safety. Branson himself had been sleeping down near the beach in a guest cottage when he heard lightning strike his hilltop home. He sprinted out the door buck naked and straight into a cactus. "No one felt sorry for me," he joked, "as everyone had more important issues to contend with." Nobody was hurt, but Branson felt a deep moment of loss. He'd raised his family in that house, and the setback gave him insight into how to weigh what's important.

The biggest heartbreak about the blaze for Branson was losing his prized notebooks. He's scribbled ideas and to-do's in a set of bound blank books in almost every meeting I've ever attended with him. He's been doing that for decades, and it has two important benefits that make him one of the happiest and most humble people you'll ever meet. Taking notes keeps him present in the conversation and able to gather knowledge rather than drifting away or indulging in holding court with celebrity-crazed admirers. "You need to have some way to stay focused on what matters, what you're learning, and what you might find important later, so track your insights in every step of your adventure," Branson says.

2. Burn Your House Down

Sir Richard's home tragedy yielded another unique insight about how to harvest failure and innovate at the same time. Here's the key idea: If you lost everything tomorrow, would you

- Rebuild your home exactly the same way?
- Fill it with all the same stuff?
- Start your career over, and in the exact same way?
- Recruit all the same people back into your life and work?

The good news is that none of this has happened today, but if you take these questions seriously for a moment, you will unleash a flood of fresh ideas about what you might consider doing, along with both regrets and gratitude about the way things are. It's a powerful way to reconnect with what and who matters to you before a crisis requires that sort of innovation.

"I'd not wish it on anyone," Branson told me, "but sometimes the best way to get clear about what has meaning to you is to imagine starting over from scratch!"

Perhaps it's time to throw a few things out that don't really work for you, or take more time to appreciate who and what you'd miss if you lost them. There can be many benefits: Branson's new home is bolder and more beautiful in ways that better reflect who he is today and what he wants to accomplish in the next chapter of his life.

3. Nobody Does It Alone

When Charles (Chuck) Schwab flunked English and was nearly thrown out of college, he said he was "humiliated because I had always thought I was a reasonably smart guy and I didn't realize how pathetic I was at the skill of reading and writing."[2] Schwab recruited friends and family to help him deliver the goods in school. His reading and writing troubles, he would later discover, were the result of dyslexia. "It might seem odd," said Schwab, "but what felt like a deficit was a real benefit." His reading disability taught him how to recruit a talented, trustworthy team and forced him to become a skilled delegator.

When it comes to building an organization, nobody does it alone. Like the blind person who develops acute senses of hearing and smell, an intelligent person with learning disabilities who is ambitious like entrepreneur Charles Schwab won't hesitate to seek help to get things done rather than assume that he can or must do it all on his own. If you're a decent reader, you might not get help. Chuck Schwab could not read well enough to stay in college, so rather than be thrown out of Stanford, he recruited study groups. Marshall Goldsmith often talks about how even the most brilliant people eventually must learn that they are expert at very few things, so the faster you learn that, the better off you will be as a leader.

Ultimately, those recruitment and delegation skills enabled Chuck to scale a business much sooner than most of his classmates at Stanford Business School. "Brilliant entrepreneurs think they can do everything, and they don't spend enough time finding the right people to grow the business," he shrugged.

None of us is an expert at everything. "When you don't know something, just say so; it will shock the hell out of everyone and help you build a team to help you," Schwab smiled.

It's perhaps the most provocative phrase anyone can say in public: *I don't know*. In fact, the Dalai Lama, the global spiritual leader of Tibetan Buddhism, who has spent his lifetime trying to build understanding among faiths around the world, has been caught unabashedly using the phrase *every* time I've interviewed him. The guru says, with a grin and without apology, "I don't know!" Nervous laughter usually creeps over the audience; then they sit in stunned silence as he smiles on stage like a bald leprechaun in orange robes and sneakers. What a shockingly simple revelation in a world where so-called experts speculate on national television far beyond their training or expertise – shouting at each other about things they do not know. Although it may not initially sound reassuring, *I don't know* is a sort of a code or catch phrase you can use to identify honest people and enduringly high achievers all over the world. It's kind of the secret handshake of integrity. When asked a question for which you do not have an answer, spend a moment looking earnest, then as folks lean forward breathlessly to await your wisdom, say, "I don't know, let's ask someone who does." It works wonders and creates a space in which learning is possible.

4. Focus on What You're For, Not What You're Against

Rather than getting sucked into a protracted, bitter feud with anyone, it's much better to let your adversaries waste their energy fighting each other. Mandela didn't go to war or terrorize his former captors. "He didn't take the bait," Branson said, "and you shouldn't, either." Virgin America, for example, didn't get distracted by turf battles and name calling, and instead focused on building a community of customers who loved its fresh, edgy vibe.

"We're too easily driven by instant gratification, both good and bad," famed educator and author of *The 7 Habits of Highly Effective People* Steve Covey told me during a long dinner at his home outside Salt Lake City.[3] Our primal brains are hardwired by fight-or-flight urges, which means that we're easily seduced by anything that feels remotely urgent rather those less-exciting things that have longer-term strategic impact. "It's tempting to behave like Pavlov's dog, leaping at anything that shows immediate threats or rewards," Covey cautioned. Be wary of urgent things that steal your time from long-term commitments.

5. You Don't Have to Be Perfect to Make a Difference

"Do not judge me by my successes," Mandela admonished. "Judge me by how many times I fell down and got back up again." When you're suffering a setback in your startup, imagine how much worse Mandela had it – and just how creative he had to be in a cramped cell every night. From dawn to dusk, he dragged stones in the blinding heat. You can't steel yourself year after year dreaming that hopeless circumstances will change, he said. You have to change the way you deal with them. Being flexible in finding a new door every time the last one slams shut is the difference between those who find their way and those who self-destruct.

I will never forget Nelson Mandela's warm embrace as he almost collapsed in my arms after midnight during his last visit to the World Economic Forum (WEF),[4] the invitation-only summit in the Swiss Alps where CEOs, presidents of nations, artists, educators, and entrepreneur billionaires convene every winter. I was executive producer of Schwab.com, and I was participating in panels at the WEF and interviewing hundreds of leaders in Davos for a reprise to the business classic, *Built to Last*,[5] by Jim Collins and legendary Stanford professor Jerry Porras. The bestselling sequel, *Success Built to Last: Creating a Life That Matters*[6] (with Porras and Stewart Emery) feels like Dale Carnegie's epic adventure *How to Win Friends and Influence People*[7] updated for the new millennium.

Almost every thought leader I met for face-to-face interviews pointed to Mandela as a perfect role model for leadership. In our conversation, the Nobel Laureate smirked and told me that perfection was never a part of his plan and that he "never achieved it." In the years before Mandela, an activist lawyer, had been sent to a death camp, he was rarely without zealous overconfidence about his mission to end apartheid. Although he initially advocated a peaceful solution, Mandela eventually took up arms when the path of peace appeared to be a dead-end. The fact that he didn't start out as a complete saint with perfect grace or humility before his long walk to freedom makes his journey even more useful to the rest of us.

"You have enduring impact not because you are perfect or lucky," Sir Richard sighed as he finished a beer, "but because you have the courage to stay focused on building a better future rather than dwell in the past."

Leaders find love in their work and life when they find the courage to turn their wounds into wisdom and their passions into purpose.

> ### Reflection Questions
>
> 1. Who do you look up to as a hero or leader?
> 2. What characteristics or actions of theirs would you most like to emulate?
> 3. Do you love your work? Your life? What elements about them might you begin to appreciate if you look at them from a different perspective? What might you want to change?

Notes

1. Richard Branson quotes from live interview with Mark Thompson, at his home on Necker Island, British Virgin Islands, 2015.
2. Charles Schwab, live interview with Mark Thompson, 2011, https://www.youtube.com/watch?v=7kpkh1pm4A8.
3. Steve Covey quotes from live interview with Mark Thompson, at his home in Provo, Utah, 2012.
4. Nelson Mandela quotes from live interview with Mark Thompson, at The World Economic Forum, Davos, Switzerland, 2000.
5. Jim Collins and Jerry I. Porras, *Built to Last: Successful Habits of Visionary Companies* (New York: Harper Business, 1994).
6. Jerry Porras, Stewart Emery, and Mark Thompson, *Success Built to Last: Creating a Life That Matters* (New York: Plume, 2007).
7. Dale Carnegie, *How to Win Friends and Influence People* (New York: Simon & Schuster, 1936).

12

The New Work of Leaders

How Does Your Leadership Narrative Show Up?

Stephanie Pace Marshall

Stephanie Pace Marshall is an internationally recognized educational pioneer and inspiring speaker and writer on leadership, learning, and the design and creation of transformative learning environments. She is founding president and president emerita of the Illinois Mathematics and Science Academy; the founding president of the National Consortium of Secondary STEM Schools; and past president of the Association of Supervision and Curriculum Development, International. She is author of over 40 published journal articles; an author for Organizations of the Future *(Drucker Foundation) and an editor and coauthor of* Scientific Literacy for the 21st Century *(2002). Her 2006 book,* The Power to Transform: Leadership that Brings Learning and Schooling to Life, *received the 2007 Educator's Award from the Delta Kappa Gamma Society, International. She is a fellow of the Royal Society for the Encouragement of Arts, Manufactures, and Commerce in*

London and a trustee of the Society for Science and the Public in Washington, DC. She serves as chancellor of the Lincoln Academy of Illinois.

■ ■ ■

Stories become testaments, old or new, that choreograph the life of a community.
                                                            —Stephen Larsen

The Invitation

In 1997, I received an unusual invitation: "Come and spend a week with a group of medicine men and women 'spirit doctors,' healers, and elders of the Pitjantjatjara Aboriginal tribe, explore the nonlinearity of ancient ways of knowing, and co-create a new, more sustainable human story for the new millennium."

Despite challenges, I accepted the invitation; the possibility of cocreating a sustainable human story with some of our oldest living ancestors was magnetic.

Months later I arrived in the Red Center of Australia, and for the first time in my life, I felt completely disoriented. I did not know how to be, belong, or think there. Everything I thought I knew, every way I had navigated and made sense of my world, was challenged. Most frightening was my loss of identity, my sense of who I was now, in this place.

I had said yes, with great clarity, and had traveled far to engage in a most elusive and irrational journey. I needed to understand why. Throughout my life, I had seen countless examples of narratives (even false ones) trumping data. I became curious and captivated by the asymmetrical power of story to change hearts, minds, and behavior.

Fortunately, before I became irretrievably lost, that quiet voice inside that often tells us what we don't want to hear, spoke up: "You came here to learn and cocreate, and you no longer know how. So you must surrender, let go of what you think you know, listen, and pay attention."

Here's what I heard and learned. Aboriginal culture has its origin in *dreamtime* or *world-making*. Aborigines believe that before the world awakened, their ancestors emerged from sleep beneath the earth and began to sing their way across the land, seeking companionship, food, or shelter. Since the earth was still forming, their wandering and singing the names of things and places into the land actually shaped the landscape, creating mountains, watering holes, caves, plants, and animals. Eventually each ancestor reentered the earth, transforming themselves into a part of its topography forever. As they wandered and sung the land into existence, each left songlines, a "meandering trail of geographic sites" that crossed the country and were the result of specific encounters, captured as story.

Songlines are musical narratives and geographical maps, "a sort of musical score of a vast epic song-story that winds across the continent, telling of the ancestors' adventures and how the landscape came into being."[1]

Aborigine children are born into and inherit a stretch of a songline; the song's verses are their birthright and the roots of their identity. It is this continuity of song and story that keeps both the land and their connection to it alive. Since songlines are maps embedded in the land, there is simply no word for *lost* in Pitjantjatjara. Walking and singing these song–stories in the appropriate cadence in which they were created tells the Pitjantjatjara where they can find shelter, food, and water; singing them in reverse tells them how to go home.

The night before we left, we were given a remarkable gift. Sitting around the campfire, we witnessed the tribal elder sing and dance a songline; then he paused and we thought he was finished, but he began to sing and dance again. Our guide was astonished: "The Elder has changed the songline," she said, "and nothing will be the same." Over time, it became clear that this new songline was the roots of a different, more sustainable human story; the presence of Western leaders and Aborigine elders had inspired and enabled its emergence. Together, we had *cocreated* a new story.

This experience profoundly changed me. I shifted how I understood the essential work of leaders and embraced a new framework for grounding our work: story, map, and landscape. I did not disavow my need to develop expertise and skills in the work traditionally ascribed to leaders; rather, I chose to stand in a different place by paying attention to both the overstories (actual events) and the understories (journey of our hearts and souls) within my organization.

Years ago, I heard a renowned photographer respond to the question, "What's the secret to taking a good picture?"

"Technique is important," he said, "but the art of taking a good picture is knowing where to point the camera."

The same is true for leadership. As leaders, we must consciously *point the camera* in places previously unheard, unseen, or unrecognized. When we illuminate our personal and organizational narratives, we see, hear, and experience them differently – and can then choose to change them.

Songlines and their seamless integration of story, map, and landscape are relevant to our new work as leaders – as storytellers and mapmakers. We, too, are *born* into a songline – a constellation of stories and identity-shaping narratives of who and how we are; as we walk these patterned stories, usually unconsciously, we feed them and keep them alive. They become our maps, whether prison or portal, and we become the stories we tell ourselves about ourselves. We become the stories we live.

During this uncommon journey to the world of the Pitjantjatjara, a profound insight unfolded for me, and it frames how I now think about my work:

- Mind-shaping is world-shaping.
- When we change the story, we change the map.
- When we change the map, we change the landscape.
- When we change the landscape, we change our experiences and our choices.
- When we change our experiences and our choices, we can change our minds.
- When we change our minds, we can change the world.

Changing the story changes everything. Leaders can create conditions by design to illuminate and unlock new stories of potential and possibility and to set them in motion so new maps can be walked.

Firestorm or Gift?

The following story illustrates how paying attention to story, map, and landscape is a powerful driver for organizational change. Several years ago, one week before my institution was to open for another year, the admissions staff had mistakenly sent letters of invitation to 32 students on the wait list.

Distraught, the staff presented a plan to address the error. They would call each family, apologize profusely, but not admit the students. I listened, but said no. We had extended an invitation and our integrity was at stake. We would admit these students and welcome them.

The news of my decision spread like wildfire. We needed everything – dorm rooms, beds, mattresses, computers, residential counselors, faculty. The buzz, both positive and negative, drowned out every other conversation. We had one week to make it all happen.

Aware that I needed to know and understand our internal narratives and what the community was feeling, I asked a trusted colleague to write down every comment she heard and send them to me anonymously. Then one evening, I read all the comments, and detected two dominant patterns or narratives. One I called *the firestorm* (a story of impending division and fragmentation); the other I called *the gift* (a story of emerging pride and generosity).

I presented two visuals: one, a blazing fire, and the other a gift box with a big bow. Each image was surrounded by the community's comments. I described these narrative patterns as two emerging stories over which we had complete control and asked my colleagues which one best defined who we wanted to be. We could choose the firestorm, grounded in a narrative of scarcity, and likely ensure we would have a dismal year; or we could choose the gift, grounded in a narrative of abundance.

As the year unfolded and the 32 students thrived, it was clear that the story we chose to live was *the gift*.

I later heard from many who wanted to embrace this story, but felt their responses were inadequate when confronted by the firestorm advocates, that the public naming of these two stories as choices gave them a place to stand and an authentic voice in cocreating our desired future. In response to negative comments, there was no argument; all they had to say was, "You're living in 'the firestorm,' and that is not my story."

This profound leadership experience yielded an epiphany: We are wired for storytelling. Facts largely activate the language areas of our brains, but stories activate and engage our brain holistically. We are relational beings, and stories enable us to identify with the experiences of others and connect them to our own. When we change our stories, we change our choices. And when we change our choices, we can change our minds.

Today, we behave as if we believe that more information, sophisticated data analytics, and additional and better strategies will predictably produce the outcomes we seek. But what transforms organizations into generative and creative environments are deeper relationships, and authentic conversations of meaning and purpose and life-affirming stories of identity: stories of who we are, what is possible, and how we want to *be* together in our work.

As leaders, we must know what to look for and how to see it, what to listen for and how to hear it, what to tell and how to tell it. We must also attend to the understory – the emotional and soulful dimensions of who we are.

"I never predict," says Peter Drucker, "I just look out the window and see what's visible but not yet seen."[2] Our work now is to point the camera on the often unseen and unspoken narratives in the collective consciousness of our organizations and shine a light on them so we can choose who we want to be. Sometimes the leader's role is to remind us of who we really are.

Lessons Learned: What Has Become Clear

Leaders and Leadership

1. We lead who we are and cannot create what we have not become. Leadership is first an *inside job*.
2. Successful leadership is not first about organizational strategy, but rather it is about personal and organizational meaning, coherence, and clarity of identity (*who* we are) and of purpose (*why* we are).
3. The greatest power we have as leaders to ignite and engage our organizations resides in the authenticity, clarity, congruence, and courage of our internal moral compass, made visible through the stories we name and live. There can be no space between what we say, what we do, and why.
4. Our current conceptions of leadership are far too small for our capacities and imagination. They are grounded in a faulty mental model; a distorted view of power, motivation, and meaning creation; and often false proxies for assessing authentic success. This dishonors who we are. As a result, we internalize a mental map that drives us to replication and modeling the strategies and tactics of traditional definitions of leadership success. This is a profound illusion. As Peter Drucker is reputed to have said, "Culture eats strategy for breakfast, and leaders create culture."[3]

5. Leaders care for the well-being of the whole. They create conditions for everyone to be seen and heard into speech; they see beyond the visible events into the organization's meaning-making capacities and identity-shaping patterns that form the essence of its mission and purpose.

6. Wise leaders illuminate both their organization's visible overstories and invisible yet palpable understories. They do so with clear intention so the unseen patterns that shape our minds and behavior do not drive decisions based on illusion, but rather on clear and conscious choices about the narratives we choose to live.

7. Leaders know where to *point the camera*, enabling us to notice our embodied narratives and guiding us to choose ones that reinforce and deepen our identity.

Storytelling and Mapmaking

1. We become the stories we tell ourselves about ourselves; we become the stories we live.

2. Our stories become our maps and as we walk them, we create our *landscape* – our experiences and choices.

3. Belonging to a community (an organization) is not a private matter; we are all connected. Within a community, there is no such thing as a random comment; every comment contributes to an emergent and unfolding narrative that either works for or against us.

4. It is the understory, the timeless and enduring story we live beneath the surface, that shapes our character and culture. When we live a story, consciously or not, it becomes our map – defining our worldview, our possibilities, and who we become.

Reflection Questions

1. How would you describe the leadership narrative you are currently living? Share a story that illuminates how this narrative shows up in your organization.

2. Reflecting on the roles of leaders as storytellers and mapmakers, have you experienced an epiphany as a leader? What made this a defining moment for you?

3. How might you begin to illuminate and name the understories within your organization?

Notes

1. David Abram, *The Spell of the Sensuous* (New York: Vintage Books, 1977), 166.
2. Robert Lenzner and Stephen S. Johnson, "Seeing Things As They Really Are," *Forbes*, March 10, 1997.
3. See discussion about quote at Andrew Cave, "Culture Eats Strategy for Breakfast. So What's for Lunch?" *Forbes*, November 9, 2017.

13 | Choose, Build, Live High Expectations!

Mel Spiese

Major General (Ret.) Mel Spiese spent 36 years on active duty. An infantry officer, he had extensive experience in formal training and education positions as a senior officer, including colonel assignments as Director of the Combined Arms Training Program, Command of School of Infantry, and Director of Expeditionary Warfare School. As a flag officer, he commanded Training Command, Marine Air Ground Task Force Training Command, and Training and Education Command, as well as serving as the Deputy Director of Strategy, Plans, and Assessments, J-5, at US European Command, and Deputy Commanding General of First Marine Expeditionary Force and Commanding General of 1st Marine Expeditionary Brigade.

Specific actions in training and education assignments include the complete restructure and redesign of Enlisted Professional Military Education, leadership development in Professional Military Education anchored in Values-Based Leadership, and institution of Values-Based Training in all Entry-Level Training programs, among many other accomplishments. He was responsible for Mission Rehearsal Training for units deploying to combat in Iraq, and the transition of Mission Rehearsal Training from Iraq to Afghanistan. He transitioned to Cubic Defense Systems upon retirement from active duty and is now consulting independently for a number of businesses, in addition to the development of Leaders Can Be Made.

■ ■ ■

While attending an *Inspired Work* workshop in 2015, I was asked by the founder (and author of *The Workplace Engagement Solution*[1]), David Harder, if the Marine Corps had a problem with workforce disengagement. We were discussing the characteristics of the younger generations – Millennials and Generation Z – and the challenges they present to employers. He was interested in aspects of work behavior and performance that had become common expectations of our generation.

I began with a laugh, "No. The Marine Corps experiences many challenges with junior members, but not disengagement."

The Marine Corps is the youngest of the military services and turns over roughly 20% of the force annually. It draws from the general population, and the demographic we were talking about has shouldered the brunt of the past 15 years of intense operations overseas.

Those who choose to be Marines are not particularly remarkable compared with the demographic at large, except for an interest and willingness to reach for something bigger inside of themselves. They come to us willing – even eager – to transform themselves. When young recruits enter the Marine Corps, they have only one thing in common: They are ordinary people seeking something more. That certainly was *my* personal story when I was 17 years old. I was living an unremarkable life on an unremarkable path. Then I was presented a remarkable opportunity, that when taken, forever changed me and the expectations I had for my life. But I could just as easily have chosen a life of low expectations.

The Marines have not lowered expectations. On the contrary, they have deliberately held onto high expectations and found a way of seeing the potential behind immediate appearances. What we commonly see in today's civilian workforce is an outcome of reduced cultural norms and low societal expectations. But the *unseen thing* as I look at society today is the potential and possibilities buried beneath those low expectations. Since the Marine Corps draws from the same demographic pool as civilian employers, the civilian workplace has the same access to the innate qualities of dedication, persistence, selflessness, adaptability, resilience, and excellence that are present in today's Marines.

It comes down to how organizations view and work with their people. It is not a matter of what may be written or said, but rather the reality of what is practiced. Is the workforce the heart of the organization to be developed and groomed? Or do members represent components to be manipulated and costs to be managed by senior executives? That answer, as it is manifested in organizational behavior, makes all the difference in the world.

What is it about the Marines that is different? The Marines *see* – and therefore believe in – the potential and innate dedication in the young civilians who present themselves to recruiters all over the United States. And Marine recruiters are trained to hold the belief that this dedication is out there in America's small towns and big cities alike.

As Wayne Dyer said so often, "When you believe it, you will see it." In my 36 years in the Marine Corps – much of which was charged with the task of turning young civilians into the best America has to offer – I knew firsthand that even in the Marine Corps, the power was in seeing what so many others overlooked in the personal lives of each of the young men and women I was responsible for and came to know.

Identity

This is the heart of Marine success. The Marine Corps has an identity, individual and collective, that reaches the best in people and elevates them to something definable and measurable that is bigger than self, not lowering to meet people where they are, nor catering to comfort or selfish gratification. It is a hard-earned identity, not given, and appeals to the highest ideals and aspirations inside of people rather than the lowest common denominators.

The Marines have not cornered the market on identity, of course, and identity is often a major element in attracting talent for companies of all sizes. We know of organizations and companies that have become institutions in themselves, and anchor their appeal on organizational identity. The difference is the nature of that identity. Is it cheap gratification of being associated with a brand? Or deep, enduring satisfaction of pulling together for a selfless cause?

Ultimately though, outcome results from input and process. If input revolves around catering to self, outcome is likely to be the same. An organization so structured will attract and develop people who have little loyalty to the larger whole, but seek other opportunities that cater to self.

For all that is hyped about organizational culture and values, words count for little; behavior and practices count for all. A review of the websites of automobile makers who made news the past several years regarding decisions that resulted in loss of public confidence and adverse governmental action reveals multiple uses of words like *trust* and *compliance*. In the end, though, those were empty words compared to the deliberate organizational actions that led to blistering results. Wonderful words, but irrelevant when it mattered.

Many companies making news today are identified as innovative and creative, yet their day-to-day experience is a culture of conformity and low expectations. The workforce is becoming disengaged, and data abounds regarding unhappiness and lack of fulfillment. This is culture and values in practice, and as outcome results from input and practices, this is not surprising.

An identity built on characteristics that uplift and elevate, that equip and develop the best in people, can free the spirit and unleash the individual. The performance of Millennials and Generation Z Marines over the last 15 years has been superb. They have lived up to defined institutional standards built over two centuries. Young people continue to be drawn to the Marine Corps, despite known adversity, risk, and challenge. It's because of the Marines' identity.

Based on my experience in the Marines, I have identified four key steps that have been proven to bring out the best in the unseen talents of Millennials and Generation Z.

1. Identify: Find and Attract the Right People

This is the first essential step in bringing new life to an organization. Done poorly, everything that follows is overtaxed, potentially wasted, and the organization tends to fail in achieving its desired outcomes. For the Marine Corps, it is its institutional life blood.

This, obviously, refers to the recruiting process, the process of *finding* and *hiring* the right people. The Marines first appeal to the individual's self-interest, in a sense, just like all potential employers looking for entry-level talent. Given that the Marines recruit from the same demographic as civilian businesses, the major difference is the nature of the individual's self-interest, that quality of being aspirational, of wanting the chance to serve a cause bigger than self. Success has required adjusting communications and messaging to the cultural norms and value set of Millennials and Generation Z, which reflects a dynamic, attentive, and responsive recruiting process.

That process cannot be superficial; a mere screening of talent and appealing to job position and compensation cannot get employers who they want if they seek something deeper in their workforce. Success lies in ensuring that you attract the kinds of people who fit the culture of the organization or its desired change. Many may present themselves, but it's up to the employer to sift through winners and mere *wannabes*.

This is also a process of transparent mutual inquiry. Employers owe it to the candidates to set real expectations and standards by which they will be measured and ultimately rewarded.

It is worth noting that at no point in the post-9/11 period has the Marine Corps come up short in getting volunteers for recruit or officer training. The quality has increased in every measurable way. This speaks to the message and process adopted by the Marines, and the nature of the generational demographic, both of which contrast the popular narrative.

2. Invest: Deliberately Develop What the Organization Values

It is unfair and unrealistic to impose an expectation on an employee that is not supported by training and consistent role modeling. This is where investment comes in. Investment turns an expectation into a reality. It can be broken down into two parts: instruction and induction.

As it relates to expectations, the Marine Corps presents and develops everything to its entering workforce that it expects as an outcome of performance. This is the willingness of the organization to commit to the individual, and the development of the qualities needed to make the individual effective within the organization.

A common objection is, "If I invest all this training in my employees, I'm just training them for my competitor. Why should I train these folks when they're just about to leave in three years?"

Concern about return on investment can be mitigated with development that is intentionally, incrementally, and strategically delivered. Investing in onboarding and training in specifically timed increments can be geared to phases of deliberate career management, presenting a value proposition that elicits professional commitment and loyalty. By the time the person is fully invested in training, you will already have had a valued run of service with the individual. Then, if the employee chooses to stay, you will have a wealth of trained talent upon which to sustain operational success and organizational culture, and that you can depend upon to onboard and develop the future workforce.

This concept becomes an organizational value and will allow potential or new employees to see that it is a community they want to be a continued part of.

This mindset is the critical element in the successful development of a workforce. It has enabled the Marine Corps to take an otherwise not highly considered demographic and elevate them to a standing that meets the image and outcome the Marines have achieved over the last two centuries.

It is obvious that the Marine Corps cannot expect people to show up with all required skills. But far more critical than job skills are the intangible, yet measurable, personal qualities, practices, and values that the institution has determined to be essential for individual and organizational success and for institutional regeneration and sustainability. Those qualities and practices that are most vital to the organization are not left to assumptions, but rather are accepted as an institutional responsibility to develop and inculcate within all of those who enter the Marine Corps.

As it invests in people, particularly in intangible but critical qualities, the Marine Corps invests in itself as an organization. This is not a contracted responsibility; it is an inherent one, and it is the institutional buy-in for ensuring that those qualities and practices are consistent outcomes in all Marines and that they permeate the institution.

3. Incorporate: Linking Functional Integration to Organizational Mission

Incorporation addresses organizational structure, processes, and practices. Even the best of processes that properly identify and invest in a workforce end as people fill their positions and begin their routine work. Incorporation implies building into the organization the means by which stated values, described culture, and individual expectations – all of which should be inculcated into new employees – come to life. This concept works on two levels: (1) the organization must reflect what it says it is in its expectations of employees and how they experience their day-to-day interaction with the organization, and (2) the organization must enable and support the qualities and behaviors it espouses to value in the workforce through the thoughtful positioning and use of its people.

This is the employer's side of the employment contract. The employee has been brought on board and educated. Now it is the employer's job to find a meaningful role for that person and set them free to do it.

Nothing is more transparent than organizational practices, particularly those tied to an organization's leaders. We see buzz words such as *trust*, *innovate*, *initiative*, and *empower* routinely touted, yet in practice, the desire to control, or adversity to risk, can often devalue that messaging, thereby eliciting cynicism and disengagement within the workforce.

Just as it is improper for an organization to place an expectation on a person who hasn't been properly trained, it becomes more damaging to place an expectation on someone that is ignored or violated by organizational process, decisions, actions, or culture.

Today's workforce has an expectation of empowerment; it is their nature. Marines are incorporated directly into functional positions tied to the organization's investment in building character and equipping them with skills. They are also empowered to perform, with a bias toward action. In the world in which they operate, they simply have to act; the alternative is not acceptable. The Millennial and Generation Z Marines have more than risen to the challenge, and have met over 200 years of unmatched individual and organizational success.

As a deliberate process, incorporation delivers the return on investment. As the organization invests in the individual, its return is the individual operating at a high capacity and committed to the organization, its mission, and its success.

4. Inspire: The Day-to-Day Intersection of Workforce, Organization, and Leadership

Inspire is to *inform* and *infuse* the individual with the shared vision modeled by organizational leaders. Tied to mission, it becomes the aspirational reminder of the bigger outcome that all are pulling toward together. It is holding, casting, and modeling, constantly keeping vision foremost in mind, resulting in perseverance to the collective goal and keeping day-to-day nuisances in proper perspective.

Inspiration speaks to the ongoing relationship between the workforce and the organization, manifested in the decisions and actions of its leadership. This is not just a structural, vertical leadership relationship, but it also includes informal and peer-to-peer leadership and influence. Inspire is both personal and organizational. This gets to practices (more than words or commands), which are those things the organization ultimately and actually prizes. Inspiration is what is valued and rewarded in recognition, evaluations, compensation, and promotions seen and experienced by the workforce. Success in inspiration is an organization that structurally encourages and supports the workforce consistent with what it has instilled in its people and espouses as important.

The Marines inspire through the reminder of high personal standards that surround each individual and that are modeled by those with the responsibility and privilege of leadership. It is done visibly, sometimes under great pressure, most often quietly. It not simply a constant in the work life of Marines, but also a glue that holds together units at many levels, and ultimately, the institution itself over time.

Conversely, as we understand aspects of the disengaged workforce, we know there is *disinspiration*, as well. It is inherently damaging to see mediocre performance, or acceptance of falling short of goals, being tolerated by leadership. If employees think, "Do I really want to be on this team? Do I trust my peers or respect my leaders?" or similar thoughts, you have a disengaged workforce. People seek inspiration from both peers and leaders. As it achieves a shared positive vision, the workforce supports and builds upon itself.

Each of these steps are inculcated in the Marines, providing the foundation for their identity and remarkable success. The Marine Corps operates in a unique environment, but its principles are ubiquitous, developed and practiced in a demanding environment, to then be practiced under conditions where failure is simply not an option.

The principles underlying the Marine approach, appropriately adapted, are universally applicable. Success requires specificity and intentionality, not vague cultural ideals, nor halfhearted commitments to unmeasurable outcomes. Well beyond that is the single critical aspect: Your people will not give more than you are willing to put into them.

As I look out into the world, and as I routinely see a negative narrative of Millennials and Generation Z, I see wasted people, efforts, and opportunities.

I am continually impressed by how these young people are performing in the Marines, whether leading a patrol in the face of an adversary, or simply as part of a crew, refueling a jet on the flight deck of an aircraft carrier, at sea, at night, in foul weather.

Look at what you are getting out of your workforce, where you have set your expectations, and how they are being met. If there is a difference, and if that difference has an impact on your mission and success, there may be some things to consider.

I spent 12 of my last 16 years of active duty in formal training and education assignments. I was often surprised by what I saw with our young Marines, sometimes positively, sometimes not. I learned that my opinion did not matter; rather, what was required was an understanding of Millennials and Generation Z, and adjusting what we were doing to ensure the success of our units deploying to combat and the institutional sustainment of the Marine Corps.

This was a sacred duty, and although we adjusted to the dynamics of the new operating environment of those joining the force, what was rigidly retained were those institutional standards built through remarkable effort and epic sacrifice over two centuries of the Marine Corps. A conclusion from my 37 years on active duty, and with respect and reverence to those who served as Marines in World War II, Korea, and Vietnam, is what is being fielded today is the finest force in the history of the Marine Corps.

If you are unable to say the same for your organization, I offer this: The answers lie within the organization, not outside of it, and are driven far more by what the organization is willing to do to alter that outcome than by those who are being hired and brought into the workforce.

Something to consider.

Reflection Questions

1. If you work with any young Millennials or members of Generation Z, what do you see as your biggest challenges with them?
2. What can you identify as some of the assets or strengths that this new generation brings to your organization? To the world at large?
3. What are some strategies that you might employ as a leader to tap into these strengths?

Note

1. David Harder, *The Workplace Engagement Solution: Find a Common Mission, Vision and Purpose with All of Today's Employees* (Newburyport, MA: Career Press, 2017).

14 | Respect, Courage, Honesty

True Leadership Traits

Jack Zenger

John H. Zenger is the cofounder and chief executive officer of Zenger Folkman, a firm that increases the effectiveness of leaders.

Jack taught at the University of Southern California (USC) and later at the Stanford Graduate School of Business. He received a doctorate in business administration from the University of Southern California. He was a trustee and board chairman for the UVU Board of Trustees, and just completed 10 years as a member of the Board of Regents of the State of Utah.

He received ATD's Lifetime Achievement in Workplace Learning and Performance Award, and was inducted into the Human Resources Development Hall of Fame.

He is the author or coauthor of 14 books, 150 articles and blogs, and he writes regularly for Harvard Business Review *and* Forbes.

■ ■ ■

When CEOs describe what they want most in people they hire, they consistently talk about honesty and integrity. Among the leadership competencies that our firm measures via a 360-degree feedback assessment, honesty

103

and integrity have consistently received extremely high scores, in first or second place in comparison to everything else.

I had an experience that gave me a whole new perspective on this important leadership attribute. The lesson did not come from any leadership guru; it came from a physician.

My son was diagnosed with stomach cancer. He was a practicing physician, specializing in pulmonary care. His cancer was not common and the optimum treatment was unclear to his physicians. He endured extensive chemotherapy, radiation therapy, surgery to remove half of his stomach, and finally a bone marrow transplant. After months of treatment, they performed a CAT scan that found no trace of cancer cells; his physicians, family, colleagues, and friends were hoping for a complete cure.

On Easter Sunday, his condition took a sudden turn for the worse. He was admitted to the hospital where they again began conducting extensive tests. The following day, I and other family members were in his hospital room when his oncologist came to review the results.

What then transpired was an incredibly honest and yet caring presentation of the facts. The tests revealed that his cancer had returned with an astonishing vengeance, now filling his entire abdominal cavity. His liver and kidneys were totally overtaken with cancer. Blood tests painted an equally bleak picture. At the end of his calm and careful recital of the test results, the oncologist asked if my son understood. After a short pause and in a matter of fact manner, my son quietly replied, "Yes, this means that I am going to die."

I sat there thinking about the many business leaders whom I've known through the years who could not muster up the courage to tell a colleague about the negative consequences of their behavior. Those conversations were about minor blips in a career. This conversation was about the biggest issue anyone could imagine, literally, life and death. It happened that my son and his oncologist were personal friends and esteemed colleagues. But even that relationship did not make the oncologist dilute his honest recital of the truth.

I recall thinking to myself that I had a great deal to learn from those in other professions. The physician had been compassionate and respectful in his delivery, but he chose not to sugarcoat this most painful of all messages. His dear friend and colleague deserved to know the truth, as did his entire family.

Two days later, with all of us at his bedside, my son passed away. There are no words that adequately describe that event and the emotions that came gushing up for me and all in the room. But words are also not adequate to describe my admiration for the doctor who courageously delivered a message that was incredibly painful for him to convey.

One of the fundamental principles of good leadership is the willingness to treat others with respect. Our ability and courage to speak honestly with one another are most certainly at the heart of treating one another with esteem. Indeed, our research[1] on leadership integrity paints an interesting picture. We found that leaders who received high scores on honesty and integrity also received high scores on five behavioral indices:

1. Approachable
2. Acts with humility
3. Listens with great intensity
4. Makes decisions carefully
5. Acts assertively

The first four of these describe how someone treats another with great respect. They are not in the mold of the leader who *smiles up and kicks down.* Nor do they characterize haughty leaders who put themselves into a different category and feel that they need not play by the rules that govern the rest of us. As I observed the oncologist talking with my son, he exemplified each of these characteristic behaviors.

The final item, acting assertively, is a bit odd. Most people would not immediately think of assertiveness being a bedfellow of honesty and integrity. I thought, however, that the oncologist attending to my son could have ducked that extremely difficult conversation in a variety of ways and with countless excuses. But he didn't, and he taught me a profound lesson about the kindness of true honesty.

Reflection Questions

1. What sort of lessons can you learn from other professionals, especially from those outside your field?
2. Why are honesty and integrity such critical traits for leaders?
3. How comfortable are you dealing honestly with your colleagues? With the people you lead? If '*not very,*' what makes such interactions difficult?

Note

1. John H. Zenger, Joseph Folkman, and Scott Edinger, "Making Yourself Indispensable," *Harvard Business Review*, October 2011.

PART III

Defining Moments

Each of us has a defining moment that has influenced what we see when we look out the window. Some of us have more than one. Defining moments are those experiences we have in which we become aware of something about which we were previously not conscious. These experiences are the shapers of our character, the inspiration for our decisions, and the starting point of our life journeys.

We open this section with an article by CEO of Best Buy, Hubert Joly, who analyzes his initial reluctance to utilize the help of an executive coach in his business life and describes how his life and career were transformed once he began work with Marshall Goldsmith. He is particularly emphatic about the critical importance of being open to feedback in order to grow as a leader. Rita McGrath then summarizes some key themes she has learned across her academic and professional career, concluding with what she has found about Marshall Goldsmith's advice that "feedback is a gift" and the practical implications of starting with a good theory. In her article, Beverly Kaye explores the importance of acknowledging your "flat side" and finding ways to move outside your comfort zone and do things to challenge yourself to grow and become a more well-rounded and effective leader. Catherine Carr draws on her many years of humanitarian experience serving around the world as part of Doctors Without Borders to explain the importance of opening one's heart to both joy and sorrow in order to expand and grow and connect to the world in more meaningful ways. Jeffrey Kuhn describes the "strategic myopia" that affects so many leaders and organizations. He draws on Peter Drucker's concept of looking out the window at what is "visible, but not seen" to suggest new paradigms and possibilities for developing your strategic eye. Prakash Raman draws on his adolescent experiences – both successes and failures – as a world-ranked tennis player to offer advice to business leaders seeking to bridge the gap between inspiration and operation in their own personal and professional lives. And Margaret Wheatley discusses the critical need for leaders to think and reflect on where they've been before deciding where they would like to go next, and describes how cultivating a new way of seeing can open up new choices. She emphasizes the need for a new type of leader in today's world and describes the crucial role of leadership at the local rather than the global level.

15 | The Power of Accepting Feedback

Hubert Joly

Hubert Joly is chairman and CEO of Best Buy Co. Inc., the leading provider of consumer technology products and services, with approximately 125,000 employees in North America and more than $40 billion in annual revenue. Mr. Joly joined Best Buy in 2012, and led the company through its much publicized Renew Blue transformation. The transformation resulted in improvements in customer satisfaction, market share gains, revenue growth, and improved margins. Now, Mr. Joly is leading Best Buy into its next phase, Best Buy 2020: Building the New Blue. In this new chapter, Best Buy is driven by a clear purpose: to help customers pursue their passions and enrich their lives with the help of technology.

Prior to joining Best Buy, Mr. Joly was CEO of Carlson, a global hospitality and travel company. Before that, he led Carlson Wagonlit Travel, Vivendi Universal Games, and Electronic Data Systems' business in France. He serves on the board of directors of several nonprofits and corporations, including Ralph Lauren Corp. Mr. Joly was awarded the Legion of Honor, France's highest civilian distinction, in 2017.

■ ■ ■

I am an avid skier who likes to ski with an instructor; I am an enthusiastic tennis player who regularly works with a tennis coach. I use a coach in both sports not just because I want to get to the front of the lift line or reserve a better court, but because I want to get better at two things I love to do. Oddly, though, it took me a long time to begin working with an executive coach. In fact, if you had told me earlier in my career that a fellow executive was using a coach I might have asked about it, and certainly would have thought, "What is wrong with that guy? What problem does he have?"

My disinterest in personally engaging a coach stemmed from my struggle with feedback. I had sat through the experience many times of receiving three or four examples of what I was doing well, only to have it be followed by areas I needed to work on. I would always appreciate the first bit of feedback and happily agree with it. It was, not surprisingly, the part of the conversation involving *personal development opportunities* that I didn't like very much. In fact, my reaction was to be defensive and try to find what was wrong with the people offering such advice. Clearly, these people did not understand me or simply did not agree with me! I was good at rationalizing (and rejecting) their feedback, finding it painful and not fun. It is fair to say that I did not do much with these *development opportunities*. On the occasion where I did act on the feedback, it was without any joy or real enthusiasm.

All this changed in 2010. I give credit to my then head of HR at Carlson, Elizabeth Bastoni, who introduced me to Marshall Goldsmith. She had worked with him when she was in HR at the Coca-Cola Company. Marshall is, of course, one of the foremost, if not the foremost, executive coaches in the world. One thing that was exciting was that he was actually working with a bunch of other successful executives. In fact, Marshall specializes in helping successful people get even better, a specialty that helped me overcome my disinterest in and distaste for coaching.

Marshall has written a book entitled, *What Got You Here, Won't Get You There*.[1] At the beginning of the book, he lists the 20 quirks of successful people. If I remember correctly, I exhibited 13 out of 20. They included the notion of thinking I had to be the smartest guy in the room or often adding *too much value* to a particular discussion or meeting. His correct assessment was that I frequently wanted to make sure people understood how smart I was and how much I could add. So, I was clearly ripe for help. What followed this epiphany was my discovery of the amazing process Marshall uses.

It starts with 360-degree feedback. He talks to the people you are working with, the people who report to you, and your board of directors. Marshall does a great job distilling their feedback and gives you two documents that he sends you separately. One document has all of the things you are doing great. He tells you to read this first and appreciate it. He then sends a second document composed of your opportunities. Now, this process does not look very different from the earlier feedback scenarios I described where you hear three things you are doing well and three things you need to work on. The only difference lies in what Marshall tells you to do next: He says, simply, *you* decide what you want to work on; *you* make the choice. This framing is brilliant because, in a sense, he makes it not about *fixing* a problem, but about deciding to *get better* at something.

In tennis, I decided a long time ago that I wanted to get better at my forehand, and in skiing, I wanted to be better in the deep powder. There is always something you want to get better at and, for me, deciding that I wanted to work on this feedback – as opposed to being told I needed to – made a huge difference.

One of the reasons I was ready to accept this change was that, over the years, I have worked with a friend, Brother Samuel, a monk in the congregation of St. John. He helped me understand that the search for perfection, whether in your personal or professional life, is *evil*. Though he was referencing the biblical story of the fallen angel who thought he was perfect and did not need anyone's help, this framework helped me appreciate that I had vulnerabilities and could be loved for them, not in spite of them. As importantly, appreciating and even coming to love my colleagues' vulnerabilities was a critical component of this spiritual journey for me.

Continuing in Marshall's process: Once you decide what you want to work on, you then communicate that to your colleagues, either as a group or one-on-one. You start by thanking them for all the great things they have said about you and, importantly, you do not talk about the criticisms. Instead, you say, "Thank you for your feedback and, against that backdrop, these are the things I have decided to work on."

You then share the three things you are going to work on. In fact, I write them down and give them to my team as a prelude to asking them for their help and/or advice. A few months later, I check in and ask colleagues how I am doing. The obvious benefit of checking in is that you will likely receive more feedback or advice. With this in mind, I will say things like: "So, how am I doing on this?" Or, "Do you have any advice for me?" When you get this additional feedback, listen, shut up, and express gratitude. Don't be defensive. Remember, the good thing about feedback is that you do not need to do anything with it. You are the decider. In fact, you do not even need to agree with the feedback. You just say, "Thank you."

Checking in with colleagues has another positive result: Knowing you are going to ask for feedback on your progress is a good incentive to actually do something. As Marshall's process reflects, human beings need structure. This reminds me of the apocryphal story regarding the difference between a pilot and a surgeon. A pilot always goes through a checklist before taking off or landing. Surgeons may or may not go through a similar checklist, including perhaps not even washing their hands as well as they should. Why do each of these professionals treat a checklist differently? For the pilot, if they do not go through the checklist, *they* may die. For the doctor, if he or she does not go through the checklist, then the *patient* may die. That's a big difference and illustrates why, in the absence of possibly dire consequences, we often need structure. Marshall's process provides this kind of structure and allows you to rinse and repeat, getting better and better. Remember, there is no such thing as being done with coaching. Just ask tennis champion Roger Federer, who still has a coach help him with his swing!

There is one last benefit of checking in that I learned from Marshall. What he explained was that changing behaviors is actually easier than changing people's perceptions of your behavior. Let's imagine I am working on not being rude in meetings. If, over the next six months, I succeed in not being rude and then ask how you think I have been doing, you will probably say something like: "Well, come to think about it, in the last six months I don't recall you being rude in meetings." This particular advantage is twofold. First, I get feedback on how I am doing. Second, and as importantly, I remind you that I have changed for the better, as opposed to allowing you to potentially remember only the previous, rude behavior.

So, what are the lessons I have learned from my coaching experience?

I no longer believe my role is to be the smartest person in the room, but instead, I understand that my role is to create an environment in which others can blossom, flourish, and do great things. I have learned to accept my vulnerabilities as well as others' vulnerabilities.

I have also learned that decisions get made by *decision makers* and that I should be at peace with the fact that this is not always me. This is a key point because, as a smart, high-charging individual, you want to be in charge of everything. No! Decisions get made by the decision makers. Get used to that and remember that, sometimes, your role is to convince people of your idea or vision. If you are not able to convince them, that is your problem, not theirs.

In summary, learning with the help of an executive coach is something I wish I had discovered sooner. Fortunately, I was already working with one when I joined Best Buy five years ago. Only four months after joining, I told my new team I was going to ask Marshall to come in and talk to them so I could continue being the best leader I could be. I explained that turning around Best Buy would require all of us to be the best leaders we could be, starting with me. It was for that reason that I was asking for their help. Indirectly, of course, what I also signaled to my colleagues was that working on your own development was okay, a lesson it is never too late to learn.

Reflection Questions

1. Do you struggle with feedback, and is working on your personal development something painful or joyful?
2. Do you feel that a lack of feedback has been an impediment to your professional success?
3. Do you feel that you genuinely want to get better at something?
4. Do you have anyone in your life or around you whose feedback you would find worthwhile and useful?
5. Do you have a structured way to solicit and get feedback?

Note

1. Marshall Goldsmith, *What Got You Here, Won't Get You There: How Successful People Become Even More Successful*, rev. ed. (New York: Hachette Books, 2007).

16 | Discovering Motifs

Rita McGrath

Rita McGrath is a globally recognized thought leader who focuses on leading innovation and growth during times of uncertainty. She works with boards, CEOs, and senior executives to help them think strategically, even in today's rapidly changing and volatile environments. She received the #1 achievement award in strategy from the prestigious management rankings group Thinkers50 and is consistently ranked in the Top 10. Her most recent book was the best-selling The End of Competitive Advantage. *She has written three other books, including* Discovery Driven Growth, *cited by Clayton Christensen as describing one of the most important management ideas ever developed. She is a regular speaker in exclusive events such as the Drucker Forum and various CEO Summits. She is working on a new book about strategic inflection points.*

McGrath has recently founded Valize, LLC, a new company focused on helping organizations get beyond innovation theater by unlocking the power of the Discovery Driven growth approach. McGrath joined the faculty of Columbia Business School in 1993. Prior to life in academia, she was an IT director, worked in the political arena, and founded two startups. She received her PhD from the Wharton School, University of Pennsylvania, and has degrees with honors from Barnard College and the Columbia School of International and Public Affairs. She is married and is proud to be the mother of two delightful grownups. Follow Rita on Twitter: @rgmcgrath. For more information, visit RitaMcGrath.com.

■ ■ ■

>## An Evaluation – and a Surprise

The year was 1993. I was a newly minted PhD student and a brand-new faculty member at Columbia Business School. At the time, a rite of passage for junior members of the faculty was to teach the core, required, full-semester course, Strategic Management of the Enterprise. Teaching MBAs is challenging enough, but teaching Columbia MBAs about strategy, at that particular time in the school's history, was grim.

For starters, about half the class had come from consulting firms and didn't think there was much they could learn from a 32-year-old academic about strategy in the real world. The other half of the class were from or were aiming to join financial services firms on Wall Street. In neither case did they think that this course was going to be useful in the near term. To be honest, they resented how much of their tuition money the course was going to soak up. It also didn't help that we were required to grade on a curve or that a big proportion of the grade depended on my subjective assessment of class participation. To say the least, it was an intimidating undertaking!

Nonetheless, I really tried. I hung in there when I was characterized as a *foil flipper* (yes, we actually used printed slides and an overhead projector – and chalk – in those days). When a student remarked that I didn't seem to be that up to date on the latest news (with two kids under five and a killer commute, there wasn't much time for reading the paper!). Another student asked something about how I would tackle work–life balance and another shouted, "She'd probably put it in a 2 x 2 matrix!" I guess I overused that particular teaching tool. I also kept my cool when, for their final project, a student team did an in-depth analysis of Larry Flynt's *Hustler* magazine empire, complete with a copy of its signature publication attached to their report!

And then came an unexpected gift in the form of course evaluations. One thing to know about me is that while I do see feedback as a gift, as Marshall Goldsmith constantly reminds me, my initial reaction is to over-react. I could have 99 out of 100 people say that I walk on water and one person could say, "Well, Professor X can run on water," and I would be devastated. As I was going through the evaluations and homing in on all the negative comments (despite the reality that there were probably more positive ones), I suddenly ran across a real gem.

"Professor McGrath," the student said, "has an uncanny ability to connect anything to anything, no matter how seemingly unrelated."

Until that moment, it hadn't occurred to me that this was a sufficiently unusual skill that a student, who may well have resented having to take the class, would remark upon it. I've now become convinced that what I see when I look out the window are motifs – the often-subtle patterns that inform how organizations and other kinds of systems work. Having that perspective suggests a good point of departure for making interventions. If you want to change a system, you need to understand the interrelationships between its components. That's the kind of work to which I have dedicated most of my research, thinking, and actions.

The "How'm I Doin'?" Years

Throughout my twenties, I was a caricature of the "young woman comes to New York City to seek fame and fortune" kind of person. With glee, I had fled the Rochester area to attend Barnard College in the Big Apple. When my parents objected to my majoring in history (each week's mail contained clippings of the awful jobs and ruined lives of former history majors), I switched to political science and fell in love. At the time, there was still room in the field for rich, narrative stories about the fascinating people, circumstances, and decisions that created the political economy around us.

I also started to work in actual political systems, with internships at the Parks and Recreation department, the City Council President's office, and in various political campaigns. I also started two businesses, one in the political arena, one not. It was addictive.

Eventually, I completed a master's of public administration at Columbia's School of Public and International Affairs, which led to a job at what is now the New York City Department of Citywide Administrative Services. Running the city then was daunting. Ironically, its many problems created all kinds of opportunities; I mean, you were hardly going to make things worse. Mayor Ed Koch was a relentless and energetic advocate for his city and pushed his agencies to take advantage of new ideas.

My big break came when the powers that be decided to computerize the then-manual procurement process. I know, it doesn't sound glamourous, but the project (which I named CLIPS, for Commodity Line Item Purchasing System) proved to be a catapult to a major new role. At the age of about 25, I found myself with a staff of 12, a team of consultants, a budget that ran into the millions, the authority to weigh in on vendor decisions, and a mandate to shepherd a project that would eventually touch every city agency and affect how all commodities purchased by the city were bought. I didn't know this was going to be nearly impossible. So, my team and I waded right in. With wise support from the department's head of IT, we pulled it off, within budget and pretty much on schedule.

This period really sharpened my motif-building skills. Computer systems touch stakeholders in unpredictable ways, and a large-scale one like this is as much about organizational change as it is about technology. Some of the most significant lessons I learned about how to promote change in organizations, how to see around corners politically, how to influence people without formal authority, and so on, were from this period.

That work, despite the long hours and occasional frustrations, was exhilarating.

So there I was – a job I loved, a decent salary, a place in Brooklyn, and, eventually, a husband and an apartment in Manhattan. What could possibly have been better than that? As readers will appreciate, it's exactly when all seems to be going swimmingly well that you are often in the greatest danger of stagnation.

A Dreadful Year

On the career front, I was beginning to realize that this happy, static situation of running the now up-and-running system could go on indefinitely, creating a very comfortable dead end. Or, I could take my skills and go to the private sector. Since we were, by then, expecting our first child, that didn't seem like a sensible transition.

I had heard that business schools were booming and needed people with PhD degrees, and that there were lots of jobs for new business PhDs. The idea of doing research, writing, and teaching appealed to me, and it seemed that a professor's job was probably more compatible with motherhood than a corporate executive's would be.

I was accepted to the PhD program in social systems sciences at the Wharton School. Baby in tow, we decided to move to the Princeton area, in between New York and Philadelphia, and my husband and I entered a new world of parenting, commuting, day care, and a new house, mortgage, and community where we knew no one.

I was miserable.

Things got even worse once I started my PhD, where it seemed that the purpose of your first year was to break down any misconceptions you may have that you know anything at all about the subjects you are studying. Remember, by then I had been managing people for some years, and you might think I knew something about management. That counted for nothing in academic circles. Every article I read felt to me as though it was part of a conversation that had begun long before I arrived on the scene and would likely continue long after I left it. Take, for instance, a classic article by John Child, which took 30 pages to make the point that *strategic choice* was important for organizational performance[1]. I thought that was blitheringly obvious from the get-go, and frankly didn't see why such an article would cause the major stir that it did (John and I later became friends and co-edited a special issue of a very prestigious academic journal together).

Light at the End of the Tunnel?

One bright spot in that difficult year was being assigned to read the entire works of Peter Drucker, a book a week, as I "learned to read like a graduate student." It left me with a great appreciation of Drucker's ability to synthesize and integrate patterns in the phenomena he observed, as well as (just as with my political science study) a joy in reading in-depth discussions of people and phenomena. This flew in the face of most academic work (even in management), which has often been described as having a bad case of *physics envy*, in which statistics and large data sets are often more respected than in-depth observational studies. The same thing happened in political science as well, as the *softer* sciences attempted to gain respect for their academic rigor.

My professor Kenwyn Smith also led a course on organizational diagnosis that was foundational for my later consulting and strategy work. "It's all there when you walk in the door," he would say, "you just can't see it yet." That is very much in the spirit of being able to *see* the deeper patterns in an organization. And this led to a major insight: what clients diagnose as their problems seldom are.

Another bright spot was working at Ian MacMillan's entrepreneurship center. After rejecting various ideas for my thesis, an opportunity provided by Citibank solved the dilemma. They wanted to do a three-year study to understand their own corporate venturing process, and commissioned us to do in-depth case studies of 23 of their successful and failed internal corporate ventures. There was a modest budget to go with that, which meant that I was once again employed. The case studies were fascinating, and I discovered my love for figuring out how all the pieces of a puzzle fit together.

"There Is Nothing So Practical as a Good Theory"

This statement from Kurt Lewin is a mantra for my life, which has to do with spotting the underlying patterns and motifs. As I've learned, a good theory has boundary conditions (when will a certain cause lead to an effect?), clear independent and dependent variables (what are we solving for?), and distinguishes between correlation and causality.

To give an example, my work on discovery-driven planning, which has now resurfaced as part of the *lean* toolkit, began with the recognition that when one is working with assumptions rather than facts, the primary challenge is learning as much as possible with as little risk as possible. That theoretical world is completely different than the world in which few assumptions need to be made because the past is a good predictor of the future.

As I reflect on my story, a few key motifs stand out. The first is that discovering what you love almost always takes you down unexpected paths, and sometimes that journey is uncomfortable. This brings me to the second theme, which is that being unhappy, mad, and frustrated comes with the territory of doing something new. Having sources of support – in my case, my husband and colleagues – who can assure you that you're not the stupidest person ever to open a management journal, is key. I think, as with strategy, finding what you uniquely do well is a matter of setting a broad direction and working really hard to go there.

And yes, Marshall, feedback is a gift.

Reflection Questions:

1. Do you really consider feedback a *gift*? In what ways?
2. When you provide feedback to others, how do they receive it?
3. Have you ever been in a work/personal situation that looked great on the outside, but in which you were not happy inside? What did you do?
4. How do you apply theories about management or leadership that you may have learned in school to real-world situations? Do they fit?

Note

1. J. Child, "Organizational Structure, Environment and Performance: The Role of Strategic Choice" *Sociology* 6, no. 1 (1972): 1–22.

17 | Is It Time to Leave Your Comfort Zone?

Beverly Kaye

Beverly Kaye has earned a reputation as a thought leader in the world of career development, engagement, and retention. As founder of Career Systems International, she has had the opportunity to build a team of committed and passionate practitioners to deliver her ideas globally to organizations of all sizes.

Her many books have become texts for HR practitioners tasked with installing career development initiatives and supporting systems in their organizations. They have helped countless managers find practical ways to obtain and retain talent, as well as reminded individuals to take responsibility for their own engagement, made the career conversation easier for managers, and helped both managers and employees reimagine the notion of career mobility. Beverly received the ISA Thought Leader Award from the Association of Learning Providers in March 2018 and the ATD Lifetime Achievement Award in May 2018.

■ ■ ■

I had relocated to California after building a life and a career on the East Coast. My work at that time was in higher education, and I held a series of positions as a member of the Dean of Students team in several prestigious universities (schools that I don't think I ever could have gotten into when I was in that application process).

I remember being fascinated by the number of students who truly believed that, if they were A students, at A schools, there would be an A life/career awaiting them. For some, that materialized, but for many others, it did not. Life just got in the way. I think my early interest in the whole career arena started back then. I sensed the importance of contingency planning in case the current track became blocked.

I had a chance to widen my thinking and consider the same kind of career contingency planning in organizations as I pursued further studies at Boston University and the Sloan School of Management at MIT.

I had no idea then that I would build my own future in the world of organizational career development. That door was opened in California when I was accepted to pursue a graduate fellowship at UCLA. That opportunity led me to study adult education and change management. The years of coursework also gave me a chance to test my early ideas and thinking by teaching in a variety of organizations and adult education centers. It all led me to finally determine that the subject of my dissertation would be how organizations could support the career growth of their employees, as well as the systems and structures that were needed to make that happen.

I was always a diligent student, studying hard for every course, always doing those extra assignments that would help me gain whatever extra credit I could. Studying, memorizing, applying what I learned, and adding a bit of my own creativity when it was needed were what I was used to doing, and doing so quickly and successfully.

I was not used to operating without an action plan. I was not used to failing. But that's what proceeded to happen, several times.

I selected a dissertation committee (from the management school and the school of education) that I knew and felt would support my efforts. I selected an approach that would enable me to design a research agenda that seemed doable and would fit my style. I wanted to take action, move quickly, report on what I had learned from the research, and move on to the next stage of my own career. (Good approach for a Jersey girl!) And it was totally within my comfort zone.

But there was the problem. My committee intuitively knew and believed that operating within my comfort zone would neither change me nor give me the growth experience that this stage of my career/education demanded. They rejected each idea that I brought to them and told me to start over. As I said, failure was not something I was used to. Hard work always had been my way of getting through whatever challenges I faced. This time it did not work.

Their request was that I use an approach called *grounded theory* or phenomenological research. They actually said that they saw my flat side (right then, I knew I was in trouble). They felt I operated from my intuition and not from a theory base. I needed to ground myself in a belief system, a theory, a conceptual model that would be pulled from my own research and that I could put into my own words. It had to be something I could stand on and stand behind. I had to do more reflection (not my natural way), and come up with a strong conceptual model that was totally my own. I had no idea how to do this no matter how much I read about this approach. Not knowing was unbearable.

The one thing that kept me going was a comment from one of my committee members (while I was in tears after yet another rejection) that went something like this: "Hang in there, Beverly. If you can do this, it will be your career development." Though I did not understand it completely then, this advice somehow kept me going. I wanted this experience to define my career and was determined to get to the other side.

I selected three organizations to study and went about my interviews with HR leaders, line leaders, individuals, and managers to understand how all of them viewed career growth. I collected a mass of data and tried (unsuccessfully) to report on that data.

The idea of phenomenological research is that when your theory holds and explains all of your data, you've got it. Each time I tried, I thought I had the theory. Alas, when I presented it, I realized it just didn't hang together. I was convinced that I could not do this. The more I told myself that this was impossible, the more impossible it became. I even pleaded with my committee not to do this to me at the end of my education. Stupid words indeed, especially for the lifelong learner that I have become since that time.

Out of desperation (and loneliness), I stumbled into my own creative learning style. I realized I was not someone who could sit with information by myself; I needed a human being at the other side of my thinking. I found someone, and I actually hired that person to sit with me and listen to me talk about what I was learning and what I had heard in all those interviews I had conducted.

Interestingly enough, the *learning partner* I selected knew nothing about my research, but knew to ask great questions. As she asked and asked and asked, I responded and responded. Having someone up close and personal to bounce my insights off of was precisely what I needed (and, over the next three decades, has become my preferred way of developing new ideas). Slowly (very slowly), my own *this is impossible* perspective began to yield to insights that surprised me. The conceptual model that I had struggled to find for so long eventually bubbled up and actually became clear to me. And as it did so, I was able to make it clear to my committee and the work could begin.

I had no idea that this stretch assignment would become my real work for several decades. I was able to develop a model and framework that guided my consulting, as well as the learning solutions that were eventually designed and developed from that consulting. Along the way I met and brainstormed with other practitioners and clients. Each conversation enhanced that framework, and each presentation I gave helped to solidify this early thinking. Although the organizational landscape has shifted many times during the years I've been practicing, I have been able to rethink, improve, twist, and turn my early ideas to connect with each shift. And it all started with moving out of my comfort zone and committing to a new approach.

So, What Did I Learn?

I created my point of view from intuition combined with some helpful trial-and-error experiences. That intuition is still vital and I listen to it! But I learned that I needed to pause and reflect more, even though this was uncomfortable for me. I needed to pull insights from that reflection and test those insights with others. I needed a combination of comfort and challenge to eventually produce something I could stand behind.

We need to build our own thought platform. When that platform is confirmed by the work we do every day, it continues to provide strength and expand. When it comes through a particularly difficult experience and is ratified by continued work, you stand on firm ground.

Collaboration is sweet. For those of us who learn best when we are in dialogue with others, we need to find those dialogue partners and not be afraid to invite them in.

All of the books I've written since my first one have been collaborations with other wonderful thinkers. I realize that my creative juices get stoked when they come into partnership with others.

The hardest experiences are the ones that teach us the most. When you are able to see the world as a giant classroom, you begin to understand that all experiences are here to teach you something about yourself. If you stay open to those experiences, no matter how tough, you grow.

Reflection Questions

1. When have you felt or said to yourself, "This is impossible!" If you were able to turn that around, how did you do it? What is repeatable?
2. What is your preferred learning style? How has that been confirmed for you?
3. Have you ever used a learning partner? If so, how did that work for you?

18 | Understanding in Moments

Catherine Carr

In 2009, Catherine Carr took her human resources and finance experience on the road and joined Doctors Without Borders. Since then she has had the honor of working on more than 10 different projects in Africa, the Middle East, the Philippines, and Haiti. Each experience has played a part in shattering her preconceived notions, teaching her to become comfortable with the uncomfortable, and deepening her connection to the world.

Catherine has a bachelor's degree in communications from the University of San Francisco and an MBA from Golden Gate University. When not traveling and working, she spends her time writing, speaking, and reconnecting with family and friends. She can be found via the usual social media means. And if none of that works, there is always her website: www.catherinecarr.global.

■ ■ ■

Life changes in moments. And since there are close to an infinite number of them, it's a crapshoot knowing when the life-changing ones will hit. In my experience, they usually happen when I least expect them and always right about the time I think I've got it all figured out.

A different culture, a new condition, an idea never considered. Sometimes gently, sometimes not, forcing me to cross over and see the view from another perspective. At times freezing me in my tracks. Other times slowly drawing me in close. Every time, bringing me closer to understanding something new and allowing a deeper and more meaningful connection to the world.

Late one afternoon in 2013, well into my fifth year with Doctors Without Borders, I was working and living in a small village in northern Syria. The team had converted an unremarkable two-story house into a small hospital. Our task was to provide emergency medical care to victims of war, civilians and fighters alike.

On this particular afternoon things were slow. No emergencies, the sun was shining, and not a cloud over the olive groves in the distance. It was the middle of winter and yet there was a sense of spring in the air. I decided to escape the crowded communal office and visit the medical teams downstairs. I patted my head, determining that my hair was more or less tucked respectfully under *the sock*, that close-fitting head-covering peeking out from under the scarf of my hijab. If I had known a moment was right around the corner, I would have checked more carefully.

After some time and a lot of laughter with the downstairs crew, I bounded back upstairs, using the typically empty stairwell. I was in a great mood, humming and taking the steps by leaps. It felt good to move and I enjoyed feeling the wisps of hair that had escaped the sock against my neck and face. My hijab had definitely slipped out of place and I didn't care.

I had rounded the corner of the first set of stairs and launched into the second set when I saw him coming down toward me. He was tall but seemed even more so because he stood at the top of the stairs. He had a full beard and wore a traditional white head covering, white pants, and white tunic, with a black vest and wide black belt around his waist. Given my geographic location, our patient demographics, and the fact that he was walking unassisted, I knew he was a fighter who had come to visit a friend in the hospital.

It is said that, "Between stimulus and response there is a space. In that space is our power to choose our response. In our response lies our growth and our freedom." A lovely theory indeed, but when standing before an unexpected reality in an empty stairwell, space has a way of collapsing in on itself.

We stood. Staring at one another. I thought about bolting back down the stairs but knew that was lizard brain thinking. I held my ground. Space collapsed and time slowed. We were functioning at our most basic levels. "Interesting," I thought, "in addition to *flight or fight*, there is also *freeze*."

Knowing lizards aren't very smart, my ego rolled right over lizard brain to take the wheel. Still not the place to be if the goal is rational thinking, but it does seem to be the path our minds take when confronted with any new situation. It's as if the brain says, "Okay. Situation safe. Now, how does this situation affect me?" Ego thinking can be a dank, dark place where decisions are made in the name of *me me me* and with the conviction that *my way is the right way*.

I will never know what he was thinking. But, assuming we were both in ego thinking at the same time, I can imagine.

Me: "Hey Mister, who do you think you are? Standing there all intimidating and making me feel uncomfortable?"

Him: "Woman, who do you think you are? Running around with your hijab out of place, not respecting our customs?"

Me: "Don't you know who I am? I am a woman from the US of A and can do whatever I want."

Him: "Have you forgotten where you are? There is a war going on outside these walls. And, and … was that humming I heard?"

Me: "Yes, that was humming and listen here. You have no right to intimidate me just because of how you look. There may be a war outside but on behalf of all women in the world, I demand…."

And on it goes, the righteously right ego thinking. Falling deeper into the well where empathy and understanding do not thrive. I saw it happening and noted we were only five or six seconds into this exchange.

Then, I saw a glimmer. It was the light of rationality. I turned toward it and thought, *Whoa!!! Catherine. You are in Syria. Your hijab is out of place and he is as confused as you are. Fix it.*

But he fixed it faster. He covered his eyes with his hands and turned his body into and against the wall. *Look at that*, I said to my ego. *By turning away, he not only honors his culture and mine, he also creates space for us to pass.*

Rational thinking now standing strong at the wheel, I slowly walked up the stairs and humbly said in a low voice, "*Shokrun*" (Arabic for "thank-you"), when I passed by him. I reached the top of the stairs and turned to see what he would do next. Nothing remarkable. He simply continued his journey down and out of the building, never once looking back.

I stood there pondering all that had happened in that less than 15-second eternity of time. I like to think that a Syrian male rebel fighter crossed paths with an American female humanitarian and together, in silence, they found space in a small stairwell to honor one another's cultures in this world. And then I wonder if somewhere in Syria, a male fighter is telling his rebel friends about the time he encountered a female humanitarian in an empty stairwell.

It is possible to find empathy and understanding in a matter of seconds and in complete silence. We can also arrive at that same place when we allow our hearts to connect over time, even if we share only a few words of a common language.

While on another assignment, this time in a small village in the Ivory Coast, I got sick. Within weeks of arriving I was puking up vibrant yellows and neon greens into the plastic garbage can by my bed.

Nothing stayed down, not even the medicine. The project doctor put me on an IV and for four days I stayed in bed, except for those infrequent visits to the pit latrine. We lived and worked in a small compound where conditions were tight and there were no secrets. My colleagues and house-mates were very kind, giving me what little space there was for my dignity when I did make those visits to the latrine, holding my head and IV bag high.

It was the first time I had ever really been sick – and sick to the point where there was talk of taking me out of the field. To do so involved re-delegating duties, a six-hour road trip with two land cruisers meeting midway, a transfer and bad roads the entire way, only to arrive at a hospital where the doctors would not know me nor have English as their first language.

As profoundly afraid as I was, I also knew how fortunate I was. The doctors in the project knew me and had come to understand my version of French. I was included in their medical rotations, along with the many children they were caring for at the hospital. I had a 10-by-10 space all to myself, a bed of my own, a fan, and intermittent electricity. I had my own plastic garbage can holding my vomit and no one else's. I was the lucky one in this situation.

I slowly got better, eventually returning to work weak but ready to see what had happened while I was out. My first stop was the infant ward. It was malaria season. Medical staff moved from bed to bed doing what they could. Babies crying out at their disappointment with life. Mamas consoling their sick infants. Because of what I had just been through, I now felt their frustration and fear of being sick at a profound level. In one bed, I saw a mama lying on her side in the shape of an *S*, breastfeeding one baby while patting the back of another who was lying in the space behind her knees. I turned around and left.

I headed to the juvenile ward. *Just a quick look*, I promised myself. As soon as I entered, my heart fell into the eyes of a little boy. He was 10 years old, and from five strides away, even I, a nonmedical member of the team, could see how sick he was. He was sitting on the edge of his bed, his knees inches from the child in the bed next to his. Draped over his lap was a well-used and once vibrantly colored piece of fabric. His legs, from knees to toes, were wrapped in bandages, his body swollen and dusty. The only areas of his skin showing his true and beautiful color were where tears and beads of sweat had rolled down, cleaning away the dust. His lips were quivering in pain and he was taking quick and shallow breaths.

Our eyes connected and rather than look away, I looked deeper. Once you know something you can't not know it. I knew what it meant to be sick. I knew what it meant to be in pain, scared, and beyond miserable.

I walked over to the little boy and sat next to him, putting my hand on his head because it seemed that was the only part of him that did not hurt. He then shared his pain with me. He raised his hands from his lap, palms up, in defeat as if to say, "I'm broken." I nodded. He was speaking a mixture of French and the local language. I didn't understand the words, but I understood the feelings. I know what *broken* feels like. He spoke until he ran out of words. Then we sat in silence, holding hands, taking deep breaths together.

At dinner, I asked the team about the little boy in the corner. They knew exactly who I was talking about. Arsene had arrived weeks ago with two broken legs. He had been climbing a mango tree, picking those now ripe and delicious palm-sized fruits, when he fell. His mother wrapped him in a blanket and carried him in her arms for a full day, navigating motorcycle and bus transportation to get to the hospital. Arsene had been through multiple surgical procedures to repair his broken legs. There were complications, and just when things were going well, he had a bout with tetanus.

Over the following weeks, I found time every day to sit with Arsene. He would just talk. I would just listen. Then we would just breathe.

And in time, because this is what healing takes, Arsene's broken body began to heal. Soon it would be time to say goodbye and I had to find a way to do it.

The solution was in my suitcase. Months earlier, while in Paris, negotiating the minefields of sidewalk dog poop threatening my city shoes, ignoring the rolling eyes of Parisian waiters, and counting my anxieties, a friend sent me a worry doll. The doll was two inches long and made of brightly colored strings. She came with the instruction that she was to dwell under my pillow at night and would take my worries away while I slept. I put her in my suitcase, figuring I'd better not wear her out too soon, for she would likely come in handy another day.

On our last visit, I explained to Arsene, using a bit of my incredibly bad French and many gestures and sounds, the powers of the worry doll. I explained that she would bring him strength as he stepped back into this vast world on his newly healed legs, that she would take from him his worries and remind him to take those deep breaths we had been practicing together. I let him know that he would always be in my heart, no matter where we were in this world. Then, knowing that children play hard and things get lost, I told him not to worry when the doll leaves. It would only mean that he no longer needed her. The doll would then go to be with the next person in need because this is what worry dolls do.

I placed the doll around Arsene's neck on a bright blue cord I used to make her into a necklace. Then we said goodbye, but not before Arsene promised to be careful when climbing mango trees and to keep going to school.

Arsene taught me that when the walls we build around us to protect us from pain and sadness crumble, it is only then that our hearts have the space to expand. Our walls may protect us from the much larger world surrounding us, but they also keep us from understanding. Hope hides on the other side of those walls. Joy hides behind sorrow. Hearts break. And then they expand, because hearts have the infinite capacity to grow and hold incredible amounts of both sorrow and joy.

You must find your growth and freedom in that space between what happens and what you do. Even when it doesn't feel like it, know that there is always space: It may be tight at times and you might struggle to create more. Other times there might be so much space that you lose yourself. Either way, it is always there, encouraging you to open your heart wide, step into another perspective, and get closer to understanding something new, to connect to the world in deeply meaningful ways.

Life is made up of moments. They swirl about and follow us around, poking and prodding, trying to get our attention. Sometimes we see them but most often we walk right by, never recognizing them for what they are. So they knock us over. Forcing us to pay attention.

But what would happen if we intentionally sought out the moments? If we made it a point to put ourselves in unfamiliar and uncomfortable situations? If we looked for occasions to be knocked over by the moments? It wouldn't be easy, but as my mom says, "If it were easy, everyone would do it."

Welcome having your views and perceptions of the world rocked to their core. Get uncomfortable. Make space for empathy and understanding. And moment by moment, invite into your heart a deeper connection to the greater world.

Reflection Questions

1. Do you have any personal experiences of cultural conflict? How did you feel? How did you react?
2. What might organizations do to prevent or alleviate cultural conflicts? What could you personally do to make intercultural communications or relationships more comfortable?
3. Have you ever experienced a *moment* when you had to decide, in a split-second, how to react? How difficult was this? What was the outcome?

19 | Brother, Can You Paradigm?

Jeffrey S. Kuhn

Jeffrey S. Kuhn, EdD, is a distinguished thinker, author, strategy advisor, educator, and speaker with expertise positioned at the intersection of strategy, innovation, growth, and organizational renewal. His work centers on helping senior business leaders develop the capacity to think and lead strategically in dynamic market environments that are undergoing profound change. He holds a doctorate from Columbia University, and has served on the faculty of Columbia Business School and Teachers College, Columbia University. He is a founding member of the London-based Strategic Management Forum and is a Fellow at the Royal Society of Arts. In 2017, Dr. Kuhn was inducted into Marshall Goldsmith's 100 Coaches.

■ ■ ■

I recently wrote an article for a business journal titled, "Strategic Leadership: A Simple Cure for Short-Termism,"[1] which explored Peter Drucker's concept of *looking out the window to see what is visible, but not yet seen* as an underlying theme.

In the opening section of that article, I drew a parallel between the worldwide myopia epidemic in school-age children, stemming from excessive time spent indoors tethered to computers or mobile devices, and the strategic myopia epidemic that is raging in boardrooms around the world – an organizational pathology in which executives fixate on maximizing near-term profits at the expense of long-term strategic thinking that bolsters the value-creating capacity of the firm.

The simple cures for both forms of myopia are remarkably similar. For children, researchers recommend spending ample time outside in natural light, away from books and computers, gazing into the distance. A similar prescription can be written for business leaders: spending ample time outside the mental confines of the organization, away from spreadsheets and detailed quarterly reports, gazing into the distant future, to identify the weak signals of change (the subtle cues that are visible, but not yet seen) that portend profound market shifts.

I examined the various causes of strategic myopia, from growing investor pressure to deliver short-term gains to growing competitive intensity that tends to drive reactive, one-off thinking – the corporate equivalent of whack-a-mole. Drawing on my research in cognitive development and pattern recognition, I suggested that there is an underlying cognitive dimension to the strategic myopia epidemic in senior leaders. After all, perception occurs in the mind. I argued that years of eking out slow, single-digit growth in mature markets has conditioned leaders to think in safe, incremental terms to protect short-term profits, producing generations of denominator managers who are adept at slashing, delayering, rationalizing, reorganizing, offshoring, and nearshoring, but who lack the cognitive capacity – foresight, curiosity, and imagination – to see the exciting growth platforms of tomorrow in their minds' eyes.

Taking a page from Professor Drucker, I concluded the article by saying, "The next time you are bleary-eyed from reading reams of quarterly reports and have a difficult time thinking beyond the demands of today, let alone the next ten years, walk over to your window and take a look outside. You might be surprised by what you see."

Prior to submitting the article for publication, I emailed the manuscript to my trusty editor Ethan for a final review. The next morning, I found the marked-up manuscript in my inbox. Most of the edits were minor fixes that I didn't quibble with. But as I scrolled to the bottom of the last page, I was baffled by a question he posed in the right-hand margin next to the very last sentence: "How exactly do we look out the window?" I've been working closely with editors for more than two decades and have had my share of off-the-wall comments, but this one took the cake.

Dumbfounded, I stared at my computer screen, shaking my head in disbelief, and thought, *You don't literally look out the window. The window is a metaphor for our minds. Looking out the window means looking at the tangle of socioeconomic trends and emerging technologies that create and shape markets.*

Nevertheless, the journal welcomed my metaphorical musings and published the article without substantive changes. But I continued to ruminate on my editor's question until it dawned on me that the point he was endeavoring to make, as odd as it sounds, was that many leaders don't know how to look out the window, meaning they don't know how to scan the broad market landscape to identify intersecting socioeconomic trends and such. They're not wired that way. They're wired to keep the organizational engine humming and execute quarterly performance targets. If by chance they do peek out the window, they're not sure what to look at, let alone how.

Paradigm's Lost

If we were to turn back the clock 100 years and look out the window, our minds would construct (i.e., see) a much different world – a mechanistic, Newtonian world that gave rise to the *organization-as-machine* management paradigm epitomized by Frederick Taylor's scientific management.

Back then, there was little need to look out the window. The external environment was relatively stable and, to a degree, predictable. Industries were composed of a handful of dominant players competing with a familiar set of rules in highly structured sectors that evolved incrementally and linearly. Competition was a clash of the titans, a game of size and structural advantage. In the event that you did look out the window, your mind would have construed an orderly, immutable universe that ran with clocklike precision, in which inputs equaled outputs, actions produced reactions, and big problems could be broken into small pieces that could be analyzed in isolation.

With the dawn of the Information Age in the 1950s, a seismic shift began to rumble. The mechanistic worldview of the Industrial Era had outlived its usefulness as the business landscape became increasingly dynamic and uncertain. Over time, the orderly universe of Newton was displaced by paradigm-busting findings in quantum physics and complexity theory.

Organizations shape-shifted from well-oiled machines into dynamic organisms that were part of a larger ecosystem. Firms no longer competed in insulated provincial markets but in unstructured global arenas with new players and new rules. Facing growing market complexity and competitive intensity, leaders began to look out the window more frequently and engage in more fluid modes of thinking and being.

Today, the twin forces of globalization and technological acceleration have created a short-cycle world that has quickened commoditization cycles and shortened corporate life spans to where they can now be measured in dog years. Low-cost digital technologies have lowered barriers to entry, giving rise to new types of competitors and business models, and creating an amorphous business landscape characterized by deep complexity, high uncertainty, and transient competitive advantage.[2] The future bears little resemblance to the past.

In a short-cycle, commoditizing world, the ability to identify the weak signals of change earlier and better than competitors has become a critical organizational capability. The more dynamic and uncertain the market environment, the greater the need to scan the horizon on a systematic basis to spot emerging trends and engage in strategic reflection and dialogue. Few leaders disagree with this on a conceptual level, but in the tooth-and-nail world of business, the idea of slowing down, reflecting, and thinking conceptually about the shifting contours of the market landscape is anathema to high-strung managers who pride themselves on delivering the goods each quarter. The annals of business history are littered with examples of storied firms that were too busy minding the store and got blindsided by stealthy newcomers from outside the industry. As Kodak and Blackberry can attest, failure to acknowledge profound shifts in the external environment and ask unvarnished, uncomfortable questions concerning the strategic health of the enterprise can have grave consequences.

The mechanistic worldview of the Industrial Era continues to cast a long shadow over the way we think and lead our organizations. Scientific management's tenets of efficiency and control have been etched into the minds of generations of business leaders. When thrust into strategic roles, operationally oriented managers often struggle with broad, imaginative thinking. They can speak at length concerning asset intensity and inventory turns (concrete modes of thinking) but lose their intellectual footing when asked to think and lead with a long-term, external perspective rather than from the short-term, internal purview of operations.

However, it's my belief that, with the right developmental experiences, leaders can develop their *strategic eye* – the cognitive capacity to look out the window and see what is visible yet not seen – with a high degree of perceptual acuity.

Developing Your Strategic Eye

To illustrate, let's imagine that you are a senior business leader at General Motors, and the executive team has asked you to speak at the next board meeting concerning the transformation of the auto industry and where future growth opportunities lie.

Your mind shifts into overdrive. What should I look at? How will I recognize intersecting trends and patterns? How will I translate what I see in my mind's eye into a set of strategic insights to share with the board?

You are not alone. Many leaders struggle with strategic thinking and regard it as an inborn trait possessed by members of the lucky gene club rather than a cognitive capability – a mind-set and muscle – that can be developed. This raises an important point: *Strategic thinkers think in the form of questions.* The better you are at framing strategic questions, the better you will be at strategic thinking. As my editor intimated, you don't just gaze out the window hoping for divine revelation. Rather, you scan the market landscape with a series of broad questions to open your mental aperture. Broadly framed questions such as, What are the key socioeconomic and technological trends in the market landscape, and how do they intersect? provide an excellent jumping-off point to guide your journey. This is a significantly different, more sophisticated way of thinking than typical execution-oriented questions such as, How can we crush our competitors and sell more cars?

As a seasoned auto executive, the first thing that you will notice when you look out the window is that the industry is in a state of entrepreneurial flux, much like it was in the early 1900s, when there were 241 auto manufacturers registered in the United States alone, and steam- and electric-powered vehicles vied with the internal combustion engine to be the dominant design. Today, a constellation of Silicon Valley tech giants, venture-backed start-ups, universities, and incumbent auto manufacturers are pioneering novel forms of hybrid vehicles, electric vehicles, and self-driving cars; new vehicle concepts such as two-, three-, and four-wheeled city cars; and innovative business models such as ride sharing (think Uber and Lyft), luxury subscription services, and fractional models in which multiple parties own or lease a vehicle.

This insight leads you to a deeper set of questions: What's creating this entrepreneurial flux? How will the industry landscape likely evolve? How will customer and economic value be created in the future? How do we get ahead of the curve so that we don't get elbowed out of our own business? How quickly will the future arrive?

Intrigued, you dig deeper into the broad market landscape and identify five strategic megatrends that are reshaping the contours of the auto industry: environmental concerns with CO_2 emissions; urbanization and the rapid growth of megacities with high population density; demographic shifts such as the growth of the global middle class and the coming of age of the millennials; emerging technologies such as new energy sources and autonomous vehicles; and seismic consumer shifts, in particular, a growing preference for access over vehicle ownership. You examine the interrelationships among these trends and it becomes abundantly clear that they are converging and creating a new mobility landscape in which fewer people own cars and mobility is consumed as a service.

From a cognitive standpoint, you would have failed to see these trends if you had looked at the market landscape through the narrow prism of your current core business of making and selling cars to customers who own and drive them. To develop a broad perspective of where the future lies, you must look at the world from outside in – not through the prism of existing products and services – and beyond immediate customer needs and near-term competitive dynamics, to the broad market landscape (see Figure 19.1).

As an organization matures from fledgling start-up to industry stalwart, the field of vision often narrows, and the organization finds itself peering at the outside world through a peephole. Individuals undergo similar life-cycle changes as they grow and mature from starry-eyed children with boundless curiosity and imagination to buttoned-up executives who interpret the future through the prism of past experiences. Left unchecked,

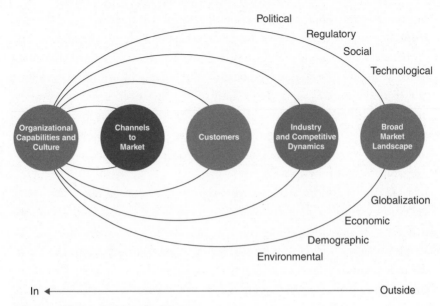

Figure 19.1 Strategic Lenses

these perceptual filters become self-limiting and self-sustaining, suppressing the long-term imaginative thinking that is essential to sustained value creation. This explains why, in incumbent firms, most growth opportunities are hidden in plain sight.

For senior leaders, spotting intersecting trends and emerging growth opportunities requires the ability to wipe one's mental windshield clean to overcome organizational orthodoxy and inertial forces that impede divergent thinking and stifle imagination. An ecological lens is also key. Expert trend spotters are like seasoned biologists who study dynamic interactions of flora and fauna in a rain forest. Markets are no different. They are based on the same principles as natural ecosystems – interdependency, dynamism, and emergence.

Help Wanted: Strategic Leaders

Drucker's dictum, while simple in form, requires an array of sophisticated cognitive capabilities to scan the market landscape and pick up subtle cues that are visible but not yet seen. Further complicating matters is a host of organizational pathologies and immune systems that function as an invisible hand influencing what we see and how we see it.

Over 20 years ago, strategy expert C.K. Prahalad[3] suggested that established firms were not resource-bound, but imagination-bound, meaning that imagination was the scarce resource. Organizations are slowly waking up to these new market realities and finding themselves in short supply of dynamic, strategic leaders with the curiosity, imagination, and entrepreneurial verve to look out the window and conceive the markets, businesses, and industries of tomorrow.

The socioeconomic trends creating the new market landscape are as structural as they are paradigmatic. Market shifts are so pervasive and subtle that they are difficult to perceive. But one thing is certain: You won't be able to *see what is visible, but not yet seen* if your field of focus is limited to the current quarter, or to fighting over a quarter point of market share with an archrival.

The leaders I've worked with through the years recognize the importance of looking out the window on a systematic basis; they just aren't sure how to make sense of what they see. But as management guru Tom Peters recently declared, "If you're not confused, you're not paying attention."[4] So, just as I suggested to readers in my article, "Strategic Leadership: A Simple Cure for Short-Termism,"[5] put down your spreadsheets and walk over to your window and look outside. You will be amazed at what you can see when you wipe the residue of industrial-era paradigms and past experiences from your lens and scan the market landscape with the curiosity and imagination of a five-year-old. Subtle cues that are invisible to the naked eye will become crystal clear when you develop your strategic eye.

Reflection Questions

1. Why is looking out the window such an important, yet unnatural, act in established firms?
2. What systems and processes does your organization have in place for monitoring the external environment? How important is this capability in your particular industry?

3. What trends in the broad market landscape should your organization be monitoring? What strategic questions should your executive team be asking?
4. In a given week, how much time do you spend looking out the window to identify market trends? Based on your role, how much time should you spend doing so?
5. What are some ways that you can sharpen your strategic eye to recognize emerging threats and opportunities in the broad market landscape?

Notes

1. Jeffrey Kuhn, "Strategic Leadership: A Simple Cure for Short-Termism," *Ambition,* July/August 2017, 34–39.
2. Rita McGrath, *The End of Competitive Advantage: How to Keep Your Strategy Moving as Fast as Your Business* (Boston: Harvard Business Review Press, 2013).
3. C.K. Prahalad and Larry Bennigson, "On Growth: A Conversation with C.K. Prahalad," *Strategy & Leadership* 24, no. 5 (1996): 30.
4. "Tom Peters on Leading the 21st-Century Organization," *McKinsey Quarterly*, September 2014, 1.
5. Kuhn, "Strategic Leadership: A Simple Cure for Short-Termism."

20 | Life Lessons from the Tennis Court

Prakash Raman

Prakash Raman is passionate about helping leaders recognize and achieve their potential to create collective success. At LinkedIn, he brings practical tools that leaders can use to help remove their own obstacles for success and happiness. He coaches, facilitates, and runs workshops focused on leading through values, connection, and shared human experience. His background enables him to take a unique and actionable approach to developing leaders. From starting his career on Wall Street to globally scaling a nonprofit, to marketing the Oreo cookie brand, he has worked through key business problems, enabling a business-rooted perspective when working with leaders. In 2016, he was selected for the 100 Coaches project created and led by Marshall Goldsmith, the world's #1 executive coach. The project aims to mentor the next generation of leader, and includes leading academics, bestselling authors, corporate executives, and top executive coaches. He also serves as a facilitator of the Stanford Graduate School of Business' course Leading with Mindfulness and Compassion and is engaged in continuing studies there. He has an MBA from Northwestern's Kellogg School of Management and a BA in economics from Rice University.

■ ■ ■

I grew up in Houston, Texas, the youngest child of an immigrant family from India. As with most immigrant families, my parents had given up everything and come to America with nothing more than a drive to provide a better life for their children. Between implicit immigrant parent expectations and the blazing Texas sun, most of my friends spent their childhood indoors focused on education. However, my years growing up were spent entirely outside mapping my future on the tennis court.

To my parents' credit, they fully supported my obsession with tennis. The minute my chubby hand first wrapped around a racket at age five, I was hooked and eager to play with my father the minute he came home from work. I would wait by the door of our brown, one-story house every day at 5:30 p.m., with my hands overflowing with the necessary gear: my dad's shiny red racket, mine with a dirty white handle, a water jug, and a can of Wilson tennis balls waiting to be cracked open.

As soon as my dad got home, I would beg and plead as young boys do best, imploring him to hurry up and change. We would play every night until the sun finally disappeared behind the trees and then proceed to walk home and discuss the evening's match at the dinner table. Even my mom and older brother would indulge me by asking what I could have done better and what my key focus areas were.

Even when off the court, my mind was on tennis. I would record every match available on national television (cable wasn't an option for my immigrant parents) and watch the tapes with feverish repetition. While most kids would sneak out of their bedrooms to play video games or watch cartoons late at night, I snuck out to watch VHS tapes of my favorite tennis players like Stefan Edberg and Andre Agassi. I studied their technique and analyzed their strategy so I might have an edge on Dad the next day. I soon gained basic competence in the sport and would valiantly lose to my dad and brother, feeling empowered by the knowledge that, with reflection, I could come back the next day and play better, even win.

Like many young players, my goal in life was to be a professional tennis player and win Wimbledon.

Resulting from my obsessive focus, I started to improve and classified myself as *pretty good*. At age 8, I was competing with the 12-year-olds, and winning. After any match (win or lose), I would reflect on what went well, and more importantly, on what could have gone better. And in this simple reality is why I loved the sport: I could break down success into the smallest of movements or the shortest of moments to see what had gone well. Each point in a match could be peeled back to reveal opportunities and corresponding microchanges to address them. Between matches, I had the power to make adjustments based on prior information to improve my chances of succeeding. While I was enamored with winning, the foundation of continuous learning truly drove me.

The results shortly followed. Fast forward a few years, and I was the #1 player in Texas, a ranking I held onto longer than anyone in Texas history. I began traveling around the United States and was soon ranked #6 in the country. I received racket and clothing sponsorships and found that my social and tennis ranking were correlated. My teenage self was seeing everything fall into place, all according to plan. By mastering this intense focus, I was giving myself a shot to achieve my dream of being a professional tennis player.

Then one day I found myself practicing a little less. I didn't want to miss out on other aspects of my life – classes, friends, clubs, dating. Even though I was practicing fewer days each week, I initially still won. My results for the next year didn't point to any decrease in ability; instead, it signaled to me that perhaps I didn't need to practice so much and I'd still win. The story I created was that I just understood the game better than my peers. Perhaps I was better than others at tennis and I could forget the obsession that had consumed me for most of my early adolescence.

I turned 16 and experienced my first loss in Texas in over two and a half years. It was a typical summer day and well over 100 degrees. I was playing someone I knew well and had beaten six straight times before. Walking on the court, I knew something was wrong. I was physically present, but my mind was already looking to get off the court. Less than half an hour later, I was down my first set ever to this familiar opponent. Was I not feeling well? Was it too hot, or just an off day? Another 30 minutes passed and I was down match point. I lost in symbolic fashion, falling to the ground while trying to retrieve the final shot.

After the match, I didn't reflect or analyze what went wrong. I instead dismissed it and didn't hold myself accountable for what had occurred. I thought, *I know I am not practicing and focusing as much as I used to. But come on! That cannot be why I'm losing. The past three years I've been better at every turn, and everyone loses at some point, right?* Not the best internal dialogue, even for a teenager.

Then the floodgates opened. I lost to more people in Texas, and I started losing early in national tournaments. I questioned my own ability, my own game plan, and started copying my peers to try and play more like them. I wondered, *Maybe they know a secret I don't. Maybe they have a better technique right now and I should hit more like them.* Needless to say, I was freaked out. But that didn't help me solve what was going on.

Losing on the court started a chain reaction in other areas of my life. I started performing poorly in school, turned in assignments late, and stopped attending my extracurricular meetings. In essence, I became self-destructive.

This state continued throughout high school. Luckily, nearly 10 years of dedicated practice enabled me to sustain a high enough level of tennis such that, despite poor performance for two straight years, I remained one of the stronger players in the country. However, I never recovered to the point of driving toward my childhood dream, and by the time I was playing Division I college tennis, the sport had become a side story, an add-on to my life as opposed to what it had been – the very core of my joy, potential, and future. The most challenging thing for me was not that I didn't reach my dream, but rather that I never gave myself a fair shot at achieving it.

While I went through this experience a long time ago, the lessons I learned serve me today in countless ways. It allows me to help business leaders bridge the gap between inspiration and operation to achieve their individual and organization goals. I would like to share three of those lessons.

1. Success Is Built on Habits, Not on Outcomes

The old adage is true: Hard work beats talent when talent doesn't work hard. My early success was built on a set of habits: focus, discipline, and consistency, all wrapped in deep intention. Prior to my downward turn, I enjoyed what I was doing whether I won or lost. I felt confident that if I lost, I would come back stronger and sharper, especially since I had a set of habits to iterate on and drive continuous improvement. Once I started seeing success, I let go of the habits and focused on the outcomes to dictate my success, and in turn, my self-esteem. Doing this led to a self-destructive pattern that began to permeate my life.

When I was at my best, my individual confidence, my sense of being *successful*, was based on measuring the consistency and discipline of my habits rather than on the outcomes. I focused on what was within my control.

We all have a responsibility to drive our own success, but our metric for success is often wrong. Any outcome or set of outcomes will always be partly based on factors that are out of our control. If we focus on what we can change and influence built on a foundation of habits, we have a chance to be successful every day. We will no longer be held prisoner waiting for outcomes to manifest. Fundamentally, success is built on habits, not on outcomes.

2. To Fully Unlock Your Potential, Reflect on Actions *and* Emotions

While I was good at reflecting on all the strategies and tactics I could use to improve my game, I never gave due time to reflecting on how I was feeling and what that may be signaling. My inability to identify my fear of failing on the court started a spiral effect of self-sabotage in other areas of my life. Being able to identify my fear, what I thought was driving it, and what part of it was real would have allowed me to take a rational and constructive approach to forward progress. I couldn't change what I felt, but I could have changed how I responded.

This lesson serves me to this day, as I put it into action through the following questions:

- What am I feeling?
- What is driving that feeling?
- What part of that is real?
- What do I want to do about those things I can control?

Doing this daily has helped me to better understand my triggers and have tangible, operational ways to address what I am feeling. Then those feelings can actively serve me as opposed to creating a pervasively destructive pattern.

It is not enough to simply reflect on your actions. By reflecting on your emotions in conjunction with your actions, you can unlock the greatest impact and development for yourself.

3. Find the Intersection of Learning from Others and Trusting Yourself

There is a difference between learning from others and trying to be like others. In my early years, I would look at the strengths of other players through the lens of my own game. How could I incorporate their strengths into my game in a way that felt authentic?

By filtering like this, I found the intersection of what others did well, what seemed to work on the court, and how I wanted to show up as a player. In other words, I was playing inside-out. This made me feel authentic. Whether I won or lost, I could go back to getting better and picking up new techniques in my own way, knowing that my own game was at the center.

However, with that in mind, as soon as I started to struggle, I went from trusting my ability and learning from others to playing outside-in and blindly following what others were doing without considering *my* game or the way *I* wanted to show up. As a result, my commitment was limited and my game didn't feel authentically me.

Learning from others is one of the greatest things we can do. The absence of trusting our own judgment, though, can lead us to live someone else's life. In his commencement speech at Stanford, Steve Jobs told the graduates, "Your time is limited, so don't waste it living someone else's life. Don't be trapped by dogma, which is living with the results of other people's thinking. Don't let the noise of others' opinions drown out your own inner voice." Find your "inner voice" to live your life of fulfillment. In doing so, you will play *your* game inside-out.

Reflection Questions

1. What do you want to achieve? What are the corresponding daily habits within your control that will allow you the chance to be successful every day as opposed to when a specific outcome happens?
2. What are the most common feelings that are getting in the way of your feeling fulfilled? What drives those feelings?
3. In what areas are you living someone else's life versus your own?
4. What are the realities that are contributing to your current success and failures? Which of those are within your control to lean in on or change?

21

The Need for Conscious Choice

Margaret (Meg) Wheatley

Margaret Wheatley began caring about the world's peoples in 1966, as a Peace Corps volunteer in postwar Korea. In many different roles – speaker, teacher, consultant, advisor, formal leader – her work has deepened into an unshakable conviction that leaders must learn how to invoke people's inherent generosity, creativity, and need for community. As this world tears us apart, sane leadership on behalf of the human spirit is the only way forward. She is cofounder and president of The Berkana Institute (www.berkana.org), an organizational consultant since 1973, a global citizen since her youth, and a prolific writer. She has authored nine books, beginning with the classic Leadership and the New Science. *Her newest book (June 2017) is* Who Do We Choose to Be? Facing Reality | Claiming Leadership | Restoring Sanity. *She has been honored for her groundbreaking work by many professional associations, universities, and organizations. She has created a website rich in resources, and her numerous articles are available to download for free at* www.margaretwheatley.com.

■ ■ ■

My newest book[1] has a question as its title: *Who do we choose to be?* I have been asking this question of leaders for several years now because it is essential that we make a conscious choice about how we will use our power

155

and influence. Are we willing to take a stand against the vicious of this time who are destroying people, planet, and the future? Or are we going to withdraw, deny what's happening, and just focus on personal success?

Until I began reflecting on pivotal moments in my career, I hadn't realized the role that choice has played in my own development; indeed, it has been the most satisfying theme of my work. In fact, I had no idea that my work could be summarized as the offering of choice until I began speaking and teaching about new science and its promise of a simpler way to lead and motivate people.

What is choice? It is the realization that we are not locked into one way of thinking or behaving, that we can liberate ourselves from the confines of our assumptions and habits of action. Ultimately, choice frees us. It offers a new sense of possibility: *It doesn't have to be this way. We can change. We can choose a different way.*

I will not forget the moment in 1990, when I was stunned with the realization that *control* and *order* were not synonyms. I was sitting at my desk, reading about the science of living systems and the capacity to self-organize into increasing levels of complexity and functionality. It was a true *aha!* moment – order could be created from interactions among parts or species or people as they each made individual decisions, but based on a shared sense of identity. The elaborate controls that were the primary focus of leaders were not only unnecessary, but they created obstacles to what complexity scientist Stuart Kauffman[2] would soon name as "order for free." Although I love Kauffman's language, I also translated this concept into my own terms: *Life seeks order, but it uses messes to get there.*

In the many years since then, I have been very clear that a new paradigm offers choice. We can interpret the world or an event or a person differently. And if we do, more becomes possible. Joel Barker's work on paradigms[3] made this very clear. He taught that what is impossible to solve with one paradigm can be easy to resolve with a change in paradigms. A new way of seeing brings with it the potential to liberate us from the prison of our assumptions.

However we see the world, whatever experiences have formed our mental models, every single one of them is woefully inadequate to perceive what's going on. We all walk around with dense blinders that filter out critical information and, as we now work faster with consuming levels of distraction, we have become truly blind. Those who take the time to think are increasingly rare, and very powerful. As an ancient proverb noted: *In the land of the blind, the one-eyed man is king.*

How many of us understand that we have choice? Consumed by tasks, addicted to distractions, avoiding thinking, we have become the most endangered of all species. And this has happened because we fail to use the essential freedom that all living systems possess: choice. Everything alive is free to choose to notice what's happening in its environment, and then free to choose how it will respond. Even though we humans still possess the highest capacities for thought and awareness, where do we see these in our actions? Failing to notice what's going on and learning from experience – failure to exercise choice – we win the award for the dumbest species as well as the most endangered. (Actually, dumb and endangered are causally linked.)

This is why I had to put choice in my book title, and why it has become paramount in my work with leaders. If we take time even for a brief moment's reflection, we can't help but notice what's happening to the people we support, the causes we care about, the families we love, and the planet we live on. Whatever skills and resources we have as leaders and citizens, how do we choose to use them? Here is a prose poem I wrote to answer this question.

What This World Needs

This world does not need more entrepreneurs.
This world does not need more technology breakthroughs.
This world needs leaders.
We need leaders who put service over self, who can be steadfast through crises and failures, who want to stay present and make a difference to the people, situations, and causes they care about.
We need leaders who are committed to serving people, who recognize what is being lost in the haste to dominate, ignore, and abuse the human spirit.
We need leaders because leadership has been debased by those who take things to scale or are first to market or dominate the competition or develop killer apps, or those who hold onto power by constantly tightening their stranglehold of fear until people are left lifeless and cowering.
We need leaders now because we have failed to implement what was known to work, what would have prevented or mitigated the rise of hatred, violence,

poverty, and ecological destruction. We have not failed from a lack of ideas and technologies — we have failed from a lack of will. The solutions we needed were already here.

Now it is too late. We cannot solve these global issues globally. We can see them clearly. We can understand their root causes. We have evidence of solutions that would have solved them. But we refused to compromise, to collaborate, to persevere in resolving them as an intelligent, creative species living on one precious planet.

Now it's up to us, not as global leaders but as local leaders. We can lead people to create positive changes locally that make life easier and more sustainable, that create possibility in the midst of global decline.

Let us use whatever power and influence we have, working with whatever resources are already available, mobilizing the people who are with us to work for what they care about.

As former president Teddy Roosevelt enjoined us: "Do what you can, with what you have, where you are."

Reflection Questions

These questions are about thinking, and they require time to think. They also ask for a *then-and-now* perspective to gain clarity about what has changed in the past few years.

1. Personally, how much time do you spend thinking and reflecting today as contrasted to a few years ago?
2. Organizationally, how much time do you spend thinking with colleagues in contrast to a few years ago?
3. How much learning from experience occurs?
4. Talk to a few staff people and get their answers to these questions. Then note whether people feel sad or wistful when they talk about time to reflect together.

Notes

1. Margaret Wheatley, *Who Do We Choose to Be? Facing Reality, Claiming Leadership, Restoring Sanity* (Oakland, CA: Berrett-Koehler Publishers, 2017).
2. Stuart Kauffman's work is thoroughly described in Meg Wheatley's book *A Simpler Way* (Oakland, CA: Berrett-Koehler Publishers, 1999). The phrase *order for free* is easily found on Google.
3. Joel Barker's initial work, in books and videos, was titled "The Business of Paradigms," published in the late 1980s.

PART IV

Be Ye an Opener of Doors

In the 1800s, great American lecturer, essayist, and poet, Ralph Waldo Emerson, said, "Be ye an opener of doors." In this section, our contributors explore the meaning of this inspiring phrase of Emerson's. What does it mean to open doors – for ourselves and for others – through which we can walk together toward a shared and positive vision of the future?

In his article, Michael Bungay Stanier dissects the "elegant simplicity" of the theory and practice of coaching as an opener to the door of great leadership. Gary Ridge offers lessons he learned about the true nature and purpose of business from his boyhood in suburban Sydney, Australia, drawing on these to advise how to develop truly "transformative" leadership and create "tribal unity" in modern organizational cultures. Brigadier General Tom Kolditz makes a powerful case for offering professional-caliber leadership development to students at the college and university level rather than waiting till they are more established in their careers. He also identifies tangible payoffs in terms of creating a cadre of young leaders well-suited to face the challenges of the "Fourth Industrial Revolution." Pawel Motyl recounts how an encounter with Marshall Goldsmith – "an expert ophthalmologist" – led him to challenge his vision of himself and reevaluate his performance as CEO of a major business magazine publisher in his native Poland. He describes how he then used the insights of Peter Drucker to realign his career path with his true personal vision. Alex Osterwalder et al. use the metaphor of a garden to describe corporate culture and how it must be cultivated and tended. A Culture Map technique is introduced as a method for helping leaders and their teams assess their current culture or design a new one. Liz Wiseman expands her previous research on leadership types to describe the Accidental Diminisher – those who unintentionally and unwittingly diminish the people they lead. She outlines several precise strategies for identifying and overcoming such tendencies in your own leadership practice, along with techniques for developing into a "great" vs. merely "good" leader!

22

The Elegance
and Simplicity of
Coaching

Michael Bungay Stanier

Michael Bungay Stanier is the founder of Box of Crayons, a company that teaches 10-minute coaching to busy managers. He is the author of the Wall Street Journal's *bestseller* The Coaching Habit, *the number one coaching book since its release. He is a Rhodes Scholar, and a member of the Marshall Goldsmith 100 Coaches. An Australian, he now lives in Toronto, Canada.*

■ ■ ■

I wouldn't give a fig for simplicity this side of complexity, but I would give my life for the simplicity on the other side of complexity.
—Oliver Wendell Holmes, Jr.

Great tools and models have an elegant simplicity to them. They provoke a paradoxical response at the same time: both, *I've never seen it like that before* and *Of course, it has to be like that.* The periodic table and Darwin's theory of natural selection are great examples of this. Marshall Goldsmith's

163

Feed*forward* process[1] and Peter Drucker's Five Questions[2] are examples in the world of leadership.

My goal is for coaching to be a practical tool for all managers, so I'm seeking the simplicity that lives on the other side of complexity in this discipline.

And there's a lot of complexity. Many hold the perception that coaching is a confusing, complex, arcane, and slightly *touchy feely* process that only HR types and people from California can master. It's frustrating. There's an increasing amount of evidence from both neuroscience and large-scale leadership studies that points to coaching as one of the essential leadership skills. Yet, progress is slow in having managers and leaders actually get better at coaching.

But it doesn't have to be so. I've seen glimpses of coaching's fundamental elegance and simplicity. One commitment and a few good questions are often all you need to be an effective coach, not just to people you manage and lead, but to everyone with whom you work.

Start at the Beginning

Let's start with the definition of coaching. There's no one clear definition of what we mean by coaching, and that means many different options have sprouted and proliferated over the years. Every expert has theirs. Every niche has theirs. Every coach has theirs. They're all similar, they're all a little different, and it all gets confusing.

Let me cut the Gordian knot. The coaching cycle is simple. A good question creates a new insight. That insight sparks action and behavior change. That behavior change leads to increased impact. Learning from that impact takes us back to a new insight. The virtuous cycle repeats.

That's *how* coaching works. The behavior that makes coaching coaching is even more straightforward to explain: Stay curious a little longer; rush to action and advice-giving a little more slowly.

It's as simple and as difficult as that.

To put that theory into action, here are four simple strategies that can help all managers and leaders lift their leadership game and improve the way they work with others.

1. Coach-like, not Coaching

Peter Block, the celebrated author of *The Answer to How Is Yes*[3] and *Flawless Consulting*,[4] once said, "Coaching is not a profession but a way of being with each other." The power in that statement is that it makes coaching something that we all can do. It's not for a few. It's for everyone.

But the term *coaching* comes with baggage. Some think about the proliferation of Life Coaching, with the occasional tendency to overdo feelings and pastels. Some go to Executive Coaching and think it's all about high-powered conversations in the corner office. Others may go to sports coaching, or ADHD coaching, or teen coaching, or mid-life coaching or – the list goes on. Whatever the reason, too many people assume *this being a coach lark is not for me.*

Reframing can make all the difference. Let's talk about our goal not as being a coach, but simply as being more *coach-like*. Now the pressure's off. This doesn't require an identity shift, but a behavior change. It's simply a way of changing what you currently do, not adding on additional burdens and expectations. And what does being more coach-like even mean? As before, simply staying curious a little longer, and rushing to action and advice-giving a little more slowly.

2. Real Questions, not Fake Questions

Most of us know that questions are the currency of coaching. Clayton Christensen[5] said, "Without a good question, a good answer has nowhere to go." The best coaching allows those good answers to show up, often, wonderfully enough, to the surprise of the person speaking the answer.

Some of us have already heard of the difference between open and closed questions. Closed questions – those targeted to get an answer of *yes* or *no* – are the weapon of every cross-examining lawyer. Open questions, on the other hand, force the person answering to work a little harder and fill in the details. Traditional coaching tends to pooh-pooh the closed question, but the truth is that both can be very useful, although on balance, you want to use open questions more often.

But that's not what I mean by fake questions.

Fake questions sound like this: "Have you thought of ...?" and "Did you consider ...?" and "Have you tried ...?" or even "What about ...?"

These, in fact, are not questions at all. They're just advice with a question mark attached.

You'll remember that the goal is to stay curious a little longer and rush to action and advice-giving more slowly. The truth is, most of us are advice-giving machines. We've been trained, praised, and rewarded all our lives for having the answer. This is how you *add value*. Even when you don't really know what the challenge is, you've probably got a solution to suggest anyway.

Some of us have become a little more cunning about the way we offer up our advice, and have learned to package our ideas as seeming questions. But let's stop kidding ourselves and begin to practice asking real questions. (I'll tell you the best coaching question in the world in a little bit.)

3. Real Listening, not Fake Listening

Those of us who've done some sort of training in coaching have most likely run into the concept of *active listening*. In fact, for many of us, that's the only remaining residue left over from the training: Nod your head a lot, make small grunt-y noises of encouragement, and look interested.

The shame is, most of us have moved into FAL: Fake Active Listening. Sure, you've got the moves down. Nodding, *uh-huh*-ing, maintaining eye contact. But are you really listening to your client? Not so much. Running through your head is not their words, but yours: "How long are they going to keep talking?" "What's the next question I should ask?" "When can I interrupt and tell them what my idea is?" "Did I leave the stove on when I left the house this morning?"

It's difficult and powerful to stay present and hear what they're actually saying. To listen without feeling the need to interrupt or make your point or add value by telling them what to do.

4. The Best Coaching Question in the World

We talked about asking real questions, not fake questions. Now you might ask me, "Michael, that's all very well, but what *are* good coaching questions?"

Well, there are many, and one of the smartest things you can do is to start collecting your favorites. When you hear someone ask a good question to someone they're coaching – say, "What's the real challenge here for you?" – you might note how it slowed down the rush to action and dug a little deeper into figuring out what the heart of the issue was. Jot it down! Or when another coach asks, "What do you want?" and you notice how that slows the conversation down and creates a moment of honesty and vulnerability and insight, you make a note to try this technique out for yourself.

But there is one question that rules them all, the best coaching question in the world.

It's just three words. And it's literally *awe*-some.

The question is: "And what else?"

What's the magic of this question? It's twofold. To start, the first answer someone gives you is never their only answer and it's rarely their best answer. "And what else?" helps them keep going and untap all that's in their head. They've got more to tell you. This gives them the chance to do that.

The other reason is that it's a self-management tool. To repeat myself and drive home the point, we're trying to stay curious a little longer and rush to action and advice-giving just a little more slowly. For the most part, however, we're not that good at this form self-control. Having "And what else?" in your repertoire is a tool to help you bite your tongue. Instead of giving them that burning answer you're desperately keen to tell them, that nugget of gold, that pearl of wisdom – hold off for just a moment. Ask them, "And what else?" instead.

Coaching is simple and it's elegant.

If you want to, you can spend months and thousands training to be a coach. And no doubt, you'll pick up some powerful and useful tools when you do. But you don't have to. Everything you need to be more coach-like is right here on this page:

- Resist giving advice.
- Stay curious and ask real questions.
- Ask "And what else?"
- Listen to the answer.

Do all of that, and you'll change the way you lead forever.

Reflection Questions

1. What is your definition of coaching?
2. What distinguishes real coaching from activities that are only *coach-like*?
3. What are some instances in your own life when you practice *fake* versus *real* listening? How might you change how you listen to be more *real* and present all the time? What would be some benefits of this in your personal/work life?

Notes

1. Marshall Goldsmith, "Try Feed*forward* Instead of Feedback," *Leader to Leader*, June 2002.
2. Peter F. Drucker, *The Five Most Important Questions You Will Ever Ask About Your Organization* (San Francisco: Jossey-Bass, 2008).
3. Peter Block, *The Answer to How Is Yes: Acting on What Matters* (Oakland, CA: Berrett-Koehler Publishers, 2001).
4. Peter Block, *Flawless Consulting: A Guide to Getting Your Expertise Used* (Hoboken, NJ: Pfeiffer, 2011).
5. Warren Berger, *A More Beautiful Question* (New York: Bloomsbury USA, 2014).

23

The Gift of Belonging

Garry Ridge

Garry Ridge is CEO of WD-40 Company. He joined WD-40 Company in 1987, and held various leadership positions there before being appointed CEO in 1997. He is also an adjunct professor at the University of San Diego where he teaches leadership development, talent management, and succession planning. He believes that in the long term, values are arguably the most important aspect of working at WD-40 Company. In 2009, he coauthored a book with Ken Blanchard titled Helping People Win at Work: A Business Philosophy Called "Don't Mark My Paper, Help Me Get an A." *A native of Sydney, Mr. Ridge holds a certificate in modern retailing and wholesale distribution and a Master of Science in Executive Leadership from the University of San Diego.*

■ ■ ■

Leadership – truly inspiring, *transformative* leadership – requires the wisdom to understand that the overarching role of business is to serve people. To give them what they need to do their jobs and smooth the edges of their days. To bring them joy. To relieve their suffering. To give them the essential tools and hope that will empower them to step into the best versions of themselves. To even ease their loneliness and isolation. While

achieving an officially conferred leadership role may take decades of diligent career building, the getting of wisdom can commence at any time
in our lives. In my particular case, I have Mrs. Peel and Mr. Knox, 1960s
residents of the west Sydney suburb of Five Dock, to thank for opening
my eyes to the true purpose of business – to lift people up in the spirit of
belonging and connection.

I was just a kid, but these two kind and caring adults taught me well.
Mrs. Peel was a lonely, elderly shut-in, and I was her 12-year-old newspaper boy. Every day I paused at her house as I made my rounds to exchange
a friendly word or two. Every Friday she would greet me at the door with
a bag of my favorite candy; we call them *lollies* in that part of the world.
Naturally, I was young enough to appreciate the sweets, but I was also old
enough to comprehend what that weekly present really meant. She had to
go through a tremendous amount of effort to procure that candy for me;
these were the days before Amazon. I learned from our weekly tradition
how powerful it can be to sincerely care about someone and pay attention to her; in return, she made me feel noticed and cared about, as well.
Our relationship took a mundane newspaper subscription to a new level of
authentic, human connection.

When I grew a little older, I began doing odd jobs at Mr. Knox's hard-
ware store. I wasn't there for more than a few months when his phone rang
with the tragic news that his father had unexpectedly died. As he rushed
out the door, he swept up the store keys, tossed them in my direction, and
said, "Here. Take care of the store while I'm gone. I don't know when I'll
be back." It couldn't have been more than a week; it's hard to remember
that far back. But what I do remember is this: His faith in me inspired me
to go the extra mile for Mr. Knox and his store. Because he trusted me,
without a second thought, in his time of greatest need, he endowed me
with the self-esteem and pride in my work that translated into an intensified dedication on my part. I was determined to take such good care of his
store that it would be in even better condition by the time he got back.

Two simple stories from an ordinary Australian boyhood. Why have
they stayed with me all these years as I ultimately became the CEO of
WD-40 Company, one of the world's most recognized and beloved
brands? I learned through these two friendships that our work life is one
critical area of our short journeys in this world where we find meaning,
belonging, welcome, and identity. While other boys my age were finding

their identity through sports and, well, let's face it, girls, I was discovering myself through my earliest of jobs. They weren't much, as jobs go. But they taught me one of my life's most valuable early lessons: I belonged, because I was valued, because I cared about the people I did business with. And because of all that, I had a place in the world.

In short, I discovered how good it felt to be needed, in a context outside my immediate family, and this inspired me to be even more valuable to the people who needed me.

This is a principle I carry with me to this day (one never outgrows the need to be valued). And this is the gift I am committed to extending to my team – my tribe – at WD-40 Company.

Ah, I see where this is going, you might be thinking right now. *We're about to talk about employee engagement, aren't we?* That would be a reasonable anticipation. For decades, we've repeatedly proven the linkage between employees who are emotionally connected to their work and better business performance. The more adept we have become in making that argument, especially being able to quantify it (as the employee engagement line of inquiry has allowed us to do), the more we enjoy talking about it.

But today I would like to invite you to consider the other side of the employee/enterprise relationship: how emotionally healthy workplaces move the individual along his or her own personal path to self-esteem, personal purpose, and, in many cases, some level of emotional healing. Does this path also result in improved business performance? Undoubtedly. That linkage is why employee engagement is a more natural and obvious conversation for CEOs to have. But for the moment, let's set aside that focus, and simply look at the thing least talked about, consequently rarely seen, even though it's all around us: the workplace gift to individuals as they seek the personally restorative, healing, growing benefits of simply showing up every day to rejoin their tribe in the mission of getting the job done. This is the gift of belonging.

Why Belonging? Why Now?

It is from this foundation of belonging that all good things begin to happen to a person, their family, their job, and the business they are associated with. This is the platform that enables the good feelings – the *positivity*, if you will – that activate trust, collaboration, improved physical health profiles, resilience, focus, bonding, even innovation, according to Barbara Fredrickson, psychologist, professor, and principal investigator of the Positive Emotions and Psychophysiology Lab (PEPLab) at the University of North Carolina.

"Positive emotions change the boundaries of our minds and hearts and change our outlook on our environment. [They] widen the scope of what people are scanning for," she said in a presentation before the Greater Good Science Center at UC Berkeley. "We see more possibilities. People come up with more ideas of what they might do next."[1]

Over her three decades of research, she has definitively linked positive emotions to an individual's (and therefore the employer's) capacity to ideate and innovate. Her phrase for this phenomenon, *broaden and build*, is now a well-accepted concept that behavioral psychologists, organizational psychologists, and consultants specializing in appreciative inquiry almost universally embrace.[2]

And yet, understanding the ROI of meeting the positive emotional needs inside the corporate community, outside the confines of the formal employee engagement conversation, is still somewhat in its nascent stages. If you consider Abraham Maslow's hierarchy of needs, *Belonging* is the first positive emotion, appearing in the middle layer of the hierarchy after the fundamental survival requirements are met. Above *Belonging* you will see *Self-Esteem* and *Self-Actualization*. All three of these emotional realms are where an individual has the emotional luxury to tap into those positive mindsets that ultimately generate innovation and contribution. Those are the realms from which any company can draw the new ideas and discoveries that will drive its future prospects. So it stands to reason that the company that exerts the effort to breathe life into that feeling of *belonging* among its employees – creating a tribal culture, if you will – will be the company that sets itself apart from its competitors, especially those who believe that simply meeting employees' needs on Maslow's lowest levels (physiological and safety/security) should suffice.

It could be that your workplace is their only source of structure, calm, solace, rewarding creativity, and feeling at home among colleagues who excite and challenge their intellectual capacity. It could be that your workplace is the one place where your employees can learn to discover their best selves, build the skills they need to navigate other aspects of their lives, and find their place in the world.

When we stop to think about modern day-to-day life, we are all beset with opportunities to feel like devalued, isolated outsiders for one reason or another. Simple, routine courtesies that provide common ground among strangers are rapidly disappearing. People interrupt each other routinely. Political differences alienate friends and family. Just keeping up with current events floods our brains with negativity and hopelessness that disempower us in other areas of our lives. As individuals change employers every three to five years, they are perpetually repositioned as outsiders and newcomers. Then, behind closed (isolating, secret-keeping) home doors, modern families are suffering devastating domestic dysfunction, such as divorce and addictions. Is it any wonder that any individual who comes to work every day is likely carrying a toxic load of isolation, loneliness, and hits on their self-esteem?

The workplace provides *psychological safety*, posits Amy C. Edmondson,[3] Novartis Professor of Leadership and Management at Harvard Business School, through providing employees with a *tribe* – maybe not the only one in their lives, but an incredibly valuable and rewarding one all the same. Her research has shown that working teams with a high degree of psychological safety – where employees can comfortably take risks and learn new things without fear of shame, embarrassment, separation, or other isolating negative feedback – show a higher likelihood for innovation and individual accountability for performance standards.

Given all the obvious benefits of living and working in the higher realms of Maslow's hierarchy, if you could create a culture that supports employees' emotional health, starting with *Belonging*, why wouldn't you?

Tribal Belonging Ignites Innovation at WD-40 Company

Like anyone in today's world, I have my own story of what it feels like to be a stranger in a strange land. I had already been with WD-40 Company for seven years when it transferred me from Australia to the United States. By that time, I had already worked in many countries in Asia while moving up the ranks at WD-40. Still, even though English is my first language, I had trouble feeling at home in a country of such unexpectedly different ways and customs.

By the time I assumed leadership as CEO in 1997, I was at home in the United States. But the concept of belonging was still top of mind as I considered the company's destiny. At that time, WD-40 was a great, successful company; yet, our culture could be best described as traditional, conservative, authoritarian, and somewhat insular.

Great was no longer good enough. We wanted to make this an even better company, on a global scale (one that would eventually touch lives in 176 countries). If we were to take our signature blue-and-yellow can with the red top to the world, we needed to give all our people not only a new focus on the product but also a new, expansive way to look at themselves (and each other). As a community, we needed to broaden our points of view, our array of possibility thinking. We all needed to see ourselves as part of something larger than our discrete roles in our current jobs. And we needed to feel free to bring forward fresh ideas without fear of being shut down for stretching beyond our prescribed confines of formal job descriptions.

In those days, companies fashionably called their cadres *teams*. But that wasn't quite right for what I was trying to create inside WD-40 Company. When I thought of *team*, I naturally returned my mind to my Australian home to the rough-and-tumble, aggressive, take-no-prisoners game of rugby. If I was looking to create a culture of performance without fear, I'd have to find a better metaphor.

Tribe ticked all the boxes. The performance emphasis is on *contributing* in the context of mutual support and cooperation – not on winning and losing at all costs. Any role you can think of within an indigenous tribe has a counterpart in the corporate community – warriors, teachers, nurturers, learners, scouts, hunters – they can all be found inside a company structure.

Equally importantly, *tribe* also spoke to me of belonging. Naturally, in a corporate setting, the possibility of termination is always an option. But in a culture that is built on a tribal philosophy, dismissing employees (we call it "sharing them with our competitors") is a last resort of such extreme circumstance; it would be almost as unnatural as it would if a tribe were to banish one of its members.

Once employees are psychologically safe in the knowledge that they truly belong to the group, they can invest their emotional energies in the tribe's mission.

The Four Keys to Creating a Tribal Culture

One of the advantages that companies have over indigenous tribes is that we can intentionally create our tribal culture – very often out of whole cloth. Because of that opportunity to be specific in our intentions, we need a framework on which to hang the characteristics of that experience we call our *tribe*.

1. *Purpose*: In the earliest days of tribal culture, its purpose was pretty straightforward: survival and proliferation of its members. Activities were basic, without much nuance, and there wasn't much choice in the matter of tribal membership: If you were born into the tribe, there you stayed, unless you were captured and enslaved by a neighboring tribe. There wasn't any need for a resume. And where time might not have been money, time was definitely calories. Wasted motion was not indulged. The range of choice was, at most, "This watering hole? Or that one?"

Now the essential thought among modern tribe members is, "Do I like the way my life feels among these people? Or maybe I should look over there?" Individuals, including individual members of corporate tribes, yearn for an experience that appeals to the higher levels of Maslow's hierarchy. They have choice everywhere. If they don't like their role within the tribe, they can lay down a plan to move into another function. If they don't like the tribe itself, or its reason for being, they can choose to change tribes at any time.

Today's tribal leaders (business executives) have to work harder at retaining members. A critical tool for rallying and retaining commitment and shared focus on a common goal is the company's *purpose*. It's up to the tribal leadership to find the most relevant, most inspiring, most uplifting and energizing focus to re-recruit their employees every day.

A purpose gives all conversation within a company a positive point of focus. Purpose is the hook on which you hang the entire experience of your workplace. As I was moving up the ranks at WD-40 Company, our focus was on removing the world's *squeaks and smells*. As long as we had no aspirations to grow or transform any further, that purpose would have sufficed. But we wanted more. So we came up with this:

We exist to create positive, lasting memories in everything we do. We solve problems. We make things work smoothly. We create opportunities.

With this single, simple purpose, we become more than stuff in a can. Anyone can make stuff in a can. Now we're about making positive, lasting memories. Now we still might be talking about a spray can and a random squeak. But now, when an idea is brought forward, we ask, "How does that create positive, lasting memories?" We're folding in the entire human experience: "How can we improve our customers' lives? How can we improve each others' lives within the corporate tribe context?"

A well-crafted purpose gives us a place in our world. It's a great tool for helping us focus on the single destination point of our shared, desired result.

It is also the most effective tool for recruiting and retaining the commitment of our tribe members. We can say to each other, "You belong to us because you're as passionate about our purpose as we are."

2. *Values*: Values are commonly regarded as *thou shalt nots* encased in happy face wrappers. But we at WD-40 Company consider our values to be providing the framework within which our people can express their freedom and do what they think is best. Our values are designed to set people free between guardrails that provide for the safety of the individual and the company.

Values, when they are well designed and thoroughly articulated, also serve as a global company's Esperanto, a language that unifies all the company's locations through a common understanding that is embraced across global cultures. As a WD-40 Company employee from, say, Shanghai, walks into a company location in Bologna, our well-defined and thoroughly articulated values eliminate the time- and energy-wasting friction so commonly experienced when strangers struggle to discover common ground.

Our six values are real to our tribe members because we have taken the time to fully describe what each one means.

1. We value doing the right thing.
2. We value creating positive lasting memories in all our relationships.
3. We value making it better than it is today.
4. We value succeeding as a tribe while excelling as individuals.
5. We value owning it and passionately acting on it.
6. We value sustaining the WD-40 Company economy.

Of the six values, number 4 speaks to our commitment to make sure that everyone feels individually supported and that they belong:

We value succeeding as a tribe while excelling as individuals.

We recognize that our collective success comes first. Our organization is a global company with many different locations and tribe members spread far and wide. But everything we do is toward the success of the entire company. Though we believe the individual can't *win* at the expense of, or apart from, the team or tribe, individual excellence is the means by which our organization succeeds, and *excellence* is defined as outstanding contribution to the whole.

3. *An Innovation-Friendly Culture*: Recall Barbara Fredrickson's *broaden-and-build* concept: When individuals operate from a perspective of positivity, their frame of mind expands their capacity to see a bigger-picture perspective and bring forward new ideas and creative solutions. Likewise, that same positivity bolsters their resilience and overall sense of well-being, regardless of the challenges immediately confronting them. This, in turn, makes them more willing to take the risks required to expose their ideas to the scrutiny of their fellow tribe members.

No one wants to look foolish. We all want to look and act our best, especially at work. And nothing makes us feel like an outsider faster than blundering in front of witnesses. It's embarrassing, for starters. A mistake might show that you're not up to speed with everyone else. This hyper-self-consciousness discourages introducing new processes, bringing new ideas to the table, questioning established practices that might be past due for improvement. To be emotionally and intellectually prepared to offer up new ideas, there must be a small part of our essential nature that is willing to look at our work with the fresh eyes of an outsider.

This requires the *psychological safety* that Amy Edmondson talks about.

As the CEO of WD-40, I addressed the challenge of making it safe to be able to put forward fresh ideas, even if they fail utterly. I set the tone by being very free and comfortable with the three words, *I don't know.*

I also instituted the concept of *learning moments*, starting with myself. The learning moment concept came from the desire to reduce the fear that naturally comes with trying something new and having it go down in flames. Fear of public humiliation keeps people from being as creative as they can be because failing in front of others can hurt a career. In another company. But at WD-40 Company, it's fodder for exploratory conversation, where everyone learns from experience. Learning moments aren't conversations about failing; they're conversations about learning from experience. And everyone benefits without having to make the same mistake themselves.

4. *Community*: A tribe is nothing without its great legends, creation story, totems, symbols, secret handshakes, and icons. Memories, especially the positive, lasting ones, build the wealth of knowledge that unites people all over the world over time. Such community markers not only tell insiders who is a fellow tribe member, but also broadcast to the world who you are and what you stand for. And they ignite the passion of outsiders (let's call them auxiliary members), as well. That, in turn, ignites pride of membership in the insider.

The weekend before writing this chapter, I was invited to a small gathering of corporate executives at a mountain ranch outside of Aspen, Colorado. Just being invited to this particular small tribe was thrilling enough. But when a GE executive found out that I was the CEO of WD-40 Company, she couldn't contain her excitement. "My father-in-law loves that stuff!" she said, asking for a picture with me. Naturally, when I got back to the office, I sent the proud father-in-law a WD-40 baseball cap and an autographed can of, well, WD-40. What else?

Conclusion

Let us not overlook the role of the tribal leader in the company tribe. It is our role to be constant learners and then teachers of our tribe members – in particular, the young generations coming up. It's not always easy, but it's critical to tribal survival.

In my homeland, the Aboriginal tribal leaders have been tasked for millennia with the job of teaching the youngsters how to throw the boomerang. When thrown properly, the weapon returns to its owner. When thrown effectively, the boomerang has made contact with an animal and the tribe will eat. Will the young Aborigine who is still learning this new skill be punished, shamed, and shunned for missing the mark?

Absolutely not. The tribal leaders teach again and again. And eventually that young man will grow up to teach the next generation.

Just as with tribal societies, as corporate tribal leaders, we have a stewardship of the lives entrusted to us in organizations. We must genuinely care about others, because what happens to our people during the day gets carried home with them when their workday ends. We must create a corporate environment that sustains, trains, embraces, and encourages our people. Their daily experience at work supports the emotional health that equips them to bring positivity back home to their core tribe – where they ultimately belong.

Reflection Questions:

1. Is there anyone in your past that had a profound influence on your ideas of business and work relations?
2. Do you feel like you are a member of a tribe at your workplace? Is there one or many *tribes* in your organization? What are their goals and values?
3. If you perceive that your organization lacks a *tribal culture*, how might you go about creating one? What would be the benefits of doing so?

Notes

1. https://greatergood.berkeley.edu/video/item/positive_emotions_open_our_mind.
2. Barbara L. Fredrickson, "Chapter 1: Positive Emotions Broaden and Build," *Advances in Experimental Social Psychology* 47 (Cambridge, MA: Academic Press, May 14, 2013).
3. Amy C. Edmondson, "Managing the Risk of Learning: Psychological Safety in Work Teams," *International Handbook of Organizational Teamwork and Cooperative Working* (Hoboken, NJ: John Wiley & Sons, 2003).

24

New Leader Development

Leadership Lessons from the Doerr Institute[1]

Brigadier General Tom Kolditz

Tom Kolditz is the founding executive director of the Ann & John Doerr Institute for New Leaders at Rice University — managing the most comprehensive, university-wide leader development program in the world. He designed the core Leader Development Program at the Yale School of Management, served as chairman of the Department of Behavioral Sciences and Leadership at West Point, and was the founding director of the West Point Leadership Center. A highly experienced leader, Brigadier General Kolditz has more than 30 years in leader supervisory positions, serving on four continents in 34 years of military service. He is a recipient of the Distinguished Service Medal, the Army's highest award for service. He is a Fellow in the American Psychological Association and is a member of the Academy of Management. He has been named a Thought Leader by the Leader to Leader Institute and as a Top Leader Development Professional by Leadership Excellence.

The author is grateful to Dr. Ryan Brown and Ruth Reitmeier for their review and contributions to this chapter.

In 2017, he received the Warren Bennis Award for Excellence in Leadership. He holds a BA from Vanderbilt University, three master's degrees, and a PhD in psychology from the University of Missouri.

■ ■ ■

My purpose is to develop leaders. I direct the most comprehensive leader-development program at any university – the Ann and John Doerr Institute for New Leaders at Rice University in Houston, Texas. The Doerr Institute is changing the world by introducing professional-caliber leader-development strategies in colleges and universities – places where leadership institutes and programs have traditionally been soft, minimally impactful, and weakly assessed. When I look out the window, I see something invisible to others: the future of leader development in providing professional quality development to young leaders early in their lives and careers. This is a somewhat contrarian approach in a field dominated by executive coaching and rarified programs for high-potential employees. Contrarian or not, the view is one I want to share with leaders in all sectors as we seek to promote leadership in our respective spheres.

The Challenges We Face

It seems like [Jim Collins] is saying that in order to be the most successful leader, you have to put the interests of the company before yours, which surprises me. I am also surprised by the emphasis on preparedness and willingness, rather than intelligence…. I tend to think of successful leaders as being more cutthroat, not open to compromise and friendship.
> —Precoaching student leader development plan, Rice University

This quotation reveals the challenges we face for leader development in the emerging global workforce. For the majority of young people, leadership is something you do when elevated to a role. Rather than an organizational commitment, leadership is understood to be a self-focused position of advantage and privilege. Leading comes with privileges and the authority to order people around. In both politics and business, some of the worst leadership role models imaginable are prominent in the news. These leaders wield great power and influence, despite lacking important leader qualities, such as personal integrity, responsibility, accountability, loyalty, trustworthiness, respect for others, and a sense of ethics. Before we can do the work of leader development, we must overcome the prevailing idea that leadership is hierarchical, transactional, and for many millennials, not held as an aspiration.

Traditional leader-development programs selectively invest in leaders many years into their careers. A common industry strategy is to focus leader development resources on developing only those identified as *high-potential employees*. This paradoxical practice causes me to wonder why companies don't identify the HR people who are hiring the *low potentials*, fire those HR people, and use the cost savings for broader-based leader development for everyone else in the organization. Focusing leader development on *high potentials* reinforces an old and debunked leader stereotype, that is, that leadership is equivalent to an elite status.

Alternatively, Frances Hesselbein, founder of the progressive Hesselbein Global Academy for Student Leadership and Civic Engagement at the University of Pittsburgh, has repeatedly made the compelling argument that being a leader is not predicated on an assigned role, but is rather a way of *being*, an element of character largely focused on serving the organization and the people in it. Similarly, in *The Handbook for Teaching Leadership*, Harvard editors Scott Snook, Nitin Nohria, and Rakesh Khurana[2] point to the former Army doctrine of *Be, Know, Do*, by subtitling their work, "Knowing, Doing, and Being."

However, the current delivery of leader-development practice typically targets a handful of high potentials who have reached the executive level – the elites who have been labeled as leaders due to their position. It's a game of catch-up. Coaching did not blossom in the senior executive space because this is the ideal point at which to develop people as leaders. It blossomed there because of a corporate focus on rationing opportunity to employees with the greatest potential, and because top leaders are ultimately responsible for the allocation of training expenses and resources, to others as well as to themselves. This state of affairs hinders the overall quality of leaders in society. It also presents a transformational opportunity for universities to impact the world by increasing the capacity of their students to lead.

The Time Value of Leader Development[©3]

Leader development among college students has the potential for having the highest payoff in terms of enduring capacity to lead. This is borne out by the best science we have. College-aged people show higher plasticity of social and emotional intelligence, memory ability, and processing speed than older adults,[4] skills that allow them to learn faster. If learning to speak a foreign language, play a musical instrument, or swing a baseball bat is best learned early in life, then why would learning to lead be postponed for late adulthood? The openness/imagination facet of the Big Five personality traits,[5] statistically correlated with higher levels of leadership, increases the most during the college years, followed by stability or slight decline in adulthood.[6] Likewise, the social dominance facet of extraversion (connected with assertiveness, independence, and social self-confidence – key aspects of leadership) is also greatest among 18- to 22-year-olds, whereas beyond age 40, no significant increases in this facet of personality appear. Finally, theory and research on identity formation suggest that the college years might be particularly strategic for leadership interventions, because it is during this period (at least in Western countries) when identity is in greatest flux, even more so than during adolescence.[7,8] The Doerr Institute consulted Professor Lara Mayeux, a developmental psychologist who teaches at the University of Oklahoma, for verification of this conclusion, and she said, "The consensus at this point is that college is the *best* time for some type of intervention, because it's the developmental period when most key elements of identity change."

Leader development also has time value because of the integration and assimilation of learning. Take the simplest example of a person growing along two leadership competencies, communication and decision making. While each has value independently, over time, being a better communicator will enhance the dialogue around decision making, and improve decision-making outcomes. Now multiply that principle across every competency improved in the developmental journey of a young person: growth as a leader becomes exponential. Leader development increases in value because of the passage of time.

Learning to Lead for the Future

The complex, transformative, and distributed nature of the Fourth Industrial Revolution demands a new type of leadership … about cultivating a shared vision for change … empowering widespread innovation and action based on mutual accountability and collaboration.

—Klaus Schwab, Nicholas Davis, and Thomas Philbeck, 2017 World Economic Forum[9]

If it makes sense to develop younger leaders, then it's also important to envision the leader skills that may be most critical for success in their future. The 2017 World Economic Forum (WEF) articulated and addressed the advent of changes related to technology as the "Fourth Industrial Revolution" (or 4IR). From the proceedings of the WEF's 2017 Annual Meeting of New Champions,[10] there is a shift in competencies that new leaders will need to master to adapt to the powerful social and economic trends in the next 10–20 years:

- *Ability to work in flat, nonhierarchical teams.* Influence without formal authority will drive team performance and be the most important leadership shift in 4IR. All team members will either exert influence or become irrelevant.
- *Flexibility in multifunctional, specialized teams of leaders.* Teams of leaders will be responsible and accountable to boards; the days of the solitary and valiant CEO leader are numbered.
- *Efficacy in distributed, multiorganizational workplaces.* Leaders of the 4IR and their teams will not be located in far-flung, isolated, suburban office parks operated by a single company, but will work in shared spaces and in multiple, nonpermanent locations as needed, befitting the increasingly decentralized 4IR leadership structure.
- *Building teams as follower networks.* It is not enough for 4IR leaders to embody a list of leader characteristics or skills; they will also need to be able to recognize, manage, and develop such qualities in other people, and to do this effectively in an extended virtual environment, beyond their formal team or immediate organization.
- *Pragmatic ethics.* Leaders will need to be savvy to deceit, malfeasance, and illegality – especially in terms of behavior conveyed by digital and informational means. They must protect their organizations in a world

disappointingly tolerant of unethical behavior. Having strong personal ethics is simply not enough; new leaders must have a strong awareness that others may not share their commitment to doing what is right.

- *Authenticity*. Technology, speed, and social media will diminish privacy in 4IR, and there will be little separation or distinction between personal and professional lives. Leaders must be living lives of integrity and consistency if they are to gain the trust of others.

- *Coward-consciousness*. Leaders must be adept at recognizing and discouraging cowardice in the face of ambiguity, volatility, and the consequences of risk. This is not just promoting courage; cowardice is a more common and a contagious quality characterized by *excessive self-interest*, not merely fear.

Doerr Institute Method: Our Contrarian Approach

Leadership is not defined by the exercise of power, but by the capacity to increase the sense of power among those who are led. The most essential work of the leader is to create more leaders.

—Mary Parker Follett

The Doerr Institute for New Leaders was designed from the outset to be a comprehensive, top-quality leader-development architecture and a model for top-tier universities. Our mission is to "elevate the leadership capacity of Rice students across the university," in order to support the university's mission to "cultivate a diverse community of learning and discovery that produces leaders across the spectrum of human endeavor." Our imperative is to better prepare graduates to lead in a world where massive change will be driven by technology shifts in artificial intelligence, big data, rapid computing, global threats, and rapid shifts in markets. Our work at Rice has application outside the context of academe, from corporate program design to self-directed leader development. The following five Doerr Institute design considerations are shared here to help readers look out through our window, see what we see, and apply a new strategy in their organizations and their personal and professional lives:

1. *Everyone Has High Potential as a Leader*. At the Doerr Institute, no one competes for opportunities for leader development. Immediately, people ask, "How can that be affordable?" It's affordable because if people

self-select into leader development opportunities, the take-rate will always be far fewer than the potential opportunity. Some individuals don't have a growth mindset and are skeptical of development. Some don't want to invest personal time in their long-term development. Some simply prefer to follow. None of those people should be consuming resources in a leader-development process, and none of them are *high potentials*, no matter what HR says about their capacity. Allow people to self-select into leader-development opportunities and grow those people to the top of your organization. The common alternative is to promote someone with technical ability who may or may not be willing or able to lead, and then ask coaches or other leader developers to make up for that – the game of catch up.

2. *Develop Leaders One Person at a Time.* When one thinks of leadership-development programs in organizations, one often thinks of group methods, tiered classrooms, and corporate universities. At the Doerr Institute, we had to devise the best approach to handle a huge array of diverse new leaders: 6,200 students across seven unique schools within the university. Our counterintuitive approach was to work with one person at a time, despite the apparent economy of scale of using the classroom. We do not steer students into leadership classes. Instead, we offer professional leadership coaching to every student in the school who requests it. Coaching individuals is far better at producing measurable outcomes in behavioral change or identity formation. Scheduling one-on-one sessions fits the work flow and demands of student schedules. We coach students in the context of activities that they are already involved in and passionate about. We do not create contrived events or experiences with entertainment value to make it palatable. Effective leader development is hard work.

3. *Ruthlessly Measure Outcomes.* Never let anyone say that leadership gains are intangible or impossible to measure. Our Institute has an independent, full-time team led by an experienced research psychologist with the sole responsibility of measuring outcomes. Never let trainers measure their own outcomes; that's like allowing the pitcher to call balls and strikes. Use rigorous measurement to guide what you undertake as development in your organization and for yourself. Don't waste resources on things that don't produce measurable outcomes. There are trendy leadership-development activities that do not produce measurable outcomes beyond temporary inspiration. Most leadership speakers, obstacle courses, leader yoga, and boot camps provide little in the way of measurable outcomes. This is one reason why people often find it difficult to measure outcomes: They are attempting to assess

events that don't produce outcomes. Do not waste time and resources on *leader-tainment*.

4. *Have a Healthy Skepticism of Single-Demographic Approaches*. We are cautious of single demographic qualifiers to the term *leader*, such as introvert leader, engineer leader, or female leader. There is no question that one can isolate and correlate leader qualities and leader challenges related to single demographic characteristics. One can also build and market programs catering to that demographic. Here is the catch: when a person actually leads, no single demographic characteristic is ever isolated – race, gender, sexual orientation, gender identity, socioeconomic status, national and cultural origin, and personal history all interact continuously. Such interaction is especially the case in global business or university settings, where cultural diversity is complex. Interestingly, our measures reveal that women, international students, and other underrepresented groups tend to participate in one-on-one coaching at slightly higher rates than does the overall student body, and to attain developmental goals at rates higher than their mainstream counterparts. Because of our highly personalized approach, we are able to consider the full spectrum of their demographic characteristics when those characteristics are important to their development or experience as leaders. We never slight the accomplishments of a leader by attaching a demographic qualifier.

5. *Don't Let Leader Development Be Displaced by Other Noble Aims*. It is important to differentiate *leader development* (increasing the capacity or ability of an individual to lead) from *training development* (teaching leaders corporate culture or policies) or *career development* (mentoring into networks, internships, or other forms of advancing a person through an industry). Close inspection of many corporate programs reveals that leader development is frequently displaced by industry-specific training development. Close inspection of university or college programs often reveals that activities cast as leader development are often mostly career development, for example, job-focused internships, mentoring by successful industry volunteers, and other career-shaping initiatives. Consider your own experience: How much time have you spent in programs that developed you as a leader, but where the content was primarily organizational training or career development?

Investing in the Future

Personalized and direct development in the university environment can change the trajectory of an individual for 50 years or longer. Early intervention with young leaders will reap dividends not only for the leaders themselves, but for the countless colleagues, direct reports, and organizations that they will work with over the course of their lifetimes. I invite you to consider the words of two Rice University students who were coached this past academic year:

> *These coaching sessions have led me to understand the factors that affect my decision making. Growing in self-awareness has allowed me to stop making rash decisions and start making strategic, goal-oriented decisions that have increased my confidence as a leader.*
>
> *I never had an opportunity before this experience to reflect on what leadership meant to me and how I could make leadership fruitful for me and those I interact with. I now realize that leadership experiences not only benefit me, but, more importantly, allow me to have the most positive impact on my community.*

I predict that in 10 years, all top-tier colleges and universities will be more serious about leader development. The rest of us can be serious right now. Lessons in cutting-edge development from the Doerr Institute are practical in their application to corporate and personal development strategies: develop only those who want to lead, develop one-on-one, ruthlessly measure outcomes, develop as whole persons, don't waste resources, don't give in to distractions. The Doerr Institute invites you to look out the window with us and join us in our mission to develop the next generation of leaders.

Reflection Questions:

1. When do you think leadership training is most effective? Why?
2. Did you receive any leadership training in college/university? How valuable did you find it then? What value has it had since then?
3. What do you consider the qualities of a good leader? An effective leader? A successful leader? How are these different?
4. Research suggests that about 30% of leaders' qualities could be inherited, but that roughly 70% of leader capacity is learned. That said, what do you think are the best ways to accelerate your learning to lead?

Notes

1. This chapter is excerpted, in part, from the author's October 25, 2017, acceptance speech for the Warren Bennis Award for Excellence in Leadership, which he received during the annual Global Institute for Leader Development conference in Palm Desert, California.
2. S. Snook, N. Nohira, and R. Khurana, *The Handbook for Teaching Leadership: Knowing, Doing, and Being* (Thousand Oaks, CA: Sage, 2012).
3. Time Value of Leader Development is a term that is a key component of the Doerr Method–early leader development for the purpose of compounding the effects over time.
4. A. Soubelet and T.A. Salthouse, "Personality-Cognition Relations Across Adulthood," *Developmental Psychology* 47 (2011): 303–310.
5. P.T. Costa, Jr., and R.R. McCrae, *The NEO Personality Inventory Manual* (Odessa, FL: Psychological Assessment Resources, 1985).
6. B.W. Roberts, K.E. Walton, and W. Viechtbauer, "Personality Traits Change in Adulthood: Reply to Costa and McCrae," *Psychological Bulletin* 132 (2006): 29–32.
7. J. Arnett, "Emerging Adulthood: A Theory of Development from the Late Teens Through the Twenties," *American Psychologist* 55 (2000): 469–480.
8. T.A. Kolditz, "Why You Lead Determines How Well You Lead," *Harvard Business Review*, July 22, 2014, http://blogs.hbr.org/2014/07/why-you-lead-determines-how-well-you-lead/.
9. T.A. Kolditz, T. Casas, I. Klett, and J. Strackhouse, *Are You a Leader of the Fourth Industrial Revolution?* World Economic Forum, Annual Meeting of the New Champions 2017: Achieving Inclusive Growth in the Fourth Industrial Revolution, 38–40, http://www3.weforum.org/docs/AMNC17/WEF_AMNC17_Report.pdf.
10. Ibid.

25

The World's
Greatest
Ophthalmologist

Pawel Motyl

Pawel Motyl has 20-plus years of experience in business, including 10 years in management consulting and executive search as well as 7-plus years in the CEO role (ICAN Institute – Harvard Business Review Poland publishing house and leading executive education firm in Poland). He is one of the leading European experts on decision making, leadership, personal effectiveness, and talent management; in 2016, he was chosen to join the 100 Coaches group, selected and led by Marshall Goldsmith.

A speaker at Harvard Business Review conferences in Poland, Pawel has delivered presentations with Marshall Goldsmith, Dave Ulrich, Andrew McAfee, Joseph Badaracco, Neil Rackham, Heike Bruch, and many others. He is a facilitator of C-level workshops and training programs and top-ranked trainer in executive education projects. As architect of consulting solutions and advisor to the management boards of leading companies in Poland, Pawel has managed and participated in numerous international assignments.

Pawel's book, Labyrinth: The Art of Decision-Making, *became a Harvard Business Review Poland all-time bestseller in just four weeks. The book won many prestigious awards in Poland, including 2014 Golden Owl, and will soon be pub-lished in English.*

More: www.pawelmotyl.com.

■ ■ ■

I never predict. I just look out the window and see what's visible – but not yet seen.
—Peter Drucker

In July 2017, I ran a quick poll among more than 30 of my friends, ask-ing for their interpretation of these words by Peter Drucker. Each of my respondents came up with a response that fell into the same category: vision-ary leaders. *Seeing things others cannot see yet* is usually interpreted as *having a vision.* Thus, the quote evoked profiles of the greatest entrepreneurs and business people (from Henry Ford to Steve Jobs and Elon Musk); inventors and scientists (Nicola Tesla, Albert Einstein, and Stephen Hawking); spir-itual, political, and military leaders (Alexander the Great, Nelson Mandela, and the Dalai Lama); and, a little surprisingly, a ski jumper from Sweden named Jan Boklöv, who back in 1986 was brave enough to introduce what we would call a breakthrough innovation today: a V-style of ski jumping.

I was not surprised. When I first came across this quote many years ago, I felt like the *Back to the Future* protagonist, Marty McFly, miraculously shot back in time to 1963 in Washington, DC, to watch Martin Luther King, Jr., expressing his compelling dream from the steps of the Lincoln Memo-rial. That dream was a vision of the country and the society that was loom-ing on the horizon, but was still invisible to many.

We have always been awed by such people.

In the years that followed, I found out that there is one more impor-tant perspective in Peter Drucker's words, a perspective that goes beyond visionary leadership and often becomes paramount to one's personal effectiveness.

Let me share a story that explains this perspective – my story.

I was born in Poland in 1975, during the Communist era, and as a teenager, witnessed the 1989 collapse of communism across Eastern Europe and the rise of a free market economy. After graduating from Cracow Uni-versity of Economics and earning a postgraduate degree from Jagiellonian University, I was accepted for an internship with the Polish office of Hay

Group. This began an eight-year journey that brought me from a junior consultant level to the team leader position, where I was responsible for the organizational research and diagnostics business in the Central and Eastern Europe region. In 2006, I decided that I wanted to understand general management better and I started looking for a CEO or a managing director position. In early 2007, after a very short recruitment process, I was appointed the CEO of ICAN Institute, Harvard Business Review Polska (Poland) publishing house.

I was proud to be part of the local edition of the world's greatest business magazine, a member of a relatively small team of 30 super-professional, dedicated people. In the following months, I was interviewed by some business magazines in Poland, and enjoyed my new status as one of the younger CEOs in the country.

Now let me fast forward to 2013. The company was doing well: in spite of the 2008–2009 worldwide economic downturn that hit the emerging markets severely, the ICAN Institute continued to grow, with both its publishing and nonpublishing businesses thriving. We became the market leaders in executive education programs and conferences, and our latest additions – management consulting and organizational diagnostics units – were helping fuel our growth. The company grew to 200 people and it showed a healthy revenue structure and margins. People kept congratulating me.

And then I made a *mistake*.

I invited Marshall Goldsmith to be the keynote speaker at ICAN Institute's November 2013 conference.

It was the first time I had worked with Marshall. He turned out not only to be extremely professional, but also amazingly open and easygoing. We had a couple of Skype calls before he came, discussing the event and the target audience. During Marshall's two-day stay in Poland, we co-delivered a workshop for 100 managers of one of the country's leading banks, had a fantastic dinner, and then worked together during the conference. The conference was an incredible success, with Marshall earning top scores in the customer satisfaction surveys. This was the highest-rated ICAN Institute's event ever!

In the evening, when the conference was finished and participants were gone, Marshall asked if I had half an hour to talk. Of course, I gladly agreed and we had a coffee. After some small talk, Marshall asked me quite a surprising question:

"Do you think you are a good CEO?"

For a moment I did not know what to say, as these were the most unexpected words I could imagine, especially after such a successful event!

Being totally frank, I said:

"I am an average one. Being a CEO is a combination of two roles: the one of a leader, which is about vision, inspiration, and people; and the one of a manager, which boils down to execution, control, and concern for order. I am good at the former and weak at the latter, which makes me – statistically – an average CEO."

And then Marshall shot the question that changed everything:

"So why do you spend your professional life doing something you are only average at?"

I was speechless. Marshall's words were so *obvious*. So rational. So true. So powerful. So unexpected. So painful.

I had to admit that being a CEO was a compilation of good times and bad. I loved working with clients, delivering workshops, and acting as a consultant, speaking at conferences across Europe, and sharing know-how through articles, podcasts, or webinars. But I hated all the operational drudgery and quite often felt unmotivated on the days that were filled with this type of activity.

Marshall looked at me with this funny spark in his eye and finally said, "Pawel, why don't you focus on things you are exceptional at?"

In a split second, I understood the truth: For many years, I had been held hostage by the expectations of other people and by the clichés that imposed a specific career path on me. The dream of each graduating student in economics is to climb the ladder to get to the position of a CEO, and then continue to move up that ladder.

Marshall's questions unveiled a new vantage point for me. I understood that for my entire professional career, I had been blind, following the dreams of other people, dreams that had never been my own. Deep in my heart, I never wanted to be a CEO or to manage a company. What I always really wanted was to create, gather, process, and share business knowledge from the world's best (sometimes counterintuitive) sources in order to help other executives become more effective and lead their companies in a better way. This was my unexpressed mission, my purpose, my professional raison d'être. And I had been compromising it because of what other people viewed as a career success.

In the nine months that followed the conference, together with the owners of ICAN Institute, I prepared a succession plan, finally resigning from my role in August 2014, with the CFO of the company assuming my duties.

■ ■ ■

It's time to come back to Peter Drucker's quote.

Obviously, it is awesome to be a successful visionary leader, and there was a common denominator in the backgrounds of all the great leaders mentioned in the beginning of this chapter: their genuine passion for what they were doing. There is another quote from Peter Drucker that I love:

Your first and foremost job as a leader is to take charge of your own energy and then help to orchestrate the energy of those around you.

Let's take one step backwards. Are we doing what we are best at? Are we in the right place? Do we realize our full potential? What are our perspectives for development? Are we happy with who we are and what we do? Do we really have genuine passion for that?

The point is, that when we look out the window, we usually see the picture that is either blurred or distorted by many triggers, both internal and external. There are expectations of others, there are stereotypes, there is our own ego. Consequently, sometimes we cannot see (or do not want to see) the truth.

In Marshall Goldsmith, I met an exceptional ophthalmologist, who fixed my sight just by asking several questions. Today when I look out the window, I can see things as they truly are. Sometimes, these are the things that others cannot see.

This is my understanding of Peter Drucker's words.

■ ■ ■

How to get there? Following are several questions and exercises that you might find useful in adjusting your own vision.

1. Where Are You?

This question seems easy, yet exploring it almost always brings some surprising outcomes.

Start with what I call the Five-Color Calendar Test.

Book at least two hours of your time, prepare markers or Post-it™ cards in five colors. Print out your agenda from the past several months and stick it to a wall. Now, move backwards in time, analyzing the events on each day at work. Mark the printed calendar entries with five colors:

1. Green for events that were successful in business terms and motivated you
2. Red for events that were successful, but did not make you feel good or made you feel unmotivated
3. Orange for events that were unsuccessful, but made you feel energized
4. Yellow for events that were unsuccessful and made you feel bad
5. Blue (or any other color) for events that were neutral

Take a step back and look. The interpretation of results is obvious: the more red and orange you see, the more concerned you should be!

Run this exercise again in four weeks. Have a notebook and pen handy, and write down your thoughts and feelings after each event you participate in at work. Mark the event with one of five colors.

Finally, talk to several people who love you, asking them a series of straightforward questions: Do you think I am happy with what I do? Am I good at what I do? Should I keep doing that? Don't be satisfied with their first answers; dig deeper. Then, ask the same set of questions to someone whom you dislike. Don't get defensive. Listen and appreciate their honesty.

2. Who Are You?

There are many psychometric tests and 360-degree assessment tools that help us understand ourselves better. But let me describe a much simpler, yet equally powerful, exercise that you can run in a short time and at no cost.

You most probably work with an organization that has a specific mission, vision, and values. These reflect the identity of the firm and become the *social glue* for employees, creating a specific company culture. Through specific associations, they are also part of the brand.

But have you ever thought about your own brand?

What would be your personal mission? What about your vision? Where would you like to be in some not-so-distant future? What values do you follow and want to be associated with?

I ran this simple exercise with many of my clients. They were usually shocked by my questions, as they had been spending much time discussing the mission-vision-values of the company they manage, but had never reflected on themselves.

There is another part to this exercise. Write down your personal mission, vision, and values and put this sheet of paper in a sealed envelope. Now go to several people you have worked with for a long time and ask them to anonymously share their opinions on the accuracy of your assessment of your mission, vision, and values. Don't forget to fasten your seatbelt before reading their replies!

3. What Else Is There?

One of the worst enemies we face today is, paradoxically, our own success. Success usually diminishes or kills our openness to and readiness for change; if things have worked fine so far, why change? A triumph of yesterday often sets a foundation for the failure of tomorrow.

Therefore, never stop exploring. Be hungry for new experiences. Force yourself to get out of your comfort zone. Do things you have never done before. Never participated in charity work? Try one Saturday next month. Never gone fishing? Check if anyone you know would take you for an early morning fishing trip. Never climbed? Find the nearest mountaineering club. That boring couple living across the street? Have a glass of wine with them.

Be prepared to abandon stereotypes and clichés! I will never forget one of my climbing expeditions to the Pamir mountain range in Kyrgyzstan, where I met a Russian guy, who – apart from being a great mountaineer – spoke very good English. We spent some time in the camps on the mountain we climbed, talking to each other pretty often. He said he moved from Russia to the United States and worked there. Automatically I had a stereotype of a blue-collar worker from an Eastern European county. We climbed and talked. It was on the last day, when I was just about to leave the basecamp, that we exchanged our e-mails, so as to share pictures taken during the climb. I could not believe what I was seeing: his e-mail was in the @Princeton.edu domain! It turned out that, over the two weeks we were together, I had wasted a chance to talk to a great applied physics specialist working at a prestigious university by continually discussing weather forecasts.

■ ■ ■

There is a wonderful scene in the 1989 film *Dead Poets' Society* when the unforgettable Robin Williams, playing English teacher John Keating, stands up on his desk in front of his somewhat shocked students, none of whom can answer his question: "Why do I stand up here?"

He explains:

I stand upon my desk to remind myself that we must constantly look at things in a different way. You see, the world looks very different from up here…. Just when you think you know something, you have to look at it in another way. Even though it may seem silly or wrong, you must try! Boys, you must strive to find your own voice. Because the longer you wait to begin, the less likely you are to find it at all. Thoreau said, "Most men lead lives of quiet desperation." Don't be resigned to that. Break out!

I was lucky to meet my John Keating on a couple of rainy November days in Poland. Remember that your personal Marshall Goldsmith might be somewhere nearby.

Reflection Questions:

1. Who has been a mentor or inspiration – a "John Keating" or a Marshall Goldsmith – in your own life?
2. What motivates you? Is your current job aligned with your dreams? Your values? Your mission?
3. What stereotypes or clichés do you hold that might be preventing you from interacting more fully with others?

26

Don't Just Let Culture Happen

Alex Osterwalder

Alexander Osterwalder is an entrepreneur, speaker, and business model innovator. He is co-founder of Strategyzer, a leading SaaS company that helps organizations develop new growth engines, better value propositions, and powerful business models via online applications and facilitated online courses.

In 2015, Alex won the strategy award by Thinkers50, called the "Oscars of Management Thinking" by the Financial Times, *and ranks #15 among the leading business thinkers of the world. In 2013, he won the inaugural Innovation Luminary Award by the European Union.*

Alex is lead author of Business Model Generation and Value Proposition Design, *which sold over a million copies in 37 languages.* USA Today *named* Business Model Generation *among the 12 best business books of all times. The German edition was named Management Book of the Year 2011.* Fast Company *magazine named it one of the Best Books for Business Owners in 2010. He crafted the first book with his long-time coauthor and former PhD supervisor Professor Yves Pigneur and 470 collaborators from 45 countries. It was initially self-published in 2009, with an innovative crowd-funded business model.*

■ ■ ■

This article was written with Dave Gray, Yves Pigneur, and Kavi Guppta.

Right now, 51% of your employees are actively looking for a new job or watching for openings. This jarring stat, from Gallup's 2016 *State of the American Workforce Report*,[1] points out that talented people are on the hunt for organizations with a future vision for growth and prosperity, where there is a chance to contribute to that future and feel engaged with the work being done.

What's going to keep talented people around? You could try to motivate people with incentives and unique perks like ping-pong rooms and free meals, but none of those approaches address the deeper issue of why employees are on the move.

We believe the answer is culture – the formal and informal values, behaviors, and beliefs practiced in an organization. Very few companies intentionally work on their culture; in fact, many companies just let culture happen. We believe that culture has to be intentionally designed and that leadership holds the power and responsibility to see this happen. Company culture can be a fuzzy conversation, but the right tools can make culture tangible and manageable. The corporation of the twenty-first century cannot just let culture happen.

What Is Corporate Culture?

When Dave Gray, founder of XPLANE, set out to design a tool to better manage culture, Yves Pigneur and I helped him create the Culture Map, a practical, simple, and visual tool.

You can use the Culture Map to map out and assess an existing culture or to design a desired culture.

Dave Gray often says that a company's culture is like a garden: You can design it, but nature will still be a force. You can't control everything about your culture, but you can intentionally take it into your own hands. Culture will emerge through constant care and nurturing.

Here's how the analogy of a garden helps leadership and teams to visualize their culture within the Culture Map. (See Figure 26.1.)

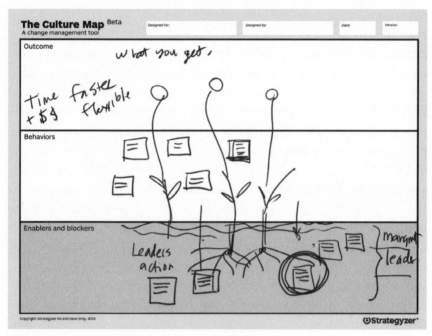

Figure 26.1   The Culture Map Garden

- *The outcomes* in your culture are the fruits. These are the things you want your culture to achieve, or what you want to "*harvest*" from your garden.
- *The behaviors* are the heart of your culture. They're the positive or negative actions people perform every day that will result in a good or a bad harvest.
- *The enablers and blockers* are the elements that allow your garden to flourish or fail. For example, weeds, pests, bad weather, or lack of knowledge might be hindering your garden, whereas fertilizer, expertise in gardening specific crops, or good land might be helping it grow. The enablers and blockers are also the only elements of the Culture Map that management can directly control. What management puts in place – policies, rituals, systems – will either help or hinder the organization and result in corresponding worker behaviors.

Shape and Nurture Culture like a Garden

Uber's recent woes – lawsuits, investigations, and leadership churn – come to mind as a negative example of what happens when culture is left untended. It doesn't just sour the brand for customers; it results in an organization that is stalled for any further potential growth. The company is now intentionally trying to transform its culture to better position it for future growth. Netflix, on the other hand, is a very different example of a company dedicated to building a great place to work where talented people contribute to a groundbreaking product. We recommend browsing Netflix's culture slideshare online to see a company that is very intentional about its positive work culture and emphasizes collaboration. Hubspot is another example of a company that is explicit about its *"culture code"* – thus demonstrating the role of a great culture in attracting talented people.

Of course, there are many different types of company cultures. Some have strong collaborative cultures, some are experimenting with flat versus hierarchical cultures, and some are purely focused on creating innovation cultures. Amazon is one example that comes to mind.

We highly recommend you read Amazon founder Jeff Bezos's 2015–2016 letter to shareholders. It's a fantastic example of how Bezos doesn't let culture just happen, but has deliberately set out to design an innovation culture. Amazon's stellar growth and constant reinvention is substantial evidence of the effectiveness of being intentional about your company culture. In Figure 26.2, we use the Culture Map to parse Jeff Bezos's letter to shareholders and unearth concrete examples of how he has built a company with a culture of constant pioneering in new spaces.

The Culture Map organizes outcomes centered on the stellar growth that Bezos desires for Amazon. These are followed by very tangible behaviors that are visibly enacted inside the organization. Lastly, these positive behaviors are driven by enablers – the space where culture can really be designed and played with. Bezos's letter to his shareholders also explicitly mentions some blockers found in most big companies that Amazon tries to avoid.

Now we can really capture the culture in a tangible way. Your culture and company will be different, but you can use Amazon as a reference for understanding what part of your existing organizational culture enables

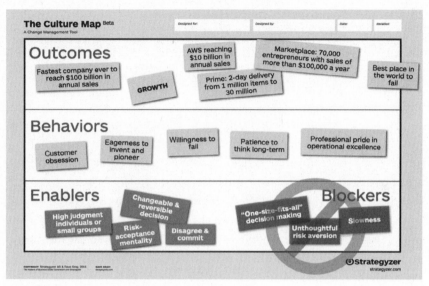

Figure 26.2 A Culture Map of Amazon

growth and what parts block it. Then you can discuss and capture how to design a future culture that better encourages growth.

How Can You Get Started?

Company culture can feel like a beast, which is why many leaders avoid having these tough conversations. But there are small ways to get started. Here are three things you can do with members of your organization to begin the conversation:

1. *10 + minutes.* Do a quick assessment to map your present culture. Think hard about enablers and blockers. Quickly capturing your current culture will allow you to carry over any existing enablers and positive behaviors that can also work in your desired culture.
2. *60 + minutes.* In a slightly longer session, you can facilitate a shared understanding of your current culture with more people contributing their perspectives. Collaboration is key. How does your Culture Map change with others sharing their input?

3. *180 + minutes.* In this long session, you can define your desired culture and kick off a conversation about how the company can move there from its current culture. Individuals, teams, and leadership can collaborate to discuss and capture the desired enablers and behaviors that everyone can begin to experiment with and implement internally.

Like a successful garden, a happy and engaged workforce is the result of an intentionally designed company culture; it's not something that you just let happen. Companies should be as intentional about culture as they are about strategy and business model innovation. We believe that a tool like the Culture Map is incredibly important for capturing and discussing organizational culture. Each one will be unique to the challenge that an organization has to face, whether that's tackling growth, crisis, or disruption. But you can't create a culture that will be effective in doing any of that without the right tools.

Reflection Questions

1. How would you describe the corporate culture of your workplace?
2. What actions do leaders at your organization take to nurture and grow this culture?
3. What elements of Amazon's organizational culture do you believe are most important to its success? Are there any similarities/differences between Amazon and your own organization's culture?

Notes

1. Kavi Guppta, "Gallup: American Workers Are Unengaged and Looking Elsewhere," Gallup's 2016 State of the American Workforce Report, Forbes.com, https://www.forbes.com/sites/kaviguppta/2017/03/08/gallup-american-workers-are-unengaged-and-looking-elsewhere/#1c178fed3e8c.

27 | The Space Between Intention and Action

Liz Wiseman

Liz Wiseman is the New York Times *bestselling author of* Multipliers[1]*and* Rookie Smarts[2]*and teaches leadership to executives around the world. A former executive at Oracle corporation, she was VP of Oracle University and global leader for HR Development. Her clients include Apple, Disney, and Google. Liz has been listed on the Thinkers50 ranking and named as one of the top 10 leadership thinkers in the world.*

■ ■ ■

The French artist Paul Gauguin once said, "I shut my eyes in order to see." My own life experiences have taught me how to see in the dark – to observe the invisible and to read the unwritten, unspoken words that reveal obscured truth. It's a skill I acquired at a young age.

My father was a gruff man who was hard on the people around him. He was raised in a good family and worked with his father and brother in the family business. But, when a disagreement about how to run the business evolved into an impasse, my father not only left the business, he left his family, vowing to never speak with them again. Tragically, he never did.

With his own family (a wife and four children), he oscillated between two modes: (1) a grumpy, curt know-it-all who told everyone what to do

205

and how to do it, and (2) a sullen and withdrawn recluse, often retreating to the TV room. He had a knack for saying the wrong thing and pushing people away. Around my father, it was easy to be offended or hurt. Some in our family viewed him as cold-hearted and unkind. Yet, for some reason, I saw him differently. While I clearly observed (and experienced) his gruff exterior, I could also see underneath it. On the inside, I saw a man who was hurt and deeply wounded: a tenderhearted, good father who just didn't know how to show love and concern. It was obvious to me that his bossy behavior was actually a misguided attempt to keep his children from making similar mistakes to his own. I can't recall ever hearing him say, "I love you" to me or anyone else, yet I always felt loved. As his good intentions became more visible to me, I was less affected by his critical behavior, and we developed and sustained a wonderful relationship. Unfortunately, there were others who didn't see beyond his behavior and their relationships didn't fare as well.

Growing up with a perpetually pessimistic and overly prescriptive father trained me to see the gap between intention and action. The empathy I gained by understanding my father helped me develop compassion for all of us who suffer bouts of hypocrisy – those moments (or entire phases) when our behavior falls short of our good intentions. It sensitized me to the disconnect that occurs when one person judges himself based on his positive intentions while others judge him on his negative behaviors. I certainly had witnessed how misunderstandings and problems can grow in the dark, dank space between intention and actions.

When I graduated from college and began my career, I encountered dozens (if not hundreds) of people like my father – overly bossy bosses and know-it-all colleagues. I saw how these leaders, determined to be the smartest in the room, actually shut down and pushed people away. In their barrage of brilliance, they diminished the people around them. Later in my career when I began to research this dynamic, I discovered that these *Diminisher* leaders got less than half of the intelligence and capability of the people who worked for them while, in contrast, *Multiplier* leaders were rewarded with the full intelligence of their employees. The economics were compelling: Compared to their diminishing colleagues, these multiplier leaders were getting twice the capability out of their people, all for the same price.[3]

As I did more research and heard from thousands of people who were stuck working for Diminishers, I realized there was more at work than just economics; these leaders left deep emotional craters. People who are shut down, limited, and bullied at work feel the toxic effects seep into all aspects of their lives. Employees with Diminisher bosses consistently reported experiencing increased stress, reduced confidence, low energy, depression, poor health, general unhappiness, and more. And the collateral damage didn't stop there; if not addressed, diminishing usually intensified. The majority of individuals also reported that they carried stress home – becoming angry and irritable, complaining more, and withdrawing socially.

Among the hundreds of comments in our study, there were two that especially struck me.[4] One person wrote, "I doubted I could do anything right, and I doubted that anything I had done had been right. I felt like I was a disappointment to my family, my friends, and my coworkers. I unfriended most everyone on Facebook/Google+, had massive depressive episodes, and even contemplated ending my life." The other heart-wrenching story was from someone who said that the stress and self-doubt got so bad, "I couldn't even take care of my dog." These short-sighted leaders were costly to their organizations and levied a burdensome tax on their employees.

The Accidental Diminisher

Many of the Diminishers I studied were legitimate bullies – the type of managers who attempt to be big shots by making others small. But as I've continued my research, it's become clear that the vast majority of the diminishing happening inside our workplaces isn't coming from these narcissistic, tyrannical jerks; rather, it is done with the best of intentions by what I call *Accidental Diminishers* – good people trying to be good managers. Just like in the movies, sometimes the good guys are actually the bad guys.

These Accidental Diminishers are well-meaning, decent managers, yet despite having the best intentions, they shut down the intelligence of others. In studying these leaders, I was struck by two findings: (1) Despite their positive intentions, the Accidental Diminisher's negative impact was often as great as that of the overt Diminisher, and (2) Very few of these well-meaning leaders understood the restrictive impact they were having on others. For the most part, they felt they were doing the right things. Many had grown up praised for their personal intelligence and had moved up the management ranks on account of their personal – and often intellectual – merit. When they became *the boss*, they assumed it was their job to be the smartest person in the room and to manage a set of *subordinates*. Or, much like the *helicopter parent*, they assumed their interventions were helping, not hurting, those in their charge.

Most of these overly helpful managers were mortified when they realized the diminishing effect their style of management was having. When one executive at 3 M recognized how her well-intentioned actions had actually been shutting down others, she went on a mission to find former employees and colleagues, apologize for her misguided actions, and better understand how her seemingly helpful actions had actually done damage.

How might we, with the very best intentions, be having a diminishing impact on the people we lead? How might our good intentions be translated and received differently than how we intended? Here are a few of the indicators that you might be having a diminishing impact, despite your best intentions:

1. *You're Always On.* You are a dynamic, charismatic leader who thinks energy is infectious. You see yourself as turning up the energy level of the team. But leaders who bring the energy tend to consume all the space and shut others down. For example, after one general manager of a $250 M division held an offsite meeting with his staff, a member of his team came to him and said, "You are sucking all the oxygen out of the room. There is no room for the rest of us." While you're trying to turn them up, others tend to tune out the "always on" leader.
2. *You're Helpful.* You're an empathetic leader who is quick to help when you see people struggling. You want to ensure that people are success-ful and protect their reputation. However, when managers (or par-ents!) rescue people too early or too often, their employees (or young charges) become dependent and suffer weakened confidence and repu-tation. Sometimes leaders are most helpful when they help less.
3. *You See the Glass as Half Full.* You are a positive, can-do leader who always sees new possibilities and great potential in others. You assume your belief in people will inspire them to new heights. But when lead-ers play the role of optimist, they undervalue the struggle the team is experiencing and neglect the hard-fought learning and work. Or worse,

the leader might be sending an unintentional message that mistakes and failure are not an option. When the leader sees only the upside, others can become preoccupied with the downside.

Seeing into the Cracks

If any of the above ring true or produce a pang of guilt, you might just be an Accidental Diminisher. But while our growth as leaders might start with a hunch based on your own insights, it shouldn't end there. You'll learn more by asking the people you lead to share *their* insights. The damage of the Accidental Diminisher is done in the dark, without awareness, which means it's hard for the manager to see. For leaders to become intentional in their impact, they must train their minds to see the effect of their behavior rather than simply the intent of their actions. Leaders must learn to view their actions through the lens of their closest customers – their employees. Here are some questions you might use to elicit this feedback:

- How might I be shutting down the ideas and actions of others, despite having the best of intentions?
- What am I inadvertently doing that might be having a diminishing impact on others?
- How might my intentions be interpreted differently by others? What unintended messages might my actions be conveying?
- What could I do differently?

Consuming Less Space

Becoming a Multiplier often starts with becoming less of a Diminisher. This usually means doing less: less talking, less responding, less convincing, and less rescuing of others who need to struggle and learn for themselves. When we feel the need to be big, let it be a signal that we need to shrink a bit and dispense our views in small but intense doses. And when our instincts tell us to help more, we might need to help less. Often the best leaders have a small footprint but a deep impact. They leave room for others to contribute and grow around them.

With self-awareness and simple workarounds, otherwise good managers can become great leaders. Here are four simple but powerful starting points for aligning your intent and your impact and leading in a way that causes others to step up rather than pull away:

1. *Tell Less, Ask More.* The best leaders don't provide all the answers; they ask the right questions, questions that focus the intelligence and energy of the people around them; questions that cause people to think deeply, step up, and assume accountability for outcomes. Instead of telling people what to do, try using your knowledge to ask insightful and challenging questions that cause people to stop, think, and rethink.

2. *Play Fewer Chips.* Rather than dominating the conversation, try dispensing your ideas in small but intense doses. Before a meeting, give yourself a budget of "poker chips," with each chip representing a comment or contribution to the meeting. Use your chips wisely and leave the rest of the space for others. As you offer your ideas more sparingly, you will not only allow others more room to contribute, your own ideas will be more influential.

3. *Give It Back.* When someone brings you a problem that you think they are capable of solving, ask them for a *fix* rather than solving the problem for them. Play the role of coach rather than problem solver. If your team legitimately needs help, offer it, but remember to return ownership back to the team by reminding them that they are still in charge.

4. *Put Others in Charge.* Instead of delegating pieces of work, let people know that they (not you) are in charge and accountable. Perhaps the easiest way to let someone know that they are in charge is by giving that person the majority vote. Tell them they get 51% of the vote, but 100% of the accountability.

Recalibrating Our Sight

As a leader, having good intentions is necessary, but insufficient. Becoming a great leader requires us to understand how our most noble intentions can have a diminishing effect, sometimes deeply so. When leaders see only their good intentions, they operate with a one-eyed view of the world, often leaving behind a wake of misunderstanding, disengagement, and unfulfilled aspiration. It is only when leaders combine self-knowledge with the perceptions and reactions of others that they can see clearly. As leaders come to realize how their best intentions go awry, their vision becomes sharper and wider, and, in the words of Robert Frost, their "two eyes make one in sight." With this insight, wise leaders both adjust their actions and clarify their intentions by reaffirming their faith in the capability of their teams.

Having better optics into this murky space between intention and impact not only presents a growth opportunity for leaders; it holds promise for our role as followers and collaborators. When we find ourselves frustrated by the actions of our leaders, we would do well to look beyond the particulars of their behavior. Instead of getting caught up in the noise, we can ask ourselves, "What might be their most noble intent? How might they be trying to help me succeed?" As Thoreau said, "It's not what you look at that matters, it's what you see." When we choose to see the best intentions of those around us, it invites both parties to work at the higher level of their intent rather than settling for the lower level of misunderstanding. As a young woman, I could have fixated on my dad's inadequacies, pining for a father who was more affirming. Instead I set my sights on the better part – the good intentions that he struggled to express. Like the traveler in Robert Frost's famed yellow wood, choosing that path has, for me, made all the difference.

When we align our actions with our true intent, we become leaders who bring out the best in others (even if it's a micromanaging boss or a difficult father). And it promises more than economic advantage; it defines our legacy. How do we want to be remembered as a leader? As someone with a big personality, or someone around whom other people grew? When employees are overlooked or underutilized, work is exhausting, even painful. But when leaders create conditions where people can contribute fully and whole-heartedly, work is exhilarating. Work becomes more than a mere job or even a career; it becomes a joyful expression of our most complete selves. Truly then is work love made visible.

Reflection Questions

1. Would you characterize yourself as a Multiplier or a Diminisher as a leader? In what ways might you be accidentally diminishing the people you lead?
2. Are your intentions usually congruent with your actions? Why or why not?
3. If your intentions and actions are not in sync, what steps could you take to bring them more into alignment?

Notes

1. Liz Wiseman, *Multipliers: How the Best Leaders Make Everyone Smarter*, revised and updated ed. (New York: Harper Business, 2017).
2. Liz Wiseman, *Rookie Smarts: Why Learning Beats Knowing in the New Game of Work* (New York: Harper Business, 2004).
3. Wiseman, *Multipliers*, 10–13.
4. Ibid., 220.

PART V

Bright Future!

Frances Hesselbein is often heard rallying all of us toward a *Bright Future!* Her vision is a "world of healthy children, strong families, good schools, decent housing, safe neighborhoods, work that dignifies, and faith that sustains – all embraced by the diverse, cohesive, inclusive community that cares about all its people."

In this section, our contributors share their hopes for tomorrow and solutions to challenges arising today that will lead us toward the bright future that we envision. Frances Hesselbein draws on her varied experiences coaching and developing young leaders – particularly in her role as CEO of the Girl Scouts of the USA – to discuss her enthusiasm and hopes for the current generation of young millennials as they rise to assume positions of leadership in the global society. She paints a picture of a marvelously Bright Future! Sarah McArthur explores the importance of communication to how we work together, the challenges of the Information Age, and how leaders can repair and prevent breakdowns in communication. David Allen suggests how a shift in perspective from viewing potential *problems* as *projects* can radically alter how we move toward our goals, not only on the personal level, but globally. He describes how to transition from victimhood to empowerment. Whitney Johnson utilizes a cheerleading metaphor – "Throw down your pom-poms and get in the game" – as an inspiration for all of us to pursue our dreams with passion instead of sitting on the sidelines of our lives and careers. Asheesh Advani describes how his early experiences as an Indian immigrant in the United States shaped his sense of optimism, self-efficacy, and unique worldview. He also reviews how he has applied these characteristics to his leadership in the Junior Achievement Worldwide program. And lastly, Annie McKee addresses the notion, so often overlooked in discussions of *success*, of truly being *happy* with your job. She outlines some specific strategies for creating – or reclaiming – this happiness in your own career.

28

Be Positive!

Frances Hesselbein

From her Pennsylvania beginnings as a volunteer Girl Scout troop leader to her rise as the CEO of the largest organization serving girls and women in the world – the Girl Scouts of the USA – Frances Hesselbein has always been mission-focused, values-based, and demographics-driven. For her transformation of the Girl Scouts in the 1970s, former president Bill Clinton awarded Frances the country's highest civilian honor, the Presidential Medal of Freedom. For more than 25 years, Frances has been at the helm of a very small but strong organization based in New York where she continues to train a new generation of leaders through leadership education and publications. She is chairman of the Frances Hesselbein Leadership Forum, part of the Graduate School for Public and International Affairs, Johnson Institute for Responsible Leadership at the University of Pittsburgh, and editor-in-chief of Leader to Leader. *Frances is the recipient of 21 honorary doctoral degrees, the author of three autobiographies, and the coeditor of 30 books in 30 languages. Frances has traveled to 68 countries representing the United States, and* Fortune *magazine named her one of the "World's 50 Greatest Leaders."*

■ ■ ■

Be careful of your thoughts, for your thoughts become your words. Be careful of your words, for your words become your deeds. Be careful of your deeds, for your deeds become your habits. Be careful of your habits, for your habits become your character. Be careful of your character, for your character becomes your destiny.

—Author anonymous

Today our work – our dialogue – is all about destiny: our own destiny, as leaders; and the destiny of all the organizations and the leaders we support. In this age of the lowest level of trust and the highest level of cynicism in my whole lifetime, my own country, and in many countries, we face new leadership imperatives. The backdrop of this dialogue is as serious, as challenging, and as difficult as any of us has faced in a long time, facing massive change all over the world, in a world at war.

In speeches, I often mention that from the beginning of our country, there are two institutions that have sustained our democracy: public education and the United States Army.

Recently, after speaking to cadets at the United States Military Academy at West Point, we had a wonderful Q&A session. As I was leaving, I encountered a group of cadets waiting for me in the back of the auditorium with many more questions. One young cadet asked me, "Mrs. Hesselbein: Why are you so positive?" I smiled and responded first with a corny joke: "Well, you see, even my blood type is B-positive." Then I went on the share with them my *B-positive* approach to leadership, which begins with my definition of leadership as "a matter of *how to be*, not *how to do*. It is the quality and character of the leader that determines the performance and the results."

People often wonder why I am so positive about a *bright future* in our own country and in communities where we are facing some of the greatest challenges the world has ever faced. In our schools and in our neighborhoods, there are families and local organizations in need, all of whom are attempting to cope with today's challenges:

- When political debates are filled with ugly and sometimes almost venomous dialogue
- When our veterans are coming home struggling with problems of health, housing, and employment
- When deaths are rising faster than ever, primarily because of opioids
- When the number of school shootings in America continues to rise

All this is part of the backdrop of our times, yet it is only part.

I continue with this bright future stuff because I have high hopes for the generation of Millennials – men and women born between about 1980 and 1995 – the first generation to come of age in the new millennium, in whom I envision great leaders with the opportunity to connect their present with a bright future.

Pew Research Center studies tell us that today's Millennials are more like those born before 1928 – the so-called *Greatest Generation* – than any cohort since. Millennials are said to be career-focused with a very high potential to lead a robust and sustainable economy. They face many challenges, as swift and exclusive policy changes are adopted that may harm large groups of them. There is a new vigor to Millennials, and the upcoming professionals of Generation Z – those born between 1996–2010. A language that includes, not excludes, which communicates in a way that reminds me of Peter Drucker's definition of communication: "Communication isn't saying something, communication is being heard."

And they are being heard! It is inspiring to join them. Remember: Every challenge is an opportunity. In these times of great challenges, the opportunities are even greater for our new generation of values-based leaders.

And it is the learning leaders who are the partners for ethical, principled, effective corporations and organizations. They will open doors. As Ralph Waldo Emerson wrote,

Be an opener of doors for such that come after thee,
And do not try to make the universe a blind alley.[1]

Recently, three young men from the Middle East arrived at my office door. They had attended our Hesselbein Global Academy at the University of Pittsburgh, a Leadership Summit now in its tenth year, bringing together 50 students from all over the world with distinguished mentors for a three-day conference. We had wondered how long it would take such a diverse group to come together, to connect, to open wonderful personal doors.

Well, it took about five minutes for all the hand-shaking and embracing to begin. They were one remarkably close group from the beginning. It is inspiring to learn how participants from our past summits have stayed connected – global as they are. The emerging leaders I meet are sending a powerful message of leadership, of building trust, of ethics in action, of the power of diversity and inclusion, of the importance of courage, of celebrating the intellect, and of service. To them, *To serve is to live* is not a foreign language.

Peter Drucker said, "I never predict. I simply look out the window and see what is visible but not yet seen." Today I hear leaders everywhere discussing the same fundamental challenge – the journey to transformation, moving from where we are to where we want to be. Our quickly changing, turbulent times do not accommodate any neat and tidy *but this is the way we've always done it* strategy. It takes courage to challenge the Gospel of the Status Quo. In our young leaders, I see that courage!

As we hurtle into the future in this crucible of massive change, there is no time to negotiate with nostalgia for outmoded, irrelevant policies, practices, procedures, and assumptions. There are no leaders of the past, only leaders of the future. The young generation of leaders will lead beyond the walls, change lives, and change our world as they are called to do. For them, and for all of us, this is a time always to be remembered. Let us honor them. We must shine a light in this age of cynicism. Our turbulent times cry out for leaders who live the mission, who embody the values, who keep the faith.

As leaders of the future in a global society, our next generation of leaders will take hold of a new adventure in learning. We look to them to take the lead into the future, as inspiring examples of the power of learning and as models of ethical global citizenship.

I have a vision of what I call the *bright future*, which I hope we are all called to share. It is a world of healthy children, strong families, good schools, decent housing, safe neighborhoods, work that dignifies, and faith that sustains – all embraced by the diverse, cohesive, inclusive community that cares about all its people. That vision shimmers far in the distance. Bright Future.

Reflection Questions

1. Are you optimistic or pessimistic about the future? What contributes to your perspective?
2. Has your vision of the future changed over the course of your personal/professional life? If it has, what factors have influenced this change?
3. What is your opinion of today's Millennials? Generation Z? How do you think they are the same as/different from previous generations of young people?
4. Does your view of today's young people have an impact on your vision of the future?

Note

1. "The Preacher," in *Lectures and Biographical Sketches*, vol. X of *The Complete Works of Ralph Waldo Emerson* (Boston and New York: Houghton, Mifflin, 1891), 224.

29

What Do People Do All Day?

Sarah McArthur

With more than two decades of experience in publishing, most prominently as a writer, editor, and writing coach, Sarah McArthur is continually striving to enhance her knowledge and expertise about the rapidly changing business of publishing and to share it with others who have a message to share.

Founder and CEO of *sdedit, her fields of expertise are management, leadership, executive and business coaching, and human resources. She has authored and edited numerous books including, Coaching for Leadership: Writings on Leadership from the World's Greatest Coaches *with Marshall Goldsmith and Laurence S. Lyons,* The AMA Handbook of Leadership, *coedited with Marshall Goldsmith and John Baldoni (chosen one of the Top 10 Business, Management, and Labor Titles of 2010 by Choice), the* Optimizing Talent Workbook *with Linda Sharkey, and* Global Business Leadership *with Dr. E. S. Wibbeke.*

In addition to her own works, Sarah has played significant roles in many other book projects including Marshall Goldsmith's New York Times *bestseller* Triggers, *all three editions of the bestselling management classic* Coaching for Leadership, *and Marshall's* Amazon.com, USA Today, *and* Wall Street Journal *#1 bestseller,* What Got You Here Won't Get You There.

Sarah holds a Masters in Publishing from George Washington University and a BA in English and Environmental Studies from the University of Oregon.

■ ■ ■

One of my favorite books is *What Do People Do All Day* by Richard Scarry. My parents bought it for me in London when I was about 5, and I studied it intensely for a year, sitting in the back of our VW van with my sister as we drove across Europe, Russia, and Africa. I still have it. It is tattered, worn, the cover is barely attached, and my young child scribble is on many of the pages – my notes for this chapter, it seems.

A mixture of written story and illustration, *What Do People Do All Day* is set in a town called Busytown. The characters are diverse. Mayor Fox, Farmer Alfalfa (a goat), the Grocer cat family, Doctor Lion, Mommy Stitches, and Abby Rabbit. Everyone plays a part in the functioning of the town. "We are all workers. We work hard so that there will be enough food and houses and clothing for our families."[1]

To me, this book is the essence of work is love made visible – working together for the functioning of society and the well-being of people around the globe. Its message is that we all contribute to society; everyone has a place, everyone is included, everyone participates. Humanity is a big network of people working together; there is no disconnect caused by poor communication.

There are chapters such as, "Building a New House," "Mailing a Letter," and "Firemen to the Rescue," which illustrate the different roles for each project. For instance, in "The Train Trip" chapter, a sweet little family of pigs takes a train to visit their cousins in the country. Along the way they buy magazines to read from the friendly porcupine's newsstand, the hard-working dog and mouse fuel and oil the train, a welcoming fox engineer drives the train, and the focused pig switchman changes the tracks, so the train goes to the right place. Busytown is a town of cooperation, organization, and productivity based on simpler times when we communicated with the people around us rather than ignoring them to scroll our feeds. You wouldn't see Abby Rabbit taking selfies and posting them to SnapChat during Algebra class.

This is what I see now when I look out the window. I see a breakdown of communication caused by information technology. While it is a great advancement for society, when poorly used it is destructive and can have significant negative consequences. The breakdown is caused by (1) the rapid pace of information technology, which among other things, causes important stories to quickly get lost in the next day's media flood; (2) a frequent lack of courtesy and respect in the social media chatter; (3) a lack of ethics on the part of some caused by the ability to self-publish and the diminishing role for the gatekeepers (publishers) who used to review our content before it went public; and (4) an addiction to a constant influx of digital information that is overpowering our reliance on each other for personal connection and passing on our knowledge.

- *Speed*: The speed of communication technology is astounding; in fact, it is exponential. "According to the law of accelerating returns, the pace of technological progress – especially information technology – speeds up exponentially over time because there is a common force driving it forward." Being exponential, as it turns out, is all about evolution.... [Ray] Kurzweil wrote in 2001[2] that every decade our overall rate of progress was doubling, "We won't experience 100 years of progress in the 21st century – it will be more like 20,000 years of progress (at today's rate)."[3]
- *Courtesy and Respect*: Frances Hesselbein famously says that the best advice she ever received is to have respect for all people. This great leader also says, "Language is the greatest motivating force. You can phrase something positively and inspire people to do their best, or negatively and make them feel worried, uncertain, and self-conscious. ... I try ... to use my own voice in a way that shows caring, respect, appreciation, and patience. Your voice, your language, help determine your culture. And part of how a corporate culture is defined is how the people who work for an organization use language."[4] The language we use in our global communications is creating our global culture. What do we want our global culture to be like? Respectful and courteous, kind and inclusive, or contrary and definitively embattled faction against faction, department against department, personality against personality (think Jolie versus Aniston, Swift versus Perry).
- *Ethics*: According to Tom Kolditz, in his essay for this book, "The 2017 World Economic Forum (WEF) articulated and addressed the advent of changes related to technology as the 'Fourth Industrial Revolution' (or 4IR). From the proceedings of the WEF's 2017 Annual Meeting of New Champions,[5] there is a shift in competencies that new leaders will need to master to adapt to the powerful social and economic trends in the next 10–20 years.... [One is that] Leaders will need to be savvy to deceit, malfeasance, and illegality – especially in terms of behavior

conveyed by digital and informational means. They must protect their organizations in a world disappointingly tolerant of unethical behavior. Having strong personal ethics is simply not enough; new leaders must have a strong awareness that others may not share their commitment to doing what is right."[6]

■ *Addiction*: Even at the time of this writing, we're still debating whether or not there is such a thing as a *social media addict*. In January of 2018, the World Health Organization announced that it will list video gaming as a mental disorder. Social media addiction has yet to make the list. Mark Griffiths at Nottingham Trent University, who has been researching gambling and internet addictions as well as the overuse of social networking sites such as Facebook, Twitter, and Instagram, believes that social media can be "potentially addictive." He has found "a technological compulsion like 'social media addiction' comes with all of the behavioural signals that we might usually associate with chemical addictions, such as smoking or alcoholism. These include mood changes, social withdrawal, conflict and relapse."[7]

Solution to the Breakdown

What can we do to repair this communication breakdown and prevent future ramifications from it? One thing that I do to repair and address this challenge is ask myself: *Am I being heard*? Frances Hesselbein often says, "Communication is not saying something; communication is being heard." I take this to heart in all of my communications, written, oral, digital. If I am not heard, I have not communicated.

How can one be heard by the most people? Three things are paramount.

1. *Have a message.* The first key to being heard is to have a message, something to say that you feel is important to be heard. Great leadership messages are most often inspirational, hopeful, and engaging. As with this section of our book, we've instilled hope and engagement with its inspiring title – Bright Future!
2. *Be courteous and have respect for all people.* I can think of no better way to phrase this than that expressed by Frances Hesselbein in *My Life in Leadership*. She writes, "Today, when we observe the lowest level of trust and the highest level of cynicism, the call for leaders who are healers and unifiers must be heard. Wherever we are, whatever our work, whatever our platform or forum, we must find the language that heals, the

inclusion that unifies. It is a critical time for leaders at every level to make the difference, and demonstrate that respect for all people is a paramount value. 'For if the trumpet gives an uncertain sound, who shall prepare himself to the battle?' should be a powerful reminder for all of us."[8]

3. *Be clear and concise.* This is a skill of the best communicators, leaders, writers, and speakers in history. It is in large part learned and in some part natural talent. Being clear and concise means choosing your words deliberately and carefully, and it leads to the simplification of the most complex ideas, so that they can be understood by the broadest audience. Clarity equals Coherence. We learn this skill from others and when we practice it in our own communications. For instance, those of us who are sensitive to our *audience* or conversation partners, pick up on nonverbal cues that we are not being heard and rephrase or pause. A coherent message and the ability to deliver it in a way that makes sense to the broadest audience is very advantageous to being heard.

Interestingly, communication breakdown is a significant challenge in the Information Age. One might think that with such incredible tools for communication at our disposal and the abundance of information at our fingertips, we would be well on our way to utopia. We're not quite hitting the mark yet, but many of us are working toward it by being positive. We are deliberately choosing our words to create an inclusive global culture and actively phrasing our language to be forward thinking, respectful, and clear. We are not engaging and indulging the rapid-fire flood of negativity that has come with these great advancements in our communication system. In focusing on the positive, we are actively creating for humanity a Bright Future and we call on you and everyone across the world to join us!

Reflection Questions

1. Do you notice communication breakdown in your personal and/or professional life?
2. What can you do to repair this breakdown and prevent it in the future?
3. How will you know if you are being heard?
4. How can you use your words to create a positive environment for yourself and those around you?

Notes

1. Richard Scarry, *What Do People Do All Day?* (New York: Random House, 1968).
2. Ray Kurzweil, March 2001, www.kurzweilai.net/the-law-of-accelerating-returns.
3. Alison E. Berman and Jason Dorrier, March 2016, https://singularityhub.com/2016/03/22/technology-feels-like-its-accelerating-because-it-actually-is/#sm.00000jlmvildgnd5uymy2x1clcu0d.
4. Sally Helgesen, *The Female Advantage* (Oakland, CA: Berrett-Koehler Publishers, June 2010), 81–82.
5. Thomas A. Kolditz, "Why You Lead Determines How Well You Lead," *Harvard Business Review,* July 22, 2014, http://blogs.hbr.org/2014/07/why-you-lead-determines-how-well-you-lead/.
6. Thomas A. Kolditz, Chapter 24, this volume.
7. Sophia Smith Galer, "How Much Is 'Too Much Time' on Social Media?" January 19, 2018, www.bbc.com/future/story/20180118-how-much-is-too-much-time-on-social-media.
8. Frances Hesselbein, *My Life in Leadership* (San Francisco: Jossey-Bass, 2011), 27.

30

What If There Were No Problems, Only Projects?

David Allen

One of the world's most influential thinkers on productivity, David's 35 years of experience as a management consultant and executive coach have earned him the titles of "personal productivity guru" by Fast Company Magazine *and one of America's top five executive coaches by* Forbes Magazine. *The American Management Association has ranked him in the top 10 business leaders. His best-selling book, the groundbreaking* Getting Things Done: The Art of Stress-Free Productivity, *has been published in 30 languages; and the "GTD" methodology it describes has become a global phenomenon, being taught by training companies in 60 countries. David, his company, and his partners are dedicated to teaching people how to stay relaxed and productive in our fast-paced world.*

■ ■ ■

The world we live in now, as experienced by the majority of its population and reported by its multimedia, is full of problems. Seemingly, there's a rising tide of things wrong or broken, ranging from situations that are merely suboptimal to those that are unbearably catastrophic.

"I don't understand what's going on in my government."
"My bank just merged with another, affecting all my personal transactions."
"There are millions in Africa now displaced and starving."
"I don't know if the school she attends is safe for my daughter."

The awareness of such things gone potentially haywire, and the publicity about them, is spreading worldwide.

Whether there is actually any greater amount of negative circumstances now than in the past is debatable. But there is definitely more perception by many more people of how many *bad* things are going on, in how many places and in how many ways. Reactions can run the gamut from resignation (mostly) to resolved action (rarely). Complaining, worrying, and criticism seem to be the de facto majority response.

I am suggesting that the world needs to change its orientation to seeing not problems, but projects. Such a shift in perspective offers a tremendous improvement opportunity at the macrolevels of national and international politics, but also at the microlevels of individual lives.

We've always been aware, to some degree, of our own personal issues and dilemmas. But now, in our jobs, our more transparent organizations are having their dirty laundry aired. We're also increasingly made aware of the problems and dangers in our living environments. The always-on press competes for our attention by portraying the most dramatic situations worldwide with the bloodthirsty perspective rivaling that paid to a Roman coliseum spectacle.

What's missing for the most part is a point of view. What's not seen is how best to see something.

What if each and every one of these *problems* was instead considered a *project*?

What?! Are we supposed to deny the things going on in our universe that we don't like, or consider terrible, unjust, immoral, or just plain stupid? Not at all. We simply need to recognize them as something we can or intend to do something about, or not. And those that we can or might do something about, we need to ensure that we are appropriately engaged with our commitment to doing so.

Because we don't see it that way doesn't mean that there's not another way to see it.

There are things we can realize that we can't change because they are immutable (like gravity, which is causing people serious injury, as you read this) or we simply don't have the resources of time or money to effect the change (such as stopping global warming or changing someone's intractable preconception about a culture). Those realities we can simply accept or ignore, perhaps just sending good thoughts that the situations turn out for the best.

What's visible yet not seen here? It is the fact that the world is simply what it is – neither good nor bad – but how we are *engaged* with that world is always our free choice, and that creates either a positive or negative experience thereof. When individuals and organizations adopt the standard of outcome-and-action orientation for each and every thing that emerges as tensions in their ecosystems, hallelujah! We would start to live in a world with resolution/solution orientation instead of one with kindergartens of whining, recalcitrant children.

The activity of complaining or worrying (which is the passive form of complaining) assumes that something should be better than it is, but avoids a positive engagement in making it so. We bother others and ourselves about what we don't like – what is going on that we wish or assume should be different. But mostly we engage in those acts of criticism when we have not personally decided or defined what, if anything, we intend to do about them. And the *if anything* factor is critical.

This is not something simply relegated to esoteric or philosophical discourse, nor to the seemingly shortsighted, self-interested, and constipated nature of many of our political climates and conversations. It affects how we all deal with the day-to-day realities of our worlds.

In my work with some of the best, brightest, and most sophisticated people in the world, we have invariably uncovered issues, problems, and opportunities that have taken up residence in their psyches. There are circumstances creating stress and internal *spin*, but no forward motion. Indeed, these are often subtle and ambiguous – a disgruntled staff person, a frustrating organizational process, an uncomfortable aging parent. Applying the simple but highly effective thought process of identifying what has these an individuals' attention, and clarifying a desired outcome and a specific next action to take, has totally reframed their outlook and relieved tons of pressure.

The primary issue is often that they are the victims of their own creativity! Paradoxically, it is usually the most aspirational, motivated, and productive people who wind up being the most overwhelmed with the *stuff* of their work and lives – things they themselves have put into motion.

Say that a senior person on your team is not performing up to expectations. Or your personal financial and legal affairs are not in order in case something should happen to you. Or you're not sure if the company's going in the right direction, you have aging parents for whose care you feel you're going to be responsible, or you know you should exercise and meditate more.

How do we create positive relationships to those things yanking our psychological chains, potentially waking us up in the middle of the night? Trying to ignore them doesn't do it. Practicing mindfulness doesn't do it. Drinking doesn't do it (though in random moments that may give you a little false courage to engage!). What's required is the cognitive practice of making some decisions about what those things are that are grabbing our attention and what we're going to do about them, exactly, if anything.

In my experience, what we're here to do and learn on this planet is simple, but sublime. We're here to become aware of and accountable for where we have placed our attention and our attachments; and to recognize who we are as creative beings, optimally directing our energies going forward.

I don't share that often with my clients. Frankly, I haven't found it necessary. If it's the truth, they'll find that out for themselves, in their own perfect timing. If it's not, then I don't have to be perceived by anyone as wrong!

What I have uncovered is a personal productivity methodology, which embodies that dynamic and gets people involved in it, but in the easiest, most mundane and practical way.

The first step is having someone identify everything that has his or her attention. The reason something would be on someone's mind is because he or she has some interest in it being dealt with, but has not yet decided exactly how to approach it.

Why is that e-mail still sitting there? What's that document on your desk asking you to do about it? Why is that receipt still in your briefcase? What are you going to do with those meeting notes?

The things we have allowed ourselves to get involved with will continually demand our attention until or unless we unhook from them completely (resign from the committee) or we appropriately engage with and commit to them (identify the desired outcome and the next action, parking reminders about those in the right places).

The simple act of deciding what you really need to do about a piece of paper on your desk or an e-mail lurking on your computer is the microcosmic embodiment of moving from being a victim of your world to being in the driver's seat.

Interestingly, I've watched how challenging it is for some of the best and brightest people to avoid that kind of thinking and decision making, about even some of the most mundane stuff.

You have four free tickets to the game; who do you invite? Even the more subtle and serious stuff remains nagging; is divorce an option for us?

And yet, how simple could this be if we reframed our dilemma as a *project* rather than a *problem*? What's the outcome we'd like to have happen? What's the next action required to move toward that appropriately? It's very simple, but often very challenging.

How many of our politicians are focused on an outcome of looking good to their constituents instead of achieving some desired result that would benefit their base? How much political activity is invested in criticizing instead of defining, clarifying, and taking real action toward some positive outcome?

What if every news story went like this: Here's the current reality. Here's who's invested in making a difference there. Here are their desired outcomes in the situation. Here's how they're approaching this.

This actually is how many stories are framed, to some degree, as in the case of a wildfire raging in the national forest. Here's what's going on, as best we see it. Here are the people and resources being allocated to deal with it. Here's their game plan.

It's not, however, how we see much of the rest of world's news positioned and delivered (and likely ingested by us). We often see terrible situations and seldom the stories of who and how people are engaged in correcting them.

There is an equal responsibility to engage appropriately with what you have accepted into your universe as you have with allowing it in in the first place.

This clarity of definition for ourselves – What's mine or theirs? Is this something I can be involved with? What's my interest or investment in doing something about this? – is key to staying optimally clear and productive.

What would it be like if this were the behavior of all of us?

What if your son or daughter wants to take karate classes or have a birthday party? Would they have come to you with a desired outcome predetermined – learn karate? Would they be taking a decided next action – talk to mom about taking a karate class? They could. Few do, though, at least not in a consistent, emotionally neutral way.

What if your parliament decides to take a different tack on handling the budget? What are we really trying to produce, as a positive outcome here? If we agree on that, who owns making that happen?

The best of the consultative and rigorous decision-making processes would buy into this approach – outcomes desired, actions required – though they often lose sight of those key foci when they get mired down in the weeds of discussions and negotiations.

But, the whole world? Why are we not trained yet to approach our experiences and our environment from an outcome and action focus? Of course, there are many things going on in the world produced by people who *do* have that focus, but toward results that we might consider *bad*. Granted. But in my experience, in the long haul most of the negative behaviors engaged in stem from insecurity – a lack of awareness of our own worth and power. There's a direct correlation between feeling the victim and being a victimizer. If, from the beginning, we were trained to see every problem as a project, that empowerment would allow us to more readily step into and express the greater goodness of who we really are.

Worrying and complaining can serve a valuable purpose. They can identify those things that present an opportunity for change and improvement. The problem may be visible, but we must also stay focused on a desired positive outcome and a path forward. In other words, we must look out the window to see what is not yet seen.

Reflection Questions

1. Consider how you view obstacles in your personal and professional lives; where did you acquire such a perspective?
2. How can changing your perspective from looking at challenges as *problems* to *projects* create a greater sense of empowerment in you? In those you lead?
3. Think about how you determine responsibility in any given situation. How do you decide who is responsible for what, and what your responsibility is?
4. How do you frame the relationship between outcomes desired and actions required? What steps do you take to move from one to the other?

31

A Cheerleader
at Heart

Whitney Johnson

Whitney Johnson brings a strategic eye and long-range vision given her multifaceted professional experience. In addition to great success as a Wall Street investment equity analyst, she co-founded (with Harvard Business School's Clayton Christensen) and managed Rose Park Advisors–Disruptive Innovation Fund. As a classically trained pianist, she has special insight into discipline, practice, and perseverance.

Whitney is an expert on disruptive innovation and personal disruption and specializes in equipping leaders to harness change by implementing the proprietary framework she codified in the critically acclaimed book Disrupt Yourself: Putting the Power of Disruptive Innovation to Work. *She's been named a Thinkers50, Leading Business Thinker Globally, and a Finalist for Top Thinker on Talent, 2015. Her guests as host of the Disrupt Yourself Podcast include such luminaries as Patrick Pichette, former CFO of Google, and Garry Ridge, CEO of WD-40.*

Whitney coaches C-Suite executives across a variety of industries and has a deep understanding of how executives can create or destroy value. Her approach to coaching is grounded in the disruptive innovation theory, based on the premise that the individual is the fundamental unit of the disruption. Building on this foundation of personal accountability, she works with executives using the stakeholder-centered coaching approach devised by Marshall Goldsmith: Change must come from within, but it is facilitated by the ecosystem.

■ ■ ■

Confession: I was a high school cheerleader.

This was a dearly held girlhood dream, an aspiration I worked hard to make happen.

Hard work wasn't foreign to me. I was a good student, and had, at a young age, been willing to get up early and practice piano. But that was more my mother's dream for me than my dream for myself.

In fact, I would major in music in college, somewhat unwillingly – mom again, inserting her ambition where mine was inchoate – and exit with a BA that was the culmination of many years of consistent effort. But I didn't possess any particular desire to perform (much less the drive demanded to be a concert pianist) or any realistic venue in which to do so. At that point in my life, being a cheerleader had been the one passion that I had articulated to myself clearly enough to make it happen.

Post-university life was headed in a different direction anyway; at about the same time I graduated, my husband completed his MS and we transplanted to New York City so that he could pursue a PhD at Columbia University. I found Manhattan intimidating; I would never have moved there on my own. But my husband's program in microbiology was going to take five to seven years. There were bills to pay and food to put on the table. I needed – and wanted – a serious job, so I turned to Wall Street.

I had never taken a course in accounting, finance, or economics. No business credentials whatsoever. No connections in New York City. Looking back, I've often marveled that I attempted something that I felt so singularly ill-equipped to do. I landed a secretarial position, a not atypical entry-level role for a woman on Wall Street in the late 1980s.

It being the era of *Liar's Poker* and *Bonfire of the Vanities*, there was near my desk a bullpen of almost exclusively male, aspiring 20-something stockbrokers. They spent their days cold-calling prospects, enduring frequent hang-ups, trying to persuade prospective investors to pounce on the stock du jour. The pressure was intense to make their numbers – phone calls logged, accounts opened, and dollar amounts sold. The hard sell was always in play. One of the default persuasions I heard them employ again and again was this: "Throw down your pompoms and get in the game."

I was offended. I was offended as a woman by the blatantly sexist tone of this challenge; quit being womanly and act like a man. But this also offended me personally as a former cheerleader, a woman for whom cheerleading had been a highly sought-after rite of passage. I hadn't come up in the era when girls' athletics were commonly available in school or community. Cheerleading *was* my sport and an important opportunity for extracurricular participation at a time when opportunities for girls were much more limited than they are today.

Then one day, sitting at the same desk, listening to the same routine of cold-calling across the way, hearing "throw down your pompoms and get in the game" yet again, I had an epiphany. Suddenly, the challenge felt personal in a different way and I thought, "I need to throw down my pompoms and get in the game."

I was, for the foreseeable future, the primary breadwinner for my family. Why would I settle for earning X, if I could earn 10X? Why would I be a Wall Street spectator, bench warmer, or cheerleader for others, if I could, with extra work and discipline, become a game-changing player? Was I looking for a supporting role or did I want to be a star?

This was a pivotal moment.

I enrolled in accounting and finance courses at night, doggedly pursuing the dream of moving from the third (or fourth or fifth) string to becoming a starter in the Wall Street game. A few years passed and the hard work was coupled with the good fortune of having a boss who was willing to build a bridge for me. I moved from support staff to investment banking analyst. From there, I moved into investment research, becoming an *Institutional Investor*-ranked stock analyst. Then I ventured into entrepreneurship with Harvard's Clayton Christensen, and now I'm an executive coach, speaker, writer, and all-around thinker about career management. I want to help put others at the helm in driving their own success stories by moving from the sideline of their professional lives to center field.

For a long time, I used the "throw down your pompoms and get in the game" experience to encourage other women and girls to do what I had done and turn a ho-hum job – or no job at all – into an exciting, growing, fulfilling career path. After all, research demonstrates that our cultural norm is still to cast women in supporting roles and that most women still feel more societal approval if they stick to the sidelines, offering support and encouragement to others, rather than leading themselves. I wanted every woman to have the tools, especially the confidence, to make their career dreams a reality. I still do, but with this caveat: Is the dream really theirs, or is it someone else's dream for them? In fact, is it *my* dream for them, rather than their own?

Today, women constitute 50-plus percent of both the workforce and the university population, and though we still lag behind men in higher-level positions across most sectors, the demographics over time favor us to continue to improve in career opportunity – for those for whom this is the dream.

But the demographics also indicate a growing loss of dreams among our male counterparts who are unemployed in unprecedented numbers; the United States ranks 22nd in male labor force participation out of the 23 developed nations in the Organization for Economic Co-operation and Development. Almost 32 percent of men 20 and older are without paid work, as reported in Nicholas Eberstadt's book, *Men without Work: America's Invisible Crisis*.[1] These are men, Eberstadt alleges, who for the most part are not seeking work. They are occasionally at home as primary caregivers to their children, but not often. They are voluntarily unemployed and for the most part, they are watchers of television and players of video games.

This is a complex problem, heavily, though not entirely, rooted in the consequences of the recent Great Recession. I am concerned that this is a symptom of demoralization in our society and want to issue a new rallying cry to these men: Throw down your joysticks and get in the (real) game. We all need to be dreaming. We need an objective to strive for, a purposeful occupation that gives meaning to our lives.

I began my career as a secretary, a cheerleader of sorts for men who were doing the really interesting work I longed to do. Once I got into the game I wanted to play, I became a cheerleader for women, encouraging them to believe in their ability to become the stars of their own stories. Now I feel compelled to be a cheerleader for men as well, challenging them to be the masters of their own destiny, the scripters of their own leading role, not junkies of the latest role-playing game.

It doesn't really matter what your dream is so long as it's something of worth. Career dreams are great. Ditto dreams for your family, your parenting, your children. Perhaps you want to invent something, start a business, or engage in an artistic endeavor. Maybe philanthropy is your avenue to stardom, or volunteerism. I have a long-time friend whose most dearly held dream for retirement is to volunteer with hospice, helping people at the end of life compose their personal history as a legacy for their loved ones and bring the curtain down gracefully on the pageant that is uniquely theirs.

Our dreams may change; they probably should. As we grow wiser and more experienced, inevitably older, we value some things more and others less than in earlier days. But our need for fulfillment, for the mystery of new horizons, the challenge of opportunities to learn and solve significant problems, to contribute to the improvement of our neighborhood or the world, in large ways and small, should never leave us. We may move from one passion project to another, disrupting ourselves again and again as one dream is abandoned or fulfilled and another takes its place. Whatever your dream(s), I challenge you to throw down your pompoms, or your joystick, and get in the game.

Until you take them up again. Because true confession: My first dream will probably be my last. I am a cheerleader at heart.

Reflection Questions:

1. In what ways are you a cheerleader for others in your personal life? In your workplace?
2. Do you have a saying like, "Throw down your pompoms and get in the game" from your youth that you apply to your present life? How is it still relevant? Have you had to adjust it?
3. Do you think that men and women face the same or different challenges in the workplace? To what do you attribute this?

Note

1. Nicholas Eberstadt, *Men Without Work: America's Invisible Crisis* (West Conshohocken, PA: Templeton Press, 2016).

32 | Silver Linings

Asheesh Advani

Asheesh is the CEO of Junior Achievement (JA) Worldwide, a global NGO dedicated to educating young people about entrepreneurship, financial literacy, and work readiness. With offices in over 115 countries, the JA network serves over 10 million students annually and is one the world's most impactful NGOs. Asheesh is an accomplished entrepreneur, having served as CEO of Covestor (a financial marketplace acquired by Interactive Brokers) and Founder/CEO of CircleLending (a social lending company acquired by Richard Branson's Virgin Group). He helped pioneer the social finance industry by working with regulators and credit bureaus to develop guidelines for peer-to-peer lending and crowd funding. Asheesh's experiences have been chronicled in case studies at Harvard Business School and Babson College. He is actively involved in the World Economic Forum as a member of the Civil Society Advisory Council and Global Agenda Council for the Future of Education, Gender, and Work. Asheesh is a graduate of the Wharton School and Oxford University, where he was a Commonwealth Scholar.

■ ■ ■

There is a short story from Hindu mythology about two brothers that my mother used to tell me when I was young. Both brothers had the same teacher and were about equal in ability. One of their assignments was to go out in search of someone who could teach them new skills. The first brother returned and said to his teacher, "Everyone I met has certain skills that I do not have, so I can learn from everyone." The second brother returned and had concluded the opposite for his teacher, "I have certain skills that each person does not have, so I cannot learn from any of them."

When I look out the window, I see a world filled with people from whom I can learn. I see a world filled with opportunities. I see a world where young people strive to become more confident by learning new things – and where most learning occurs by interacting with others. When I look out the window, I feel impatient and think there is so much more to learn, so much more to do.

Seeing the world in this manner does not make me a popular person at dinner parties. I'm too optimistic and don't have much capacity for gossip. Seeing the world in this manner does not make me a great project manager. I usually assume that employees who miss deadlines have good reason for doing so and seek to understand their need before passing judgment. Seeing the world in this manner does not make me the best husband. My wife, whom I've been with since our freshman year of college, does not appreciate my sunny outlook when she's had a bad day and needs someone to commiserate with rather than look for silver linings. (I once made this comment, for example: "Even though your 7 a.m. meeting did not show up today, at least you got a chance to have breakfast alone to plan your day.")

When I look out the window, I see a constellation that includes optimism, gratitude, and a thirst for learning, which are linked together like the Big Dipper. Let me explain.

Optimism is not something that you're born with. It is learned over time. Gratitude – being thankful for what you have – breeds optimism. In my family, we have developed a practice of telling each other three things that we are thankful for on a regular basis. My wife started this exercise with our kids while driving them to the school bus each morning. The first one or two things are easy to identify – a good grade on a test, a goal scored in a game, a dinner that was followed by a favorite dessert. It becomes harder to find a third thing and nudges the mind to turn neutral and otherwise negative experiences into positive ones, for example, missing the school bus, but still getting a ride to school; dealing with a health issue for a loved one, but still being able to care for them. The mind starts to develop the habit of looking for the positive in everything.

I don't fully understand why I look at the world in this way. My friends once tried to figure it out. I'm part of a forum group of eight friends who meet monthly, organized as part of the Young Presidents' Organization (YPO). During a forum retreat, we hired a professional moderator who asked us to dig deeper to understand each other. In my case, the group explored my relentless optimism and *learn-from-everyone* outlook on the world, asking questions about my past, probing my childhood experiences, seeking inner demons that would explain my behavior traits. The conclusion was that, as a young immigrant from India, I had tried hard to fit into my adopted homeland of Canada. Growing up, I watched movies and tried to emulate the main characters. I was like a sponge, learning from everything and everyone I could, so that I could fit into my new surroundings, particularly during my teenage years. Therefore, I must have inadvertently turned each negative experience into a positive experience as a coping mechanism to avoid unhappiness. This created a habit at an early age that became a lifelong, ingrained practice. I don't really know if this psychoanalysis is accurate or not. For example, I don't understand why others with a similar immigrant experience would have had different outcomes and behaviors. It seems clear to me, however, that optimism, gratitude, and a thirst for learning are inextricably linked in my personality.

I am currently working as a leader of a nonprofit organization that teaches young people to have a similar can-do attitude that I developed in my youth. The organization is called Junior Achievement (JA) Worldwide. Founded in 1919, it has grown substantially over the years and has spread to over 115 countries – as diverse as Gabon and Sweden – with programs reaching over 10 million young people per year. We like to say that JA *activates* youth for the future of work. I am convinced that one reason for the growth of the organization is the hunger and desire for entrepreneurship and self-confidence that pervades today's youth. I travel a lot for my job and everywhere I go, I find that young people love learning if it is presented to them in the right way – as a game, a field trip, a business start-up project, or a chance to *shadow* a manager or leader in the workplace. Young people crave positive feedback and they want to learn how to become confident, if someone would just tell them how to do it.

Self-efficacy is a multiplier, a skill that makes all other skills possible to learn and master. Some people call it self-belief or self-confidence, but the

meaning is similar enough. Stanford psychologist Albert Bandura[1] tells us
that there are four ways to increase self-efficacy:

1. Mastering skills through hands-on experience
2. Observing others with self-efficacy achieve success
3. Hearing that others believe in one's ability to succeed
4. Rerouting negative thoughts into positive ones

Of these, the first (mastering skills) is overwhelmingly correlated with
learning self-efficacy, and that makes sense: success begets success. If students practice setting a goal, working toward it, staying with it in spite of
setbacks, and achieving it, they'll learn that such a process will work in the
future. The next time they need to learn a skill, they'll believe they can.

I see this every day in my work at JA, especially though the JA Company Program. Middle- and high-school students roll up their sleeves and
start a flesh-and-blood company, complete with a business plan, company
officers, a product that has to be manufactured or assembled, suppliers to
source, bills to pay, and customers to woo. The JA Company Program is
often a student's first experience being a CEO, CFO, CMO, or any number of other jobs, and instead of reading about famous entrepreneurs like
Steve Jobs, they're creating real products with real colleagues and earning
real revenues. Living it and experiencing it give them a taste of what's possible in a manner that can't be fully digested from a textbook. And each
success (individual ones and those shared by the team) sets the stage for the
expectation of future success.

Students also learn self-efficacy by observing others achieving success,
but the correlation is a bit less strong than with hands-on skill mastery.
Still, whether observing their peer groups or adults, students who see others believe in their abilities to succeed – and then actually do so – are more
likely to believe in their own future successes.

Until I met Marshall Goldsmith, I didn't fully understand the power
of daily routines to improve self-efficacy. Marshall's book, *Triggers*,[2]
is a prescription for taking personal responsibility for behavior change
and recognizing environmental and psychological triggers that set you
back. One of Marshall's recommendations is to use a daily routine of
"active questions" that measure our effort, not our results. For example,
if you're facing a challenging relationship problem with your friend, don't

blame your friend, your social circumstances, or your bad luck. Instead, he recommends asking yourself daily (daily!) what you have personally done to address the issue. Self-efficacy is borne from personal responsibility.

When I look out the window, I see a world filled with people who I can learn from. I see a world filled with opportunities. I see a world where young people strive to become more confident by learning new things – and where most learning occurs by interacting with others. When I look out the window, I feel impatient and think there is so much more to learn, so much more to do.

Reflection Questions:

1. How does your view of the world compare to that of those around you? What impact does this have on your relationships?
2. How important do you consider an optimistic attitude in your life? In your work? Do you have such an attitude?
3. What elements in your life contribute to (or diminish) your sense of self-efficacy? What strategies can you take to foster your feelings of self-efficacy when it is low?

Notes

1. Albert Bandura, *Self-Efficacy: The Exercise of Self-Control* (New York: Worth Publishers, 1997).
2. Marshall Goldsmith, *Triggers: Creating Behavior That Lasts – Becoming the Person You Want to Be* (New York: Crown Business/Random House, 2015).

33 | Are You Happy at Work? (And Why It Matters)

Annie McKee

Annie McKee, PhD, is a senior fellow at the University of Pennsylvania Graduate School of Education and a best-selling author, speaker, and advisor to top global leaders. Her latest book, How to Be Happy at Work: The Power of Purpose, Hope, and Friendship *(Harvard Business Review Press, 2017) follows several HBR bestsellers, including* Primal Leadership *with Daniel Goleman and Richard Boyatzis, and* Becoming a Resonant Leader. *As a coach to executives in Fortune/FTSE 500 companies and public sector institutions, she uses a person-centered approach to help leaders develop their emotional intelligence, enhance their strategic thinking abilities, and build resonant cultures.*

■ ■ ■

Are you happy at work? If you are, you are one of the lucky ones. You have trusting, warm relationships with colleagues. You feel that what you do is important and your daily actions are an expression of your values. Your future is bright, and work is an avenue to your dreams. Your life is richer, fuller, and more meaningful than if you are bored or miserable at your job – as so many people are. After all, we spend nearly a third of our lives working, and for many of us it's more than that. If those hours are full of stressful interactions with people you're not sure you like and who may not like you either, or if you feel that you aren't making a difference or that the future is bleak, it is very unlikely that you will feel the deep and abiding enjoyment that all of us yearn for in life.

Common sense tells us that happiness matters at work just as much as it does in the rest of life. We now have research to back this up: Happy people are better workers. We are more creative, committed, and engaged when we are fulfilled by our work. We are more adaptable, we learn faster and better, and we are more successful, too.[1]

Happiness Matters

With both common wisdom and research pointing to the same conclusion, it is baffling to me that so many of us are not happy at work. The now-legendary Gallup statistics paint a dismal picture of boredom and disengagement – not exactly a recipe for happiness (or success).[2] And in my own experience with people all over the world, I've heard a common refrain: "I want to love my job. I want to be happy at work. But I am not, so I am holding back." This is often followed up with the first reason why so many of us aren't happy when they say, "And does it matter anyway? Isn't work supposed to be tough? Do I even deserve to be happy?"

It's time to debunk these myths. Happiness is a human right – a right that can and should be available to all of us, no matter where we work or what we do. Happiness impacts the quality of our lives, our health, and our relationships. It also impacts our success at work.

Our performance suffers when we are disengaged, dissatisfied, and unfulfilled at work. The destructive emotions that take over when we are in this state – emotions like fear, frustration, and anger – interfere with our reasoning and kill innovation. They also compromise our health and our relationships. And it's not only our personal performance that suffers; our companies do, too.[3] In fact, companies with happy and engaged employees outperform their competition by 20%.[4]

How to Be Happy at Work

I have been truly unhappy at work twice in my life. In the more recent situation, there were two issues that pushed me from delight to misery. The first problem was that I had been overworking for so long that I burned out.[5] The second (and related to the first) was that I'd made some decisions and allowed some things to happen in our workplace that were contrary to my personal values.

Stress, I found out, is a happiness killer. There is virtually no way for us to enjoy our daily lives when every moment is filled with worry, or too much work for any one human being to do. Unfortunately, I am not alone in having lived like this for so long that stress became burnout and burnout led to bad decisions and feeling trapped.

I know how this happened to me and I know I am not alone. We live in an always-on world where it is possible to work all the time. In some companies, we are expected to be available around the clock, on weekends and on vacations. How, then, can we step off the path and make sure we remain healthy?

Reclaiming Happiness, Step One: Emotional Intelligence

Avoiding burnout – or pulling back from it – starts with self-awareness in the form of a foundational emotional intelligence (EI) competency.[6] For me, tapping (back) into my knowledge about myself – what I needed emotionally, physically, and intellectually at work – took some time and effort. Like other leaders I've worked with, I had to take a good, hard look at what had happened to me over the many years of working so hard. This wasn't easy and, frankly, it took courage. Then, I had to make tough decisions about things that affected me, my colleagues, and others that I worked with. I had to pull back. Again, this took effort, and self-management, another EI competency. It's not easy to change patterns we've created and that others have gotten used to. With growing awareness of the negative impact of stress on my life and my work – not to mention my happiness – I was ready to move proactively to make things better.

Reclaiming Happiness, Step Two: Bring Values Back to Work

To start, I had to look at some of the fallout from burnout – most importantly, that I'd gone along with some decisions in the business that were counter to my personal values. This wasn't as easy or as clear-cut as it sounds. There was no lawbreaking going on in the consulting project we were working on, and some would say there were no ethical violations, either. But for me, what the company was doing was wrong. For a long time, I had justified our collective actions, telling myself, "We are helping people, at least," or, "You can't throw stones from the sidelines – get in there and try to fix things." These justifications were sensible and reasonable, at first. But, over time, I realized that our company's activities weren't truly helping people or making things better. Instead, our efforts were a cover, making it look like the client wanted to make positive changes when, in fact, it became quite clear they did not.

The lesson of this story for me was that if we let go of our core values, or compromise our beliefs, we can't possibly be happy. And, as it turns out, at this same time we were studying quite a lot of organizations around the world in terms of their leadership, culture, that sort of thing. As I began to look at these many studies, I found that, yet again, I wasn't alone in what I needed in order to reclaim happiness: We all want to know that our efforts are making a positive difference and that we are living our values at work.

I learned even more about what makes us happy at work as I delved into the studies of the people and companies who asked us to help them improve their cultures. These insights helped me understand what had gone wrong for me long ago in another job that ultimately made me unhappy.

Reclaiming Happiness, Step Three: Improve Your Relationships

A long time ago, I worked for a man who didn't like me. Of course, I didn't realize this at first; he'd hired me, after all, and must have seen something redeeming in me and my qualifications. But within a matter of months, it was clear that he didn't respect, trust, or care about me.

I tried everything to make the situation better. I worked harder, tried to be as pleasant as I could be, found solutions for his workplace problems. But it just kept getting worse. In retrospect, he may have been threatened by me, or maybe he really didn't like working as part of a team. In the end, it didn't matter why he treated me that way. What mattered was that I became so frustrated and fearful that I started losing my edge. I stopped being able to do my best work. I lost my energy and creativity. Ultimately, I got sick.

Happiness is impossible when our relationships are toxic. Unfortunately, there are far too many people like my old boss in our organizations – and they get away with murder. There's hope on the horizon, however, as a growing body of scholarly and practical research is showing beyond a shadow of a doubt that relationships impact individual and collective success.[7] We need love – companionate love – at work *and* in life.[8] We need to both feel cared for and to share our care and concern with others, to help them and support them, too. We need to feel we belong – that people like and respect us for who we are.

We do need friends at work. We also need to be able to see how what we are doing with people in our workplaces feeds our dreams, our very personal hopes for our future.

Reclaiming Happiness, Step Four: Reach for Your Dreams

In order for us to be truly happy at work, we need to see our work as an integral part of our present *and* our future. We need to feel that what we do at work helps us to get somewhere – and not just to the next rung on a career ladder.

When I was unhappy in those two jobs, it was difficult to see where I was heading. During my lowest points, I felt stuck and couldn't see past the misery of the present. I realized, though, that to lose hope is to lose life. So, even when things were really bad, I tried to focus on what I wanted in my life, what I wanted in my job, what I wanted in my relationships. I tried to hold on to hope, to have an optimistic vision of the future, and to make plans. And in both situations, it was this vision and acting on my plans that got me through to the other side – and back to happiness at work.

My experiences of being unhappy at work led me to make some decisions about what I would put up with going forward – and what I would not. I also sought to understand the essence of what I'd learned and have come to some conclusions about happiness at work:

1. We must feel that our work is meaningful and tied to a purpose we see as noble. Work, it turns out, needs to feel like a calling, not just a job. As research has shown, we can experience work as a calling no matter

what we do; it's all about how we frame our experience and how we engage with our daily activities and with people.[9] So, if we're cleaning hospital hallways, we're keeping patients healthy. If we are entering data for an insurance company, we are helping people get payments they need so they can go on with their lives. If we are lucky enough to manage people, we are helping them reach their potential. Whatever job we have, it's up to us to see the noble purpose in it, to find ways to live our values, and to have a positive impact on people and the planet.

2. We need friends at work. We are fundamentally social beings; we need each other and we need to enjoy one another, too.[10] Trust is important, as are respect and feeling safe enough to show people our true selves, our true natures. This doesn't mean that we must share every detail of our personal lives with people at work, but it does mean we need to care and be cared for. Today, our organizations are our tribes and we need to know we belong.

3. We need hope. We need a personal and compelling vision of the future that includes, but is not only about, work. A hopeful and inspiring vision of where we want to be, what we want to be doing, and how we want to live gives us energy to face today's trials, keeps us focused, and helps us to stay the course through good times and bad.[11]

It's not always easy to be happy at work; I have learned this the hard way. But if we focus on purpose, friendships, and hope, we can find and stay on a path that fits who we are and what we want, while helping us to reach our potential and contribute to others and to the greater good.

Reflection Questions:

1. How important is *being happy at work* to you?
2. How do you define *being happy at work*? What factors contribute to or diminish your happiness at work?
3. If you're not happy at work, does it really matter? Can you keep working at your job despite not being happy? If so, what are the costs? The benefits?
4. Using some of the conclusions here about what contributes to workplace happiness, are there any areas you could work on to improve your own happiness?

Notes

1. For research and perspectives on the relationship between emotions, happiness, and effectiveness, see: Annie McKee, *How to Be Happy at Work: The Power of Purpose, Hope and Friendships* (Boston: Harvard Business School Press, 2017); Shawn Achor, *Before Happiness* (New York: Crown Business, 2013); George E. Vaillant, *Triumphs of Experience: The Men of The Harvard Grant Study* (Cambridge, MA; London: Belknap Press of Harvard University Press, 2012); Barbara L. Fredrickson, *Positivity: Top-Notch Research Reveals the Upward Spiral That Will Change Your Life* (New York: Three Rivers Press, 2009).

2. Annamarie Mann and Jim Harter, "The Worldwide Employee Engagement Crisis," Gallup, January 7, 2016, www.gallup.com/businessjournal/188033/worldwide-employee-engagement-crisis.aspx.

3. For information on the impact of emotions on cognition, competence, and health, see: His Holiness the Dalai Lama and Archbishop Desmond Tutu, with Douglas Abrams, *The Book of Joy: Lasting Happiness in a Changing World* (New York: Avery, 2016); Jane E. Dutton and Gretchen M. Spreitzer, *How to be a Positive Leader: Small Actions, Big Impact* (San Francisco: Berrett-Koehler Publishers, 2014); Richard J. Davidson with Sharon Begley, *The Emotional Life of Your Brain: How to Change the Way You Think, Feel and Live* (London: Hodder, 2012); Annie McKee, Richard Boyatzis, and Frances Johnston, *Becoming a Resonant Leader: Develop Your Emotional Intelligence, Renew Your Relationships, Sustain Your Effectiveness* (Boston: Harvard Business Press, 2008).

4. David Sirota and Douglas Klein, *The Enthusiastic Employee: How Companies Profit by Giving Workers What They Want* (Indianapolis: IN: Pearson FT Press, 2013).

5. Sarah Green Carmichael, "The Research Is Clear: Long Hours Backfire for People and for Companies," *Harvard Business Review*, August 19, 2015, https://hbr.org/2015/08/the-research-is-clear-long-hours-backfire-for-people-and-for-companies.

6. Richard Boyatzis and Annie McKee, *Primal Leadership: Realizing the Power of Emotional Intelligence* (Boston: Harvard Business School Press, 2002); Richard Boyatzis and Annie McKee, *Resonant Leadership: Renewing Yourself and Connecting with Others Through Mindfulness, Hope, and Compassion* (Boston: Harvard Business School Press, 2005).

7. Daniel Goleman, Richard Boyatzis, and Annie McKee, *Primal Leadership: Realizing the Power of Emotional Intelligence* (Boston: Harvard Business Press, 2002/2014); V. S. Ramachandran, *The Tell-Tale Brain: A Neuroscientist's Quest for What Makes Us Human* (New York: W.W. Norton and Company, 2011).

8. Sigal G. Barsade and Olivia A. O'Neill, "What's Love Got to Do with It? A Longitudinal Study of the Culture of Companionate Love and Employee and Client Outcomes in the Longterm Care Setting," *Administrative Science Quarterly* 59, no. 4 (2014): 551–598.

9. D. Rosso, K. H. Dekas, and Amy Wrzesniewski, "On the Meaning of Work: A Theoretical Integration and Review," *Research in Organizational Behavior* 31 (2010): 91–127.

10. Daniel Goleman, *Social Intelligence: The New Science of Human Relations* (New York: Bantam Books, 2006).

11. Shane J. Lopez, *Making Hope Happen: Create the Future You Want for Yourself and Others* (New York: Atria, 2013); Richard. E. Boyatzis and K. Akrivou, "The Ideal Self as a Driver of Change," *Journal of Management Development* 25, no. 7 (2006): 624–642; A. Jack et al., "Visioning in the Brain: An fMRI Study of Inspirational Coaching and Mentoring," *Social Neuroscience* 8, no. 4 (2013): 369–384; Annie McKee, Richard Boyatzis, and Frances Johnston, *Becoming a Resonant Leader: Develop Your Emotional Intelligence, Renew Your Relationships, Sustain Your Effectiveness* (Boston: Harvard Business Press, 2008).

Index